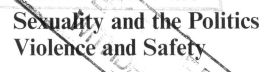

# Sexuality and the Politics Violence and Safety

*Sexuality and the Politics of Violence and Safety* offers a timely and critical exploration of issues of safety and security at the centre of responses to violence. Through a multi-disciplinary analysis that draws on feminism, lesbian and gay studies, sociology, cultural geography, criminology and critical legal scholarship, this book offers to transform the way we understand and respond to the challenges raised by violence. It breaks new ground in its examination of the rhetoric and politics of violence, property, home, cosmopolitanism and stranger danger in the generation of safety and security.

Using interviews, focus groups and surveys with lesbians and gay men, *Sexuality and the Politics of Violence and Safety* draws upon 'real life' experiences of safety and security. It raises some fundamental challenges to the law and order politics of existing scholarship and activism on homophobic hate crime.

**Leslie Moran** is Professor of Law at Birkbeck College, University of London.
**Beverley Skeggs** is Professor of Sociology at the University of Manchester.

# Sexuality and the Politics of Violence and Safety

**Leslie Moran and Beverley Skeggs**
**with Paul Tyrer and Karen Corteen**

 Routledge
Taylor & Francis Group

LONDON AND NEW YORK

First published 2004
by Routledge
11 New Fetter Lane, London EC4P 4EE

Simultaneously published in the USA and Canada
by Routledge
29 West 35th Street, New York, NY 10001

*Routledge is an imprint of the Taylor & Francis Group*

© 2004  Leslie Moran and Beverley Skeggs
with Paul Tyrer and Karen Corteen

Typeset in Times by Exe Valley Dataset Ltd, Exeter
Printed and bound in Great Britain by
TJ International Ltd, Padstow, Cornwall

*British Library Cataloguing in Publication Data*
A catalogue record for this book is available
from the British Library

*Library of Congress Cataloging in Publication Data*
Moran, Leslie J., 1955–
    Sexuality and the politics of violence and safety / Leslie Moran and
Beverley Skeggs, with Paul Tyrer and Karen Corteen.
        p. cm.
    Incudes bibliographical references and index.
    1. Violence.   2. Violence–Prevention.   3. Gays–Crimes against.
    I. Skeggs, Beverley.   II. Title

HM1116.M67  2003
303.6–dc21                                                2003008588

ISBN 0–415–30091–6 (hbk)
ISBN 0–415–30092–4 (pbk)

# Contents

# Acknowledgements

This book draws upon research that was undertaken as part of the 'Violence Sexuality, Space' project, one of twenty projects that made up a major research initiative on violence promoted by the UK government funded Economic and Social Research Council (ESRC) (award No L133 25 1031). Full details of the project can be found at http://les1.man.ac.uk/sociology/vssrp.

First and foremost our thanks must go to those who shared their everyday experiences of safety and security with us. A special thanks also goes to Professor Betsy Stanko, the Director of the Violence Research Programme, for her support and enthusiasm throughout the length of this project and beyond. Paul Tyrer, Karen Corteen and Lewis Turner worked as the project's research staff. Their energy, dedication and determination were fundamental to the project's success.

Papers based on the research have been presented to various audiences over the last four years in universities and conferences in Australia, Canada, Germany, the UK and the USA. The experiences have always been challenging and contributed to the genesis of the text presented here.

## Acknowledgements from Leslie Moran

Special thanks to current and past colleagues and friends who offered support in many and various ways during the course of this project: Richard Collier, Derek Dalton, Tor Docherty, Costas Douzinas, Dominic Janes, Morris Kaplan, Elena Loizidou, Fiona Macmillan, Derek McGhee, Shaun McVeigh, Daniel Monk, Gail Mason, Dirk Meure, Tim Murphy, Steve Myers, Suresh Nanwani, Susan Paterson, Mariana Valverde, Andrew Sharpe, Bev Skeggs, Julie Wallbank and last but not least my Mum and Dad, Annie and Alec Moran.

Particular thanks are due to Paul Passavant who arranged my visit to Hobart and William Smith College, Geneva, New York as visiting fellow in the Fisher Centre for the Study of Men and Women. Special thanks to the members of the centre, Betty Bayer, Susan Henking, Dunbar Moodie and Lee Quinby who provided such a warm welcome and a stimulating and convivial environment. Finally, thanks to Dirk Meure for his hospitality and Professor Chalmers for the invitation to be a visiting fellow at the Law School, University of Tasmania, Hobart.

## Acknowledgements from Beverley Skeggs

Thanks to those who have read all the sections of this book. I am truly grateful. Laura Doan, Mike Savage, Sallie Westwood, Andrew Sayer, Jon Binnie, Betsy Stanko, Sally Munt, including the great 'queer' reading group 'Comings and Goings', with Lisa Adkins, Nicole Vitellone, Sarah Green, Don Kullick, Eleanor Castella, Penny Harvey. Thanks also due to my fantastic ex-colleagues who remain influential: Celia Lury, Jackie Stacey, Sarah Franklin, Maureen McNeil, Sara Ahmed, Lynne Pearce, and, of course, my new colleagues who have had to cope with a very stressed head of department as I finished this book. Thanks especially to Les for tolerating the stress too.

Especial thanks and apologies to my mates: Valerie Atkinson, Nickie Whitham, Graham Day, Jean Grugel, Stuart Baron, John Hobbs, John Phillips, Pat Kirkham, Jeanette Edwards, Krystal Packham and Henri Kreil. I know some have lived the pain of this book with me. Sorry. And of course, thanks and apologies to my amazing parents: Doreen and Ken Skeggs, who continue to sustain me when I should be sustaining them. I really do appreciate the care and loving that all the above have provided.

# 1 Violence, sexuality and cultures and spaces of safety

This is a book about violence and safety. Our primary focus is the nature and practices of safety and security, not violence, a departure from most contemporary writing on violence. The focus on safety can be explained simply. Safety and security are at the heart of reactions and responses to violence, yet violence is predominantly represented as being in opposition to safety. But this is a very partial and limited representation of the relationship of violence and safety. The loss of safety and insecurity – the threat of, the drama, the anxiety, the possibility – shapes the whole public imaginary of violence.[1] Violence, we suggest, is also *for* safety and security.

In taking safety and security as our point of departure, it is not our intention to suggest that work which gives priority to violence, is either invalid or has no urgency. Nor do we seek to distract attention from the perpetrators of violence. Our study builds on pioneering lesbian and gay scholarship (Blumenfeld 1992; Comstock 1992; Herek and Berrill 1992; Mason and Tomsen 1997; Valentine 1989) and activism (Butler 1997b); Greater Manchester Lesbian and Gay Policing Initiative (GML & GPI) 1999; Kuehnle and Sullivan 2001; Mason and Palmer 1996; National Advisory Group 1999; National Coalition of Anti-Violence Programmes (NCAVP) 1999; Sandroussi and Thompson 1995; Morrison and Mackay 2000), which documents violence previously denied or ignored. Though debate continues as to whether this work documents previously unrecorded levels of violence or reports an explosion of 'new' violence (Jacobs and Potter 1999; Moran 2000), it is clear that lesbians and gay men experience a wide spectrum of heterosexist violence, from physical assault to harassment and verbal abuse, on a day-to-day basis.

The nature and form of safety and security is frequently an unexplored and unquestioned dimension of work on violence in general, and violence against lesbians and gays in particular. In part, this may be explained by the immediacy of the impact of violence and the urgency of the need to respond to its damaging effects. Critical reflection on the assumptions of safety and security at play in the response to violence may, in this context, seem to be something of a diversion, a luxury, which is at best out of place. In the specific context of violence against lesbians and gay men, the absence of critical reflection also needs to be situated in the political context in which debates and interventions, focusing on violence, have arisen. An urgent priority has been, and in many instances remains, the struggle to ensure that this violence is recognised and taken seriously as a threat to good order. Critical reflection on the nature and form of safety and security also tends to be overshadowed by a focus on the individual and social causes of the violence where the primary objective is to bring violence to a more speedy and successful end.

Safety and security also remain marginal and unexplored for another reason. Much work on violence emphasises the failure of security and the lack of safety. In part this focus reflects the immediate political context of the intervention: the demand that a wide network of individuals and organis-ations (both official and voluntary) take violence seriously and provide services to promote safety and security. It is not our intention to suggest that this approach has no validity. Our objective is to question the assumptions about safety and security that inform this work. We want to expose the silences and question the marginalisation of perceptions and practices of safety and security that takes place in this politics. Safety and security, we argue, are too important to be left as assumptions operating in the shadow of violence.

Various factors suggest that this is a matter that demands urgent atten-tion. There can be little doubt that the oppressive and destructive dimensions of heterosexist violence are a key factor informing the task of the manage-ment of violence by lesbians and gay men. However, as Gail Mason (2001) has demonstrated, the management of violence also has another dimension. It is one context in which lesbians and gay men *take control.* Both dimen-sions inform the nature and day-to-day practices of safety and security produced by lesbians and gay men. In turn both are at work in the sexual politics of violence and safety that turns to the state in general, and its institutions of crime control in particular, in attempts to counteract the everyday reality of heterosexist violence. An emphasis on insecurity and the lack of safety denies this complex state of affairs. There is considerable irony in silencing and marginalising the practices of safety and security by those who are particularly vulnerable in society. Lesbian and gay people have long had primary responsibility for their own sexual safety, and in the face of day-to-day hostility it is a remarkable success story. The priority of insecurity threatens to ignore this fact, pushing the nature and practices of sustainable safety and security developed by lesbians and gay men out of the political frame. At best, the sexual politics of safety takes the form of unspoken assumptions at the heart of interventions relating to violence. At worst, the priority of insecurity may reinforce vulnerability and disempower.

Wendy Brown (1995) captures another of our concerns. She warns of the 'perils of pursuing emancipatory political aims' (p. ix), suggesting that pro-gressive and emancipatory political projects may, contrary to expectations, generate reactionary and conservative political effects and affects, producing unfreedom in the name of freedom. Safety and security, we argue, is one context in which a progressive and emancipatory politics of sexual violence may in fact reinforce modalities of subordination and exclusion. Our reference to the lesbian and gay experiences arising out of a sexual politics of violence and safety does not seek to single out that politics or experience of violence and safety for particular criticism. Nor is it to suggest that it has unique problems. Our objective is to use the lesbian and gay experience to explore the limits of contemporary political projects of violence and safety more generally.

This book will offer evidence in support of our argument that, in the absence of critical reflection on safety and security, political projects which demand that violence be taken more seriously will at best be flawed. A failure to address the nature and form of safety and security that is being produced in response to violence, we argue, threatens to limit and undermine the very objectives of freedom and justice promoted by that politics.

In developing a critical understanding of the nature and form of experiences and practices of safety and security we may be in a position to more actively define, influence and determine the satisfaction of our present and future safety and security needs. In turn it may help to draw attention to the dangers and limits of a political agenda founded upon safety and security which may close off the possibility of understanding the significance of regimes and perceptions of safety and security that inform a perpetrator's acts of violence. Violence is not the antithesis of safety and security. As we demonstrate in Chapter 2, violence is a key practice *of* safety and security. An analysis of safety and security will enable us to better understand violence and its relation to social order. Finally, we are concerned that without critical reflection on safety and security the future of lesbian and gay social order will, in our name, be imposed on us by default, rather than as the result of our active participation in determining its manner and form.

## Cultures of safety

Before we turn to analyse current experiences and practices of safety and security we make some comments about the wider social and cultural contexts and concerns that inform the sexual politics of violence and safety. The backdrop to contemporary sexual politics of violence and safety is changing economic, social and cultural conditions. These have been variously described as a shift from Fordism to post-Fordism; modernity to postmodernity, tradition to de-traditionalisation; a movement from the politics of redistribution to recognition politics, and the vision of a society based on hyper-commodification and the immateriality of culture, generated through various formations of ambivalence, risk and reflexivity. All represent an attempt to understand the present through both continuity and change. And whilst these reported changes are often at the level of rhetoric, polemic and suggestion, in this study we want to explore how they are changing the landscape for how we can understand violence, safety and the politics of sexuality. For instance, David Garland (2001) documents how the structures of criminal justice, a set of state institutions dedicated to security, safety and order, have changed in important ways, arguing that the most important aspect in the 'history of the present' are the cultural assumptions that animate them. He identifies a new crime control culture that embodies a reworked conception of penal welfare, a new criminology of control, and an economic style of decision-making, formed through new administrative strategies and institutional domains. Yet, this crime control culture is not just shaped by the mechanisms through which it is institutionalised, it is also shaped by much wider issues of sexuality, gender, race and class.

Sexuality informs and reworks what we know as culture through the increasing presence of lesbian and gay issues on a public agenda. An objective of this study of violence and the cultures of safety is to examine *both* the politics and strategies that produce sexual subjects in this context and to explore how these particular sexual subjects impact politically through the use of culture. Garland (2001) and Young (1999) suggest that crime control has been shaped by two underlying forces, the distinctive social organisation of late modernity and the free-market socially conservative politics, that came to dominate UK and US politics in the late 1980s. We want to know how these forces simultaneously shape and are informed by new political organising and new demands on the state and markets.

The demands made by a variety of different groups, such as lesbian and gay demands for safety and security, need to be set, we propose, in the context of new patterns of association between political, economic and civil institutions that are currently being forged, such as those illustrated in the new debates about governance,[2] a term that designates rather loosely a field that takes in debates over private interest government, neo-corporatism, mesocorporatism, private interest, government, socio-economics and associative governance (Slater and Tonkiss 2001). Studies of governance focus on issues of policy problem-solving, questions of institutional design, mechanisms of representation and particular objects of regulation – such as crime control – constituted through the very discourses and practices that seek to govern them. One aspect of new debates about governance is that cultural goods and cultural logics have become increasingly more significant in generating both economic value and mechanisms of social order. How the public imaginary is shaped in terms of how people think they can relate to and make use of violence and state institutions is also significant. This is why new forms of governance are central to how political claims can be shaped. To explore this further we now turn to the claims that have been made by lesbian and gay politics for recognition.

## Recognition politics?

Nancy Fraser (1995) documents a shift from the 1980s politics of redistribution (concerned with inequality, economy and class) to a politics of recognition (concerned with difference, identity and culture). This shift means that in order to have access to the protection of the law, or any rights, one must be 'recognised' as legitimate. Visibility and the relation of the visible to the invisible are central to recognition politics. Eve Sedgwick (1990) suggests that the relation of visiblity/invisibility is the 'defining structure' for lesbian and gay oppression. We would add that it is also central to the lesbian and gay recognition politics of freedom. In the context of violence and safety various techniques such as crime surveys and auto-biographical accounts of violence,[3] have had particular significance in the production of new visibilities.

Patricia Williams (1991) documents that for black people in the United States pathology or invisibility are the ways in which they are legally seen. They are not just misrecognised (as pathological), but often not recognised at all. This is the violence of judgement where one is delegitimated. Yet law's violence, as McVeigh *et al.* (2001) note, developing Derrida, is that it can be distinguished from 'numb force' because it opens an opportunity to respond to the call of justice. All recognition claims are claims for justice, an appeal to be heard and seen and not misrecognised. So the demand for recognition is always a demand for justice. One of the demands made by lesbians and gay men is that they become visible before the law and therefore can access protection. There are various techniques for producing this visibility (such as crime surveys, as will be discussed below). Yet recognition politics is always reliant upon a scopic economy, that is, it assumes that groups can be made visible, want to be made visible and that visibility can enable a claim to be made on the state. But the demand for law through visibility may produce paradoxical effects. It may generate forms of visibility that, when rendered through law, generate very restricted representations of lesbian and gay experience (Robson 1998; Phelan 2001).

The demand for law always forces groups to become visible (otherwise their demand could not be seen). Any demand for law brings into focus the values that have been attached to the groups who are making the claim for recognition and state protection; values previously attached through various forms of symbolic economy. Alison Young (1996) charts the institutional-isation of visibility, which 'mark the time of the criminal by marshalling a citizenry against her as the subject-to-be-looked-at; all mark the face of the citizen as the subject-who-looks, in an ever present state of watchfulness' (p. 210). It is through these scopic economies that an 'us' and 'them' can be imagined. But who is the 'us' and 'them' when complicated by sexuality?

So whilst recognition may enable claims for law, justice, resources and legitimation to be made, it may also be premised upon misrecognition, and by attaching negative values to the groups who demand recognition, the subject may be fixed in new exclusions and pathologies. Part of the struggle we see in the demand for law is premised upon both making visible and trying to engage a shift from misrecognition (negative value attribution) to recognition (positive value attribution)[4] via culture and identity. To participate in recognition politics, categories have to already exist, or have to be made, that have some sense of value and are inhabitable by those who are meant to occupy them.[5] So, for instance, as Sara Ahmed (1998) has shown in relation to being black, and Beverley Skeggs (1997) has shown in relation to being white and working-class, and Mariam Fraser (1999) has shown in relation to queer, some categories of visibility are brought into recognition with only negative value attached to them.

When the political landscape is shaped by visibility/invisibility who and what can be seen (and how) becomes highly significant. This is particularly acute for the politics of sexuality, as Mason (2002) demonstrates. Examining the visual and discursive nature of violence, she details how violence infiltrates not just the daily experience of lesbians and gay men, but also the knowledge systems through which we construct and recognise sexual identities. She also shows how homophobic hostility functions through the ambiguous trope of visibility. Using the metaphor of visuality, Mason argues that violence is itself a spectacle, a bodily experience and practice through which we see and thereby come to know certain things. Violence, she argues, also makes a 'statement' about the disordered, or dislocated nature of lesbian (and we would add gay) sexuality. Different repertoires of meaning operate as mediums through which violence is experienced.

> The act of violence is a spectacle. This is not so much because violence is something that we observe, but, more, because violence is a mechanism through which we distinguish and observe other things. In other words violence is more than a practice that acts upon individual subjects to inflict harm and injury. It is, metaphorically speaking, also a way of looking at these subjects.
>
> (Mason 2002: 11)

One of the central techniques of mobilising identity to generate recognition is the use of pain to make a claim. Violence is the inscription of pain, but then pain is also used to assuage and control violence and to demand a different violence. Brown (1995) contends that the injuries, insults and agonies embodied in the politicised subject become a necessary fetish for gaining visibility and credibility in late modernity (Taylor 1994); the subject, in effect, is what she feels, and she desires recognition of her pain as her primary identity. For Brown, as a result of this complete identification with pain, the politicised subject is either unable or unwilling to break its hold or envision a less self- absorbing and retributive politics, leading her to argue that it is ultimately neo-conservative because it does not project into the future.

## Locating recognition: being in and out of place

The sexual politics of safety and security in particular, and recognition politics in general, we argue, is always a matter of location: of being in and out of place. We want to draw attention to two connections between recognition and space. The first concerns the relationship between recognition, visibility and space. The work of Castells and Murphy (1982) suggests that place is a precondition for the visibility of marginalised groups. They argue that excluded groups need to symbolically occupy a given territory if they are to have any impact upon the transformation of the urban structure. However, at the same time, to make oneself symbolically visible always invokes systems of knowledge, classification and disciplinary power. Visibility is always spatialised and dialogic. As Zukin (1990) notes, the production of place depends on decisions made about what should be visible and what should not, who should occupy the space and who should not. Pile and Thrift (1995) describe the way in which, within scopic regimes, visual practices fix the subject into the authorised map of power and meaning. The institutional landscape of the inner-city, Keith (1993) contends, creates a cultural reality that in part defines the frames through which mapped subjects are rendered legitimately visible. Visibility is about a recognition of being in or out of place that invariably invokes regimes of placement. Symbolic territorialisation depends on an investment in a present and a future belief of knowing where one's place should be and making claims for that space. The chapters that follow examine a number of different rhetorical and political regimes through which the everyday experience of place as located safety (being in place) and in security (being out of place) are produced. Beginning in Chapter 5 we examine the significance of property. In Chapter 6 we turn to explore the deployment of ideas of comfort and home. The distinction between the local and the cosmopolitan is the focus of Chapter 7. Finally we turn our attention to the spatial and corporeal dimensions of the stranger and the uses of estrangement in production of locations of belonging (safety) and being out of place (danger).

The work of Ghassan Hage (1998) on the nation offers a second illustration of the significance of space within the context of recognition politics, through an analysis of the practices of belonging. The practices of nation, he argues, assume, first, an image of a national space; second, an image of the nationalist himself or herself as a master of this nation; and third, an image of 'ethnic/racial [and we add sexual] other' as a mere object within this space. Their combination generates a spatial-affective aspiration. This aspiration enables practices to take a shape that can be recognised as making a contribution to and not detracting from the value of the imaginary nation. Various examples can be used to illustrate the point. In the 1980s, in the UK, legislation prohibiting the 'promotion of homosexuality' (known by its paragraph number 'Section 28') and its accompanying media campaigns demonised and 'outed' teachers and public workers whose gayness was represented as a threat to the future value of the nation (Smith 1994). In this case the national imaginary was generated through a particular body that gives symbolic priority to (national) insecurity: the figure of the 'innocent child' in need of protection from dangerous lesbians and gays. More recently this same body of insecurity has come to represent and shape the nation under threat in relation to a different monstrous sexual other; the paedophile.

Against this constant pathologisation, groups who are positioned outside, or as the contagion within, have to work to generate a sense of what Hage defines as 'governmental belonging'; the belief in one's possession of the right to contribute to the internal and external politics of the nation. It is the management of this belief in contribution to national practices, the feeling of entitlement, which enables the nation to be figured as 'one's home'. The discourse of 'home' is one of the most pervasive and well-known elements of spatial practices of belonging in general and of national belonging in particular. 'Entitlement' is a theme we explore in Chapter 5. We will also return to the theme of 'home' as a location of belonging, in Chapter 6.

The ambiguity of being simultaneously inside and outside leads Hage to argue that practical nationality is best conceived of as question of resources and a matter of the accumulation of resources (cultural capital).[6] For example, it is the process of establishing a white heterosexual national order that reciprocally valorises the very whiteness and heterosexuality that operates as its principle of organisation.

Hage's work draws attention to the need for caution in any analysis of the inclusion/exclusion dichotomy. For example, sexually marginalised groups may be both pulled in *and* pushed out; their cultural capital as middle-class, for instance, may generate a sense of belonging and entitlement to the state, whilst they are simultaneously defined as being out of place and denied entitlement because of their sexuality. The tension between the two enables us to examine how those who are marginalised and figured outside of the nation, or even as its threat, can also feel entitled to make claims on the nation.

In working this entitlement Berlant (2001b) offers an illustration that has particular pertinence within contemporary politics of violence. She argues that the privileged are now able, through the mimesis of an affect of suffer-ing (insecurity), to utilise the technique of telling trauma to make a claim for their own belonging to the nation. In this process, she argues, the nation becomes refigured, so that new forms of emergent US national personhood require stories of trauma (insecurity) in order to establish legitimate national existence. This has the effect, she concludes, of effectively eroding the everyday non-traumatic stories of suffering and survival which become marginalised from the national imaginary as those who have access to the circuits of symbolic domination and legitimacy are able to establish the agenda for their composition of capital. Particular techniques – such as confession or telling of trauma – are used to claim a form of cultural capital (a demand for security) though injury, by those who were previously denied the public position of value through their suffering in their personhood.

Being and belonging are significant themes within the spatial themes of the sexual politics of violence, safety and security. One spatial distinction connoting safety and danger has long dominated this politics: the private (safety) against the public (danger). While this spatial distribution of safety and danger is now highly contentious (a matter we explore in Chapter 6) the predominance of the public/private distinction continues. In some respects the dominance of this particular spatial distinction is unsurprising. As Sedgwick (1990) explains, the public/private binary does phenomenal cultural work in western liberal democratic societies. It occupies an exceptional place in the way we make sense of belonging and being in and out of place. However, this does not suggest that other spatial themes are absent from contemporary lesbian and gay scholarship. Spatial categories of community, nation, state (Altman 1996; Cooper 1994; Kinsman 1987) have some popularity, occurring in debates about sexual citizenship (Bell 1995; Bell and Binnie 2000; Evans 1993; Stychin 1998; Waaldijk 1993; Wintermute 1997), and in connection with other spatial themes, especially the international, supra-national and global. Work informed by urban studies (Adler and Brenner 1992; Castells 1983; Castells and Murphy 1982), cultural and sexual geography (Bell and Valentine 1995; Brown 2000; Duncan 1996; Ingram *et al.* 1997) and architectural studies (Betsky 1997) has elaborated and deployed a rich diversity of other spatial categories which include place, site, environment, the urban, suburban, and rural, closet, queerscapes, locality, liminality, utopia and heterotopia, ghetto, region, neighbourhood, building and home. However, this diversity ought not to detract from the long-standing dominance of the distinction between the private and the public (Lauristen and Thorstad 1974; Mason 1995; Mason 1997a; Moran 1996). Such is the range of meanings produced through the public/private distinction that, warns Sedgwick, it threatens to make it difficult to not only differentiate that distinction from, but also to imagine, alternative spatial categories. It is therefore not surprising that in the context of lesbian and gay politics these many other spatial tropes have been over-determined by the public/private distinction. One of the concerns of this book is to further challenge the dominance of this spatial distinction.

Elizabeth Grosz (1995) draws attention to an important characteristic of spatial language: the space/body interface. In general, she argues, this interface is a matter of representation, of metaphor and metonym. Spatial categories, as metaphor and metonym, produce the body as a sign of location: being in place and/or out of place. In turn, Grosz notes, the body also works as a metaphor and metonym of space. The body as metaphor may be deployed in both positive and negative terms, as the space of good order or its apotheosis. An important term that joins them is the boundary.

The boundary dominates much of spatial thinking. Place, location, urban, rural, metropolis, home, and so on are terms that connote different spaces as bounded phenomena. In turn bodies are also imagined as bounded entities. For example, the skin is represented as the boundary par excellence; between inside and outside, between one person and another (Ahmed and Stacey 2002). As metaphor and metonym boundary not only produces the body as location, but as delimitation *and* as connection. It produces these characteristics of bodies and spaces by way of a parallel between the body and the spatial. We first explore the significance and nature of the boundary in Chapter 5, in the constitution of order (safety) and disorder (insecurity) in the context of a particular rhetoric and politics of belonging: talk of property. Jennifer Nedelsky (1991) argues that it is in this context that the boundary has come to occupy a central place in contemporary conceptual and institutional frameworks not only of security and safety but also of anxiety, fear and insecurity. Like Nedelsky (p. 168) we would argue that the image of the boundary is not limited to talk of safety as a matter of property: it has a much wider significance. The boundary metaphor is implicated in all of the various rhetorical and political regimes we examine in the following chapters: comfort and home, the local and the cosmopolitan and estrangement.

While the growing recognition of the importance of space and the diversity of spatial categories through which power and desire are enacted is to be welcomed, various authors have expressed concern over this development. We share their concerns. Smith and Katz (1993) draw attention to the need to carefully examine the relationship between space and language. In particular they warn of the way spatial (and we would add corporeal) metaphors in general and that of boundary in particular connote fixity and stability, thereby erasing the contingency of space and bodies and the political struggle by which different spaces and bodies and spatial and corporeal categories come into being. For example boundary connotes a line that divides, separates and distributes. It suggests a limit that has clarity, is impermeable, stable and fixed. Smith and Katz point to the ways in which these connotations threaten to erase interconnections, proximities and instabilities and make us blind to the political dimensions of boundary sites and boundary events. One of the effects of this de-politicisation is that while spatial themes proliferate, the different spaces and bodies remain under-documented, analysed and theorised (Retter 1997). In response to these dangers spatial themes demand detailed consideration. The chapters that follow offer a detailed analysis of the various regimes of meaning that shape, invest and are shaped by metaphors of boundaries.

The spatial dimensions of safety and security, order and disorder also have another significance, in law. Analysis of the spatial themes within law is a recent enterprise. Existing work has drawn attention to the juridical significance of key spatial metaphors such as territory, jurisdiction and sovereignty (Blomley 1994; Cooper 1998; Goodrich 1990, 1992; Johnston 1990). Moreover, in a study of the legal landscape of constitutional law in the USA, Nedelsky (1991) draws attention to the spatial trope of boundary as limit in law; as boundaries, jurisdiction and sovereignty connote the juridical as limits of power, authority, rule, legitimate violence. In turn, Nedelsky notes that these limits are intimately associated with security and order. Law, she suggests is coextensive with space and constitutive of particular spaces.

The spatial dimension of law therefore creates safety and security as matters of location. Law is always already located, spatially distinct, subject to limitation, parochial: it is a rooted practice (Beck 2002). We should take that parochialism seriously in order to avoid grand distinctions between safety and a lack of safety, security and insecurity. A rooted approach demands that particular attention is paid to the spatial politics that inform that location. It also demands that we be sensitive to the complexity of the parochial. Law as a juridical space is not a singular but a location made up of multiple spatial categories superimposed and interpenetrated in a particular juridical place of order and security. This suggests that the locatedness of belonging in general and its juridical manifestations in particular needs to be understood as both a singularity, a multiplicity, and as the space (in)between different spaces. While the chapters that follow separate out various dimensions of place both juridical and non-juridical it is essential also to imagine their simultaneous operation.

Finally, the corporeal is never far away from the spatial themes of law. A powerful image in which the spatial, the corporeal and the legal are woven together is the 'body of law'. The Sovereign as body is one long-standing manifestation of this idea (Kantorowicz 1957). Here law may be personified in the body of the current Sovereign, the reigning monarch, or in a more abstracted image, of Leviathan, or in a republican image of a body politic as 'the people'. Common to all is resort to the image of the human body. The body is a spatial metaphor of law. In the bounded body order is totalised and rendered coherent in the perfected corporeality of the (King's/Queen's) body. The body is also an image of law as unity. As the Sovereign's body is a corporeal metaphor of law and order so in turn the body of the individual is made subject as a ruled and bounded order. De Certeau (1984) maintains the idea of the boundary plays a particularly important role. The body is articulated and defined, he suggests, by way of delimitation. As such the truth of the body's belonging in and through the law is produced through the inscription of boundaries. Bringing together the spatial, the legal, recognition and the use of accumulated cultural capital to make claims of belonging, we now explore how they become a matter of personal responsibility, articulated through the discourse of choice. This discourse, when used in relation to safety and security, enables individuals to take responsibility for the violence they experience through the imperative to govern their own selves.

## Choice and compulsory individuality

Anne Cronin (2000a) asserts that we are now in a historical period of 'compulsory individuality'. She uses the work of Marilyn Strathern (1992) to document how discourses of choice are central to the western production of ideas of 'individuality', providing what she calls 'proscriptive individualism'. Thus, forms of control are manifested in inner-directed technologies of the self, which in consumerism are expressed as technologies of choice. An individual is defined by the 'innate' capacity of 'free choice', and this choice expresses the inner authentic individuality of that person. The abstracted notion of 'choice' becomes an inherent ideal as well as the route to the expression of individuality. Yet, as Strathern notes, within this politics of choice, we have no choice but to choose, if we are to express ourselves as individuals and if self-expression is the cornerstone of the politics of identity. Cronin maintains:

> The expression and enactment of choice (and the capacity of choosing) is framed as a compulsory choice: individuality is not an option but rather the compulsory route to selfhood . . . Choice does not merely represent a pre-formed self imbued with potential. Rather, it is a performative enactment of self, invoking the category of selfhood, or the potential of individual selfhood, in the temporality of interpretation and agentic choice (or search for self-knowledge).
>
> (2000: 279)

The neo-liberal social theory of Anthony Giddens (1991) and Ulrich Beck (1992)[7] promotes individuality not only as a necessary, but also a moral prerogative. As Nikolas Rose (1992) reveals, self-management through choice is framed as an *ethical duty* to self and society. Yet, the self is not a pre-constituted, neutral category, but must be performatively produced through the very discourses of 'choice'. But many are excluded from this choice because they do not have access to the requisite resources to enable them to become and be seen to be 'good responsible self-governing selves'. Respectability, therefore, becomes central to the production of the neo-liberal individual who can show that they have a right to belong, be recognised and be protected by the state. We show, for instance, how propriety is central to claims of ownership and belonging in gay space, but also how crime control literature and policy *insists* upon the responsible citizen. The responsible citizen 'chooses' to manage their own safety.

## Organisation of the book

We finish with a brief description of the chapters that follow. The book is loosely organised into two sections; the first explores institutional responses by lesbians and gays to violence. We begin by exploring how violence can be used as a resource, to make a claim on the state, by those who are also positioned by violence. In Chapters 2 to 4 we explore the consequences of a demand for law, arguing that homophobic violence is a violence for the social order, not a violence of social disorder; a 'legitimate' violence through which the social order is (re)produced. The lesbian and gay sexual politics that demands violence addresses and questions the heteronormative status quo, seeking to revalorise heteronormative violence as *a violence of social disorder*. The challenge here then is to make the legitimate into the illegitimate, what Ann-Jannette Rosga (2001) identifies as an attempt by lesbians and gay men to turn the state against itself.[8]

This challenge to the state, through the demand for law, takes and makes different forms and strategies. It is not only the claim for recognition that uses emotions and affects but also the law itself. In Chapter 3 we explore how criminal law institutionalises certain feelings of anger, resentment and hatred, and ask if the demand for the violence of the law is informed by the very emotions that it seeks to condemn. Exploring an economy of violence, we show how punishment is frequently organised as a 'debt' paid to the state/society, the 'creditor' (Solomon 1999). This economy attributes value to different crimes; in the case of homophobic violence it is represented as both exceptional and a sign of an epidemic of violence.

We explore this economy of violence in more detail in Chapter 4 through specific crime control policy. From this we can see how it is being both re-imagined and re-organised. The sovereign state is no longer to be thought of as either the only, or the primary, provider of safety and security in response to violence (Garland 1996). Instead, the new institutional landscape of crime control is one of 'partnerships' and 'networks' of public and private institutions. A key dimension of this new model of crime control is private responsibility; the morally responsible individual (or self) becomes a key provider of safety and the state becomes a provider of *advice* to individuals (Donzelot 1979). This making of responsible citizenship not only enables the transfer of responsibility for crime control from the state but establishes a range of personal requirements that have to be performed and seen, adding to the possibilities for ontological (in)security.

The second section of the book explores a range of personalised responses to violence, showing how the demands and responsibilities established in relation to the state are lived. We examine in depth the private and individual acts of safety, security production and management that have been, and continue to be, important for lesbian and gay safety. The chapters in this section draw upon some empirical data we collected for a study entitled 'Violence, sexuality and space'.[9] We analyse four dimensions of contemporary lesbian and gay politics and practices of safety and security; first, the uses and limits of the rhetoric and politics of property, which has particular significance in the context of claims for recognition and is intimately connected to claims upon the state for improved safety and security. Second, we explore comfort and home not only as a strategy of dealing with ontological insecurity, but also as a rhetoric and politics that shapes belonging. This exploration offers a challenge to existing scholarship on safety talk, drawing attention to the significance of belonging in the generation of experiences and practices of safety and security. By examining these problems, we explore how they are resolved on a day-to-day basis. Third, we explore safety and security as responses to violence through debates about cosmopolitanism. This feeds into the final theme of 'new strangers and new dangers'. We explore how estrangement, belonging and comfort cohere in the management and fabrication of safety and security against violence in its many different forms, showing how a significant amount of the public imaginary of safety and security is shaped by the threat, the fear, the experience, the drama and the anxiety. But also, how the imperative to manage one's self, including the monitoring of one's sexuality is, as Mason (2002) notes, an imperative to manage that which is ultimately unmanageable. Living with violence requires a range of strategies and resources that are deeply embedded in culture and which are reshaping what and how we can be in the world.

# 2 Violence for safety

## Law at the heart of the matter

Law is an important theme in contemporary lesbian and gay politics of violence and safety. Framed in terms of activism around 'hate crimes', Jenness and Broad (1997), writing about the USA, suggest that only through the adoption of new law can hate, 'become a meaningful term and the victimization associated with the problem of hate crime [be] rendered apparent and clearly defined' (p. 172; see also Jenness and Grattet 2001). A different angle, also drawn from the USA, is found in Shane Phelan (2001) on gay and lesbian citizenship. The problem of violence against gays and lesbians, she explains, is perhaps the clearest manifestation of the denial of law:

> The most minimal elements of legal or 'negative' citizenship, in which citizens trade obedience to the laws in exchange for protection, are thus denied to legal citizens who fail to meet the sexual/gender requirements for effective membership.
>
> (Phelan 2001: 23)

For Phelan, law is central to this particular form of citizenship. Legal citizenship demands individual obedience to law and gives access to the state machinery of law enforcement for use against those who violate the law. Failure to comply with the law results in the denial of access to the safety and security that the state provides. Heterosexual sexual/gender prerequisites make compliance at best difficult, at worst impossible for lesbians and gay men. As such, safety and security is made difficult if not impossible, being exposed to both individual violence and the violence of the state.

In these two examples law is the solution to violence. A demand for law is at the heart of this lesbian and gay politics of violence and safety (Moran 2001). This demand for law appears to have been most persistent, and some might say most successful, in the USA. In that jurisdiction, to date, legal solutions have taken various forms. Laws have been enacted to introduce new reporting requirements that seek to improve official data on levels of violence. The Federal Hate Crimes Statistics Act 1990 is perhaps the best-known example. Other reform initiatives have focused upon the introduction of new laws of 'hate crime' and 'bias crime'. These fall into two main types of law reform. Some reforms introduce a requirement to increase the sentence attached to already existing (parallel) offences. Others create new offences (Jacobs and Potter 1998; Lawrence 1999); neither having their origin in a politics of sexual identity. However, through tireless lesbian and gay activism, they have been deployed with some success. The inclusion of sexuality and sexual orientation in the list of categories of 'hate' or 'bias' is at the core of this politics of law reform (Jenness and Broad 1997; Jenness and Grattet 2001). Whilst our examples come from the USA, the priority given to law within a sexual politics of violence is not unique to that context, or limited to the particular formulation of activism that adopts the objective of 'hate crime' reform (Mason 1997b; Thatchell 2002).

Another context in which the sexual politics of violence and safety has become framed as a matter of law is by the crime paradigm. Victim surveys, as Stanko (1997) demonstrates, have played a significant role here. Their widespread use has represented homophobic violence in and through a 'crime paradigm', at both the local and national level (see, for example, GML & GPI 1999; Group 1999; Kuehnle 2001; Mason and Palmer 1996; Morrison and Mackay 2000; National Coalition of Anti-Violence Programmes (NCAVP) 1999; Sandroussi 1995). Through these surveys violence is made intelligible as a breach of the (criminal) law, as a wrong against the individual, against the community.

Victim surveys represent violence in very specific ways: as *hidden violence* and *unreported violence*. This making invisible by the production of absence is significant in various ways. First, it draws attention to the fact that homophobic violence is a form of law-breaking that most people do not perceive to be a breach of the law: it does not have symbolic space. Second, victim surveys highlight the fact that this is unlawful violence, largely absent from official representations of violence. As records of 'hidden' violence, victim surveys document the institutional inability of the state to recognise particular acts as instances of violence, and thereby point to the failure of the state to take violence and disorder seriously. This failure of the state (and thereby of law) is indicated by the absence of police reports of violence against lesbians and gay men. It takes the form of a lack of investigations against those who are officially known to the police as perpetrators of homophobic violence. It is marked in the dearth of prosecutions and convictions. In short it is not recognised.

Law and the state institutions that administer the law are allocated a key role in the demand for change. This may take the form of the improved application of the existing criminal law, making demands for changes and improvements to the existing administrative infrastructure of criminal justice, in particular policing and prosecution practices. Proposals for change are various (Metropolitan Police 2002; Streetwatch 1994; Thompson 1998). For example, the police should take the violence already reported and thereby known more seriously. They should pursue known offenders more vigorously. New reporting mechanisms that will encourage wider reporting should be developed and promoted. New policing responses that are more sympathetic to lesbian and gay victims of violence need to be established. Specialist training and dedicated officers should be created to realise these objectives. Sometimes it takes the form of demands for changes to these laws, including a demand for new laws.

While victim surveys have been an important context in which the 'crime paradigm' has been set in motion, its significance is not limited to that particular context. It has also been given priority through particular incidents of extreme violence. Examples include activism provoked by the brutal murder of Matthew Shepard in the USA (Loffreda 2000), the murder of George Duncan in South Australia (Baird 1997) and in the UK, the bombing of The Admiral Duncan (a gay pub in London's Soho), which resulted in the death of several of its occupants (Bowley 2000).

Our objective in this chapter and the two chapters that follow is to raise a series of challenges to these demands for law in general and the demands for criminal law and criminal justice in particular.

We begin our exploration of the relationship between lesbians, gay men and violence that is being produced in this sexual politics of violence and safety by focusing upon the dominant representation of the relationship between lesbians, gay men and the state. Our particular concern is to question the assumption that informs the law/violence relation that is to be found in contemporary sexual politics. It is a relation of *either/or*: either law or violence.

In order to address these issues we begin with an analysis of scholarship on law's violence. We then turn to examine how law's violence is addressed (or ignored) in current lesbian and gay scholarship. We conclude this chapter with an examination of one exceptional attempt to think through the relationship between lesbians and violence by Robson (1998). Her point is that, 'violence mediates all relationships between lesbians and the law' (p. 15). She aims,'to claim violence as an attribute of lesbianism' (p. 16). Her work offers a rare example of an attempt to address the question of the use of violence as a lesbian (or gay) resource (cf. Scalettar 2000).

## Challenging the politics of violence and safety

Our first challenge is concerned with the relationship between lesbians, gays and violence. One image of this relationship dominates the literature on homophobic violence: lesbians and gays are overwhelmingly represented as objects of violence (Comstock 1992; Herek and Berrill 1992; Mason 1997a; Perry 2001). Lesbian and gay individuals and the lesbian and gay communities are portrayed as victims and survivors of violence. This relation between lesbians, gays and violence is also central to victim surveys. In both types of literature violence is presented as that which destroys and makes impossible the safety and security of lesbians and gay men. Violence is separate from and in constitutive opposition to lesbian and gay. We want to argue that this is an inadequate and partial picture. Our challenge is to add another dimension: lesbians and gay men as subjects of violence.

In adding this other relation between lesbians, gays and violence it is not our intention to diminish the great importance of, or the need to document, report or understand homophobic violence as a life-threatening and life-destroying form of violence. Victim surveys in particular have done much to draw attention to the fact that this violence is part of the everyday experience of lesbians and gay men. Rather, we argue, the sexual politics of violence and safety is producing lesbians and gays not only as objects of violence, but also as subjects of violence. Our objective is to add, engage and problematise a forgotten dimension to the relationship between lesbians gay men and violence.

Our challenge is different to that found in work by Lobel (1986), Taylor and Chandler (1995) and Leventhal and Lundy (1999), which has begun to explore violence within lesbian and gay domestic relationships and legal responses to it. While this is important work, our concerns focus on a different use of violence by lesbians and gay men. This brings us to our second challenge. We want to examine and challenge lesbian and gay demands for access to the protection afforded by the state's violence. This requires us to question the dominant understanding of the relationship between lesbians, gays, violence and the state which informs this demand for state violence. In the context of homophobic violence lesbians and gays are portrayed as the objects of the violence of the State.

The state has been, and in many instances continues to be, an ensemble of institutions though which violence against lesbians and gays has been performed. This violence has been used to fashion and sustain the social order as a heteronormative order (Warner 1993). A wide body of scholarly work offers much evidence in support of the long-standing use of state violence against lesbians and gay men (Duggan 2000; Green 1999; Hart 1994; Kinsman 1987; Smith and Katz 1983; Wotherspoon 1991). In the service of this objective, state violence has been used to fashion and enforce the idea that same-sex relationships are a threat to individual and collective well-being, integrity, safety and security. State violence is a form of violence that has been deployed as the result of unrelenting surveillance and the minute scrutiny of individual and collective behaviour. Through these mechanisms and obsessions state violence has been used to proscribe same-sex relationships, outlawed as dangerous and disorderly, as deviant and dysfunctional as they are pathological (Mason 2001; Moran 1996), radically unthinkable, and beyond possibility. Through these state practices many individuals have been subjected to a civil and physical death.[1]

This representation of the relationship between lesbians, gays and the state is also present in the attempt to explain the low levels of lesbian and gay reports of homophobic violence and harassment to the police. This lack of action is explained as the effect of the long lesbian and gay experience of the police and the criminal justice system as perpetrators of violence, rather than as providers of safety and security in response to violence. It is informed by the continuing fear of state violence giving rise to a lack of trust and confidence in the state institutions of safety and security.

We do not seek to deny this state of affairs. Our challenge instead is to expose some of the limits of this way of thinking and add a new dimension to it. Lesbian and gay demands for access to state violence generate a relation between sexuality and violence, and sexuality and the state. In the past these relations were unthinkable, and in the present have been at best, largely unaddressed and, at worst, ignored. Lesbian and gay demands for access to State violence are being forged by the demand for law that is at the heart of lesbian and gay politics of individual and collective safety and security.

These demands for state violence take many forms. They are to be found in calls for the more rigorous use of the existing criminal law against those who perform acts of homophobic violence, at the heart of demands for new criminal laws such as the demand to include homophobic violence within the parameters of the new legal concept of 'hate crime', demanding enhanced punishment for those who commit acts of homophobic violence.

This brings us to our third challenge. Law is central to the contemporary articulations of the lesbian and gay politics of violence and safety that rely on recognition. Discursively identity demands promote a good society, in which they juxtapose violence as the problem and law as the solution to the problem of danger and insecurity. In crude terms these demands represent violence as bad over and against law as good. In these claims, law is not merely juxtaposed with violence, but, in the first instance, it is presented as the opposite of violence. In this scheme of things law is rule and reason over and against violence. Here violence is disordered, unruly, un-ruled and irrational, in a claim for recognition within the representation of the good and rational state. We want to challenge the approach to the state that is found in this politics of recognition. In particular we want to challenge the idea of the relation of law to violence that informs it, disrupting the either/or that structures the dominant way of imagining the law/violence relation and the chain of binary relations that inform it: either law or violence; either order of disorder; reason or unreason.

The demand for law, we want to suggest, is a demand for violence, albeit a particular form of violence: legitimate violence, good violence. More specifically the demand for law that is at the heart of the sexual politics of violence and safety is a demand for good violence in and through the state institutions of criminal justice. This demand for law and order (crime control) is of special significance in various ways.

Criminal law and the institutions of its administration, policing in particular and criminal justice more generally, offer perhaps the clearest instance of the violence of law (Cover 1986). Criminal justice is a manifestation of law, not so much as an absence of violence (in opposition to violence) but more a particular *institutional practice of violence*. In the guise of criminal law and criminal justice law is a violence associated with order, safety and security rather than with disorder, danger and insecurity. It is a good or legitimate violence over and against bad violence.[2]

The violence that flows from an application of the criminal law is perhaps most readily apparent in those jurisdictions that retain the death penalty. However, the violence of the law is neither confined to that particular act of official violence, nor is it a quality of law limited to those particular legal systems. Law's violence takes many other forms including the enforced loss of liberty and freedom, loss of property and wealth and the loss of children and other loved ones. But it is not just loss but the enforcement of everyday exclusions from belonging, from access to the entitlements of the state that frames this institutional form of the violence of the law. It is to the matter of law's violence as good violence that we now want to turn.

## Law's violence

> Legal interpretation takes place in a field of pain and death.
>
> (Cover 1986)

So begins Robert Cover's analysis of the relationship between law and violence. His observation is useful here in various ways. It points to the link between law as rule and reason and law as violence. Via interpretation the text of law, the rule, (language and reason) is turned into an action, a practice. The 'legal' context of interpretation gives that transformation a specific institutional context; it is violence realised through a specific institutional ensemble. The institutions of the administration of law connect the act of practical understanding to the physical acts of violence and coercion of others (who carry out the judicial decision), 'in a predictable, though not logically necessary way' (Cover 1986). This violence takes many different forms including the execution of an individual, the termination of a person's liberty and freedom, the removal or denial of property, the cessation or prohibition of particular social relations.

Derrida, in his essay 'The Force of Law: The Mystical Foundations of Authority', explores the law/violence relation through a reflection on the connection between law and 'force':

> The word 'enforceability' reminds us that there is no such thing as law (*droit*) that doesn't imply *in itself, a priori, in the analytic structure of its concept,* the possibility of being 'enforced' by force. There are, to be sure, laws that are not enforced, but there is no law without enforceability, and no applicability or enforcement, physical or symbolic, exterior or interior, brutal or subtly discursive and hermeneutic, coercive or regulative, and so forth.
>
> (1992: 6; emphasis added)

Derrida suggests here that law and violence (force) are necessarily related. Cover (1986) echoes similar sentiments in his observation that, 'Neither legal interpretation nor the violence it occasions may be properly understood apart from one another' (p. 1601). As such, the meaning and the truth associated with legal interpretation is produced in and through the relation to violence. 'Legal interpretation', Cover concludes, 'is either played out on the field of pain and death or it is something less (or more) than law' (pp. 1606–7).

Law's violence, Cover suggests, is a violence that is both world-destroying and world-making, 'Law is the projection of an imagined future upon reality' (p. 1604). Legal interpretation justifies not only violence that is about to occur but also violence that has already taken place.

Derrida, in a reflection on Walter Benjamin's argument that the violence of law is of two kinds, offers another insight into the nature of law's violence. Benjamin suggests that law's violence takes the form of a 'founding' or originary violence that institutes and positions law, a law-making violence, and a violence that conserves, ensuring the permanence and enforceability of the law. Derrida (1992) challenges the distribution of this distinction. He points to the connection between these two kinds of violence, '. . . the very violence of the foundation', he suggests, 'must envelop the violence of conservation' (p. 38). This, he explains, is the 'paradox of iterability':

> Iterability requires the origin to repeat itself originarily, to alter itself so as to have the value of origin, that is to conserve itself . . . This iterability inscribes conservation in the essential structure of foundation.
>
> (Derrida 1992: 43)

Iterability has particular significance for law: legal interpretation is a practice of repetition that has the characteristics of both novelty (declaring for the first time) and a saying again (a reiteration). The novelty might be the novelty of the context of interpretation (the particular case), as well as the novelty of a meaning 'found' in the existing language of the rule but previously unimagined. At the same time that novelty must always take the form of saying the same. It must be a meaning generated through the existing authorised language of law, or by reference to previous acknowledged interpretations of the law. As such, each moment of law's violence is the operation of a double violence: a reference to the founding moment of violence that established a particular regime of legitimate violence and an instance of the violence of conservation, its enforcement and thereby its perpetuation.

Finally, Derrida notes that European law tends to prohibit individual violence, He contends that this is not because individual violence poses a threat to particular laws, but because it threatens the juridical order. Law, he concludes, has 'an interest' in the monopoly of violence. This is not a

monopoly at the service of any particular justice or legal ends but a monopoly that strives to protect the law itself. Again it is an a priori of law.

## Lesbian and gay perspectives on law's violence

In many respects lesbian and gay activism and scholarship has long worked
to draw attention to law's violence and to document its operation in the
context of same-sex relations. In turn lesbian and gay politics has long been
undertaken as a practice of resistance to this legal violence. Many of the
demands made by gay and lesbian politics take the form of a call for an end
to and liberation from the violence of law. The long-standing and continuing
demand for the decriminalisation of prohibited genital acts between men in
private is perhaps the best example of this mode of engagement with law's
violence.

In some instances these initiatives also involve a different relation to law's
violence. On some occasions law's violence has been called upon to facilitate
decriminalisation. This call to law's violence has been made in order to
challenge the legitimacy of a law. This use of law's violence takes a common
form. One regime of law, national law, is challenged by way of another
(superior) legal regime, usually in the form of supra- or inter-national legal
provision (Wintermute 1997). It is here where claims for recognition
challenge the nation state and formations of national belonging. Examples
can be found in different jurisdictions. In the UK and Ireland the European
Convention on Human Rights was used to achieve decriminalisation of
genital relations between men in Northern Ireland and in the Republic of
Ireland respectively (Moran 1996). In Australia, the United Nations Convention on Civil and Political Rights was used to promote decriminalisation in
Tasmania (Stychin 1998). In the USA, decriminalisation at the state level has
been demanded (albeit with limited success) by resort to the Bill of Rights
amendments to the Federal US Constitution.[3]

The demands for criminal law, in response to homophobic hate, suggests
a rather different lesbian and gay politics of law's violence. It is a more overt
politics of resistance through the law (Merry 1995), a political strategy of
recognition that advocates the adoption and adaptation of existing legal
categories and practices to achieve the creation of new legal categories and
re-evaluation. A significant difference is that this politics, rather than taking
the form of a challenge to law's violence, takes the form of a demand for full
access to law's violence and to the use of law's violence against the status
quo. As such it is a demand that seeks to use legitimate violence to challenge
legitimate violence. Little activism or scholarship has addressed the question
of the relationship between lesbian and gay political claims-making and
violence that is being forged in the context of these demands for law.

The work of Robson (1998) offers a rare explicit analysis of the relation
between lesbian political demands for law and violence. One context in
which she pursues this approach is the politics of violence and safety. She

offers a critique of lesbian (the arguments are also relevant to gay) engagement with the law in the context of reforms associated with homophobic hate crime: the US Hate Crimes Statistics Act 1990. She argues that this law reform has both positive and negative effects for lesbians and gay men. The positive is associated with the successful incorporation of 'sexual orientation' as a category of 'hate crime' that must henceforth be recorded in Federal Statistics. At the same time, Robson also suggests, the Hate Crime Statistics Act (re)produces certain negative effects. These are to be found in qualifications added to the Act in response to the inclusion of 'sexual orientation' as a recognised category of hatred. Those hostile to the incorporation of 'sexual orientation' as a category of 'bias' and 'hate' were successful in their attempts to include a statement in the legislation that the reference to 'sexual orientation' was not to be interpreted as a positive reference to lesbian or gay sexuality. Nor, they argued, was it to be taken as a legislative basis for new anti-discrimination claims. Law reform, Robson argues, that may promote greater state protection for lesbians and gay men is also implicated in doing violence against them. It does violence to their experiences and in the enforcement of the new law perpetuates and reinforces their exclusion.

A second aspect of lesbian and gay subjection to law's violence occurred, Robson suggests, in the context of distinctions that are made in the legislation between various identities. The enactment of identity categories installs a logic of either/or (either lesbian or black, gay or latino) that does considerable violence to experience of violence that is read through identity, failing to take the multiplicity and complexity of these experiences seriously. More generally, Robson argues, they connect the demand for law's violence with the normalisation of sexual (in this instance lesbian) identity. Identity categories in law become a nexus of criteria through which distinctions are generated to differentiate good lesbians from bad lesbians, deserving lesbian from undeserving lesbians, respectable from un-respectable (Phelan 2001). As such, they work to produce new exclusions at the same time as they produce new dimensions of social inclusion. Robson's analysis warns us that what might appear in the first instance to be lesbian and gay access to good violence (turning the state against heterosexual violence) against bad violence, may at the same time be an experience of state violence as bad violence. This state violence is also violence against lesbians and gay men.

A strength of Robson's analysis is that it draws attention to the ambivalence of law's violence as a means to an end. Having exposed the contradictory and unstable relation of lesbian (and gay) politics to the violence of law, in the final instance, much of her analysis represents law's violence as bad violence. Here lesbians (and one could add following her analysis gay men), are objects of law's violence. In many respects this reproduces a well-established relationship between lesbians (gay men) and violence. But her analysis does not stop there. This does not lead her to abandon violence; rather, she takes a different turn and this is the novel feature of her work.

Robson seeks to retrieve an idea of good violence for lesbian politics. Her point of departure is that, 'violence mediates all relationships between lesbians and the law' (p. 15). She then turns her attention to the relationship between violence and lesbianism and declares, 'I want to claim violence as an attribute of lesbianism' (p. 16). It is in this context that her work offers a rare example of an attempt to address the question of the use of violence as a lesbian (or gay) *resource.*

The first step in her attempt to forge a link between good violence and sexual identity is to re-name that violence as 'fire'. In part, her resort to a different metaphor of violence is a response to the negative associations connected with violence, 'To posit an identification between lesbianism and violence implies that lesbianism is bad [since violence is negative]' (p. 16). 'Fire' is offered as an alternative metaphor in an attempt to retrieve an idea of good violence. At the same time Robson notes the ambivalence of 'fire' as violence: it connotes both 'good' violence as well as 'bad' violence. Fire may not only damage and destroy but it also strengthens and replenishes. Her choice of metaphor is not arbitrary: 'fire', she argues, has strong historical and cultural associations with women in general and lesbians in particular.

She proceeds to explore the terms of the lesbian/violence relation as inherently violent, explaining it in various ways: lesbianism is violence over against the violence of the law, which is a violence of 'heterosexual hegemony'. It is a violence that not only challenges that law but a violence that offers resistance to it. It is also a violence that is, she argues, 'non-negotiable'. As a violence that is a challenge to law it is, she suggests, a violence that provokes an emancipatory change in contrast with the violence of law that conserves and is conservative.

How are we to make sense of Robson's characterisation of lesbianism as violence? A return to Derrida's essay on 'The Force of Law' is useful here. He suggests that:

> The state is afraid of fundamental, founding violence, that is, violence able to justify, to legitimate or to transform the relations of law, and so has to present itself as having a right to law. This violence thus belongs in advance to the order of a *droit* that remains to be transformed or founded.
>
> (1992: 34–5)

Robson's makes use of lesbian violence as a violence that challenges the status quo. It is a challenge that takes the form of founding violence and as such is always/already of the order of a *droit.* The reference to its 'emancipatory' potential gives it the attribute of a potential to 'transform' and thereby to present itself as having a 'right to law'. As such it is a good violence that is in the image of the good violence of law.

Robson's analysis is significant in various ways. It is exceptional in the way it points to lesbian (and gay) politics as violence, and lesbian (and gay) politics as a demand for good violence. A second insight is how she represents violence as ambivalent, both good and bad. However, it is in this context that Robson's analysis begins to falter. Her thoughts on lesbianism as violence give priority to that violence as a founding or originary violence. Little or no attention is given to the conservative aspect of that violence.

A second problem is in Robson's ability to sustain the ambivalence of violence; both good and bad. Ambivalence is difficult to sustain (a matter we return to in Chapter 5, 'The rhetoric and politics of property'). There is a tendency to manage ambivalence by separating out the contradictory attributes that inhere in each particular instance by way of time, space and function. The repression and displacement that is produced by temporal spatial and functional divisions feeds a logic of either/or that further perpetuates the denial of ambivalence. In Robson's analysis the displacement and repression tends to take the form of lesbian violence as good violence in contrast to law's violence as bad violence. Perhaps the clearest example of this functional division is the suggestion that lesbian violence may be emancipatory (good) over against the violence of law that conserves and is conservative (bad). We should remind ourselves of Derrida's insight that the two are always intimately connected. Lesbianism as violence is both good violence (emancipatory) and bad violence (conservative) before the law, as a challenge to law and as the law. The logic of either/or also ignores the specific political context in which social and cultural differences are (re)produced and deployed.

## Conclusion

We appreciate that this chapter will be viewed by some as a highly controversial departure from the orthodox position of contemporary sexual politics of violence and safety. We make no apologies for raising difficult and troubling issues. Our objective is to expose the lesbian and gay demands for access to state violence that is at the heart of the sexual politics of violence and safety, in order that a dialogue can begin about these demands. The failure of scholars to make explicit law's violence is problematic. At best, the law/violence relation appears in an unarticulated form: as the a priori of law (identified by Derrida above). In turn, this may make lesbian and gay scholars unthinking participants in the reproduction of an appeal to the 'official' story of law as reason and rationality over against violence as that which is an always threatening presence outside the law (Sarat and Kearns 1991). This is particularly troubling. Lesbian and gay scholars are in danger of promoting a position that threatens to render invisible one more time the violence of law that they have so persistently and diligently exposed. In turn as an unarticulated assumption it fails to address a key aspect of contemporary lesbian and gay politics which is the demand for law, the demand for violence.

Ruthann Robson's work offers one of the first, albeit problematic, attempts to take the idea of lesbian and gay resort to violence as good violence seriously. Yet further work needs to be done. A rereading of some gay and lesbian scholarship, which has documented some of the effects of law's violence being produced through lesbian and gay demands for law, with and alongside Robson's work on law's violence is a useful point of departure. One context in which lesbian and gay scholars have turned their critical attention to a consideration of the effects of 'resistance through the law' is in reflections upon demands for the incorporation of lesbian and gay demands into the legal practices of civil and human rights. Their work, we would argue, is about law's violence. In general this work draws attention to the various ways in which the violence of rights has imposed new and sometimes unexpected limits and exclusions upon those who have championed law reform (Herman 1994; Stychin 1998; Phelan 2001).[4] More recently, scholars have explored demands for law's violence in the context of claims for lesbian and gay access to anti-discrimination provisions and legal recognition of same-sex partnerships in the USA (Goldberg Hiller 2002; Keen and Goldberg 2000). A particular focus of this work, we would argue, has been to examine not the lesbian and gay claims for access to law's violence in these different setting but to explore the political reactions against these initiatives. In general, the hostile responses to these initiatives seek to limit lesbian and gay access to the violence of law. One attempt to limit access to the violence of law in the anti-discrimination context has been to characterise these initiatives as claims for extra-ordinary or 'special rights'. Another position, particularly one associated with the Christian Right, has been to argue that lesbian and gay access to law's violence poses a more general threat to the legal and social order (Herman 1997).

Our objective is to facilitate a move away from, an at best oblique and at worst opaque consideration of, the law/violence relation in lesbian and gay politics of violence and safety. We seek to interrupt and question the dominant assumption that the relationship between sexuality and violence is one only of violence against lesbians and gay men. We want to expose a lesbian and gay will to forget the political demands for access to the violence of the state that are being made in response to violence.

The need to expose and question the lesbian and gay demands for access to state violence that are otherwise being silently promoted has a particular urgency. These demands are not merely an engagement with the state institutions of heteronormative violence, but an attempt to transform that heteronormative institution(s) for another, a different, sexual order.

We have no illusions as to the size or scale of the problems that lesbian and gay politics might face in this context. Perry (2001) captures the nature of this challenge in the following observation. She notes that '[i]n a generally . . . homophobic culture violence motivated by hatred *is not deviant behaviour*. In fact it conforms . . . It is an affirmation of the gendered [and sexualised] . . . hierarchy that constituted the "legitimate" social order' (p. 35; emphasis added). In a heteronormative social order homophobic violence is 'normal' everyday, commonplace, routine behaviour, a legitimate and legitimated violence. Homophobic violence is not associated with exceptional (dysfunctional or pathological) individuals or exceptional settings or disorderly social structures; rather it is ordinary violence performed by ordinary people as part of the routine of day-to-day living. The ordinariness of homophobic violence is perhaps best captured in its particular invisibility. Homophobic violence is a violence for the social order not a violence of social disorder that is understood as a threat to social security and safety. It is a 'legitimate' violence through which the social order is (re)produced. The lesbian and gay sexual politics of violence addresses and questions this heteronormative status quo. It seeks to revalorise heteronormative violence as *a violence of social disorder*. The challenge here then is to make the legitimate into the illegitimate. Rosga (2001) suggests that this project, which seeks to work in and through the institutions of the state, is an attempt by lesbians and gay men to turn the state against itself.

A lesbian and gay sexual politics that demands access to this state violence faces particular problems. Brown, writing in the context of feminist engagements with the state, articulates one of the basic problems by posing the following question:

> What are the perils of pursuing emancipatory political aims within largely repressive, regulatory, and depoliticizing institutions that themselves carry elements of the regime whose subversion is being sought?
>
> (1995a: ix–x)

It is to one of the 'perils' of pursuing emancipatory aims through a law and order agenda that we now turn.

# 3   Attachment to hate
## The emotional dimensions of lesbian and gay crime control

### Introduction

Our analysis of lesbian and gay demands for law's violence as good violence now shifts to introduce another challenge, which arises in the specific political context of the contemporary demands for safety and security: law and order. Brown (1995a) poses a question that is at the heart of our challenge to the lesbian and gay politics of violence and safety. She asks, 'What kind of attachments to unfreedom can be discerned in contemporary political formations ostensibly concerned with emancipation?' (p. xii). We want to raise some questions about the nature of the emotional attachments being made within contemporary lesbian and gay politics of violence and safety in and through a law and order politics.

The challenge we raise in this chapter does not seek to detract from the urgency of the need to take homophobic violence seriously, rather we offer it as a critical intervention. Nor does our challenge suggest that criminal law or criminal justice is necessarily an unfitting focus for lesbian and gay politics. In part, our objective is to make the terms of that engagement more apparent and thereby more open to debate. The challenge we pose in this chapter centres upon the range of emotions that are produced and invested in the focus on criminal law and punishment. Murphy and Hampton offer the following insight into some of the emotional investments commonly associated with the criminal law, arguing that:

> criminal law institutionalizes certain *feelings of anger, resentment and even hatred* that are typically directed towards wrong doers, especially if we are the victims of those wrong doers.
>
> (1988: 63; emphasis added)

The appearance of 'hatred' in this list is of particular interest. A significant focus of recent lesbian and gay law and order talk and activism has been on 'hate'. However, far from being an emotion associated with the lesbians and gay men, who advocate the application and reform of the criminal law, hate is represented only as the target of their concern. More specifically, hate is associated with violence against lesbian and gay men, which is characterised as a 'hate crime'. No mention is made of the possibility that hate (albeit a different hate) might be associated with the advocacy of legal violence (Rosga 2001).

The demands that emerge in the context of these attempts to characterise homophobic violence as a hate crime usually take three forms. The first is not so much a demand for law reform, but a demand for the administrative reform of the day-to-day operations of the institutions of policing and criminal justice more generally. The objective here is to improve the machinery of criminalisation and wider safety provision. The other two demands focus more specifically upon law reform. The first is a demand for enhanced punishment that may apply to a wide range of already existing (parallel) offences. The second is a demand for new punishments by way of new offences. The objective of these various demands is formally to bring hate to an end. In this scheme of things 'hate' is associated with crime, 'hate' is in opposition to law, 'hate' is the problem, law the solution.

Our challenge, following Murphy and Hampton's insights, is to problematise the relation between the emotions, in particular hate, but also anger, resentment, and we would add fear, and the law. Law, which is used to bring hate to an end, we want to argue, may be informed by and give shape to emotions, such as hate, albeit a different kind of hate. Our particular concern is to explore the ways in which these various emotions become insititutionalised. Our first challenge then is to pose the following question. Is the demand for the violence of the law informed by the very emotions that it seeks to condemn?

In order to answer this question we first set the lesbian and gay politics of law and order in the wider context of law and order debates. This is particularly important as it is within this wider context of contemporary politics of law and order that the emotions that Hampton and Murphy associate with the criminal law and criminal justice are being promoted and celebrated. Our analysis draws upon David Garland's (2001) work, *The Culture of Control: Crime and Social Order in Contemporary Society*. Garland raises some provocative questions for lesbian and gay law and order politics. In general, his study is concerned with changes in the institutional landscape of crime control. He suggests that one feature of the new crime control landscape is an acceptance of the limits of the sovereign state. In that context a renewed emphasis upon the punitive aspects of criminal law and criminal justice emerges. Garland describes this as the rise of punitive segregation. The objective of the traditional state institutions of crime control is retribution, revenge and segregation. Rehabilitation and the welfare of wrongdoers decline in significance.

It is not our intention to argue that lesbian and gay demands for law's violence, and the emotions produced and invested in those demands, are merely vehicles for these wider concerns. But we maintain that lesbian and gay resort to the politics of law and order is not totally remote from them.

From this point of departure we offer an analysis of the emotional investments currently associated with criminal law and criminal justice. We analyse
how these emotional investments are legitimised and therefore, rendered
invisible in the sexual politics of law and order being developed by lesbians
and gay men. This allows us to examine the conditions through which the
fabrication of sexual identity as good violence is being produced. It also
allows us to explore how sexuality is lived as an affect through violence.

## The wider political and structural context of law and order

We begin with an analysis of the wider political and structural context out of
which the lesbian and gay sexual politics of law and order has emerged.
Several commentators have noted this is a political domain undergoing
major transformations (Bauman 2000; Garland 2001; Taylor 1999; Young
1999), connected with wider revolutions within western neo-liberal capitalist
democracies. These include changes in capitalist modes of production in late
modernity: the move from a Fordist to a post-Fordist political economy; the
growing importance of the market and consumption; and the forces of
globalisation, which impact in various ways upon the social and cultural
order of societies. Young (1999) has described this as the rise of the 'Exclusive
Society', which, he argues, is being born upon the ruins of a social order
that, characterised itself in terms of inclusion, a movement from an inclusive
society of stability and homogeneity to an exclusive society of change and
division.

He argues that the inclusive society has been destroyed with the restructuring of capital, generating economic exclusion, which takes the form of mass
unemployment and the production of a new underclass. Alongside economic
restructuring, Young suggests, the inclusive society has been challenged by
the introduction of new social divisions. Those who previously experienced
the social and cultural distinctions, such as race, gender, sexuality, ethnicity,
upon which that inclusive society was constructed, have promoted attempts
to revalorise these categories of exclusion, through a politics of recognition.
Rather than being remote from the transformation of capitalist relations in
society, Young suggests, these changes are closely connected to them, in
particular the changes are associated with the rise of consumption and
individualism.

Thus, the demand for the violence of the law is framed not only by
recent neo-liberal shifts, but also by new shapes of state formation. There
is the shift, identified by Charles Taylor (1994) and Nancy Fraser (1995,
1997), from the politics of redistribution, based on economy, class and
inequality, to the politics of recognition, based on identity, culture and
rights. Recognition, they argue, is the new grammar for political claims-
making. It is the way in which demands for law in general and criminal
justice in particular can be articulated. Fraser argues that to be misrecognised:

is not simply to be thought ill of, looked down on, or devalued in others' conscious attitudes or mental beliefs. It is rather to be denied the status of full partner in social interaction and prevented from participating as a peer in social life – not as a consequence of a distributive inequality (such as failing to receive one's fair share of resources or 'primary goods') but rather as a consequence of institutionalized patterns of inter- pretation and evaluation that constitute one as comparatively unworthy of respect or esteem. When such patterns of disrespect and disesteem are institutionalized, for example, in law, social welfare, medicine and/or popular culture, they impede parity of participation, just as surely as do distributive inequities.

(1995: 280)

Being recognised as 'something' has been used by certain groups to mobilise claims for political recognition: for instance, the debates on race and ethnicity being undertaken in the context of multiculturalism in the US (Goldberg 1994), on gay (Berlant and Warner 1998) and transgender (Halberstam 1998). All these struggles suggest that recognition is one of the primary motivators of contemporary western political action. The desire to be recognised as having value is important to how we in the west conceive of ourselves as human subjects (Honneth 1995). Taylor (1994), likewise, argues that because individuals are, in part, constituted by their cultural positioning, then the basic protection provided by the state should extend to the protection of their cultures. He promotes culture-protective and culture-promoting legislation within a diverse liberal state. He draws significant boundaries between economics, politics and culture. This echoes the distinction used by Nancy Fraser, between culture and economy, which relegates sexuality to the 'merely cultural' (see Adkins 2002; Butler and Savage 1995; M. Fraser 1999; Rorty 1994): 'merely' in need of state protection.

Of particular interest here is the distinction and the relation drawn between these economic, social and cultural changes and the law and order politics of crime control. Zygmut Bauman (2002) argues that the growing importance of crime control is connected to the rise of demands for safety and security, generated in response to perceptions and experiences of insecurity and disorder that flow from these wider changes. So, whilst political claims are being made on the basis of cultural positions and fragmentation, the changes in cultural formation are also leading to a demand for more security. Crime and fear of crime has become a key sign of disorder and insecurity that may stand metonymically and metaphorically as a sign of other experiences of economic, social and cultural disruptions and trans- formations. It is by way of crime and fear of crime that disorder and insecurity may become embedded in everyday life. It is through what Garland (2001) identifies as a 'criminology of everyday life' (p. 16) that a law and order politics offers an analysis of, and solution to, the problem of insecurity in a very specific context. When crime is the sign of wider social ills, policing and criminal justice gain particular importance as the solution to these problems. The turn to institutions of policing and criminal justice reflects the fact that in the epoch of modernity these are the social institutions that have been particularly associated with internal security and good order (Neocleous 2000).

Garland (2001) examines how state institutions of internal safety and security have been affected by and responded to the changing state of affairs. He maps an important paradox of a contemporary crime control politics of law and order. On the one hand, there is the political centrality of crime control that emphasises the role of the sovereign state as guarantor of safety and security. On the other hand he argues that at the same time, there is an increasing recognition of the limits of the state to provide this safety and security. Yet the recognition of the decreasing impact of the state does not stop demands being made of it. Safety and security become part of the package of recognition claims that are made. To be recognised also means to be afforded protection.

## A criminology of the bad culture and bad choice

Garland pursues his analysis around two themes. The first is 'the criminology of the other' and the second is 'the criminology of the self'. Both have significance for the lesbian and gay politics that seeks access to legal recognition. We explore the 'criminology of the self' in Chapter 4. In this chapter we focus attention on the 'criminology of the other'.

A key dimension of the 'criminology of the other' is the politics and practices of 'punitive segregation'. This, Garland argues, is a law and order politics that connects individual and collective well-being with enhanced punishment, selective social exclusion and confinement. It involves the promotion of more severe state violence, which takes various forms, including demands for earlier resort to imprisonment in preference to other non-custodial sentences, longer terms of imprisonment and more brutal regimes of punishment. Punitive segregation is shaped by the history of nation-formation: in its most extreme forms it produces mass imprisonment (Garland 2001), and includes demands for the death penalty. Retribution and revenge are central and connecting themes. In the USA, scholars have described the move to punitive segregation as a turn towards punishment as an institutional form of vengence (Sarat 1997), and a practice more akin to institutionalised cruelty (Simon 2001).

While retribution is a dominant theme other rationales are also significant. For example, longer terms of imprisonment are promoted as a way to enhance the isolation, incapacitation and containment of those who threaten social order through crime. Enhanced punishment is also associated with deterrence, whilst the role of punishment as a mechanism for social change or the correction of prior social injustice is seen to have less significance.

These forms of imagined and physical segregation associated with crime and criminal justice echo wider trends. Another context in which they have been identified is in recent research on contemporary racism, which shows how racism is now legitimated, not through biological essentialism as it once was, but through spatial segregation. The national imaginary and the practice and political rhetoric that constitute this imaginary, enable both the cultural and physical segregation of those defined as not belonging to the nation (Balibar 1999; Hage 1998; Taguieff 1991). Stolcke (1995) demonstrates how this 'new' racism, rather than interiorising the 'other', exalts the absolute, irreducible difference of the 'self' and the incommensurability of different cultural identities (Young 1999).[1]

This culturalist rhetoric, often called 'cultural fundamentalism' (Stolcke 1995), is distinct from racism that reifies culture conceived as a compact, bounded, located, and historically rooted set of traditions and value. Instead it brings into play a definition of the other and the self as a necessary prerequisite of each other. Sociopolitical inequality and domination are thereby attributed to the distribution of differentiation itself, namely, 'their' lack, is in 'their' race. As a doctrine of asymmetric classification this racism provokes counter-concepts that demean the 'other' as the 'other'. Mutual recognition is denied precisely because the 'racial' defect, being relative, is not shared by the 'self'. And that is the point. The 'self' in this culturalist rhetoric does not need the other for its own formation, as in prior concepts of race (e.g. Fanon); rather the self and other become absolute and recognition is based on those who can claim a self that belongs to the nation (Skeggs 2003).

Crime control as punitive segregation evidences a similar politics. It is a demand to spatialise this lack and difference (now signified in and through the criminal act), to demean the other (the criminal), to separate that person physically from the self and to show distance from that person. In this claim for control through differentiation and spatialisation the 'other' as lack is made beyond criminal justice and punishment as redemption, reform, rehabilitation, social justice, civil and human rights. The absolute object often is physically produced and institutionalised through punitive segregation.

Garland notes that, against punitive segregation that emphasises the state's monopoly of violence, there is, in simultaneous operation, another very different landscape of crime control. Here the emergence of everyday crime is connected to a different set of responses. The 'everyday' of crime, Garland suggests, gives a, 'new focus . . . upon the supply of criminal opportunities and the existence of "criminogenic situations"' (p. 16). Attention centres not upon individuals but on:

> the routines of interaction, environmental design and the structure of controls and incentives that are brought to bear upon them. The new policy advice is to concentrate on substituting prevention for cure,

reducing the supply of opportunities, increasing situational and social controls, and modifying everyday routines.

(Garland 2001: 16)

When crime is ordinary and everyday deviation is less a sign of either the pathology of the individual or of a dysfunctional social system/structure, it becomes instead a matter of rational choice, routine activity and opportunity (Bauman 2002; Garland 2001). Crime therefore brings wrongdoers to the wrong choices. By imputing bad choice on to those who are seen to require control, recent developments in crime control display striking similarities with the wider trends identified by Marilyn Strathern (1992). She argues we are now beyond nature as a legitimating force for understanding people's actions. Rather, we are now in an era of compulsory individuality and compulsory choice, where all we have to legitimate our actions is 'choice'. Those 'in need' of crime control are read as having made the wrong choices. Choice, she argues, becomes the very essence of individuality, requiring no external control; rather it is a form of 'prescriptive individualism', or what Taylor (1994) calls 'self-expressive choice' in which the expression and enactment of choice is framed as a *duty to the self*. As Anne Cronin (2000a) shows, choice makes a 'compulsory individuality' in which choice does not merely represent a preformed-self; it is a performative enactment of self, invoking the category of selfhood in the 'moment' of expression. Some people make the wrong choices because they are located in a culture that does not give them access to the 'right' choices. Thereby de-legitimation is located in themselves; they are bad selves as opposed to the good selves who can make the right choices and take responsibility (for their own security and safety). It is their own bad choice that produces them performatively as bad individuals, because they cannot govern themselves and produce themselves as ethical beings (Rose 1992). This logic displayed in and through punitive segregation produces punishment as a regime concerned with compliance, promoting and reinforcing the status quo. So, how does this connect with lesbian and gay law and order politics?

## Punitive segregation and lesbian and gay politics of law and order

Crime control has been given particular priority in the sexual politics of violence and safety bringing together what is frequently characterised as the more progressive politics of identity with the more conservative and reactionary contemporary politics of law and order (Jenness and Broad 1997). Various commentators (Bauman 2002; Garland 2001) have noted how the current priority given to crime control is generated through a politics of law and order in general and a victim politics in particular. It would be wrong to conclude lesbian and gay demands for access to state violence for safety and security are reducible to the law and order politics of 'punitive segregation' outlined above. For example, in the first instance lesbians and gay men are making demands to have access to long-denied mechanisms of safety and security. As such there is no necessary connection between lesbian and gay demands for the particular state violence associated with punitive segregation. It may be just an asymetrical historical alignment.

In some respects lesbian and gay demands for state violence seem to be remote from some of the characteristics of punitive segregation. In particular, they do not so much promote the status quo as offer a significant challenge to one of its key dimensions, *heteronormativity*. However, at the same time the lesbian and gay claims offer to reinforce a different status quo: the priority of a law and order politics that places violent crime as *the* problem of social disorder and a more brutal regime of criminal justice as *the* solution. There is a logic to this equation that corresponds to the reproduction of the culturalist rhetoric outlined above.

This is further supported (as the opening chapter showed) through the promotion of an identity politics which is premised upon converting experience of social positioning into an epistemological claim for moral authority (Bar On 1993). That is, in claiming that one's experience as gay or lesbian gives a special access to knowledge, which is better and more authoritative than other forms of knowledge. This produces the experience of culture (via positioning) as the determining factor in knowing and being able to make political demands. So there is good culture and bad culture which enables demands on law to be made. It is culture, it is argued, that is enhanced by recognition and by the use of criminal law and criminal justice to control those who threaten this culture. The struggle is again symbolic (and which struggle is not?) in which cultures are pitted against each other as worthy, and different moral designations are given to cultures which need control and those which need recognition through assimilation. Violence becomes evidence, a marker of a culture that lacks, that cannot be assimilated or legitimated. Unlike those in the last chapter who could use violence as a resource to mobilise their victim status to make a legal claim, here violence is read off the culture, not as a resource but as a bad choice. This is culture that cannot be used to make a recognition claim for law.

The most explicit alignment of a lesbian and gay sexual politics of violence and safety with the themes of punitive segregation is to be found in the context of demands for the addition of sexual orientation and sexuality to new laws that create parallel 'hate' or 'bias' crimes. These reforms advocate the introduction of more severe punishment for those who commit an existing offence of violence with evidence of the proscribed 'hate' or 'bias', the logic being that it is their culture that makes them hate, biased and violent; it is their inability to govern themselves, it is their lack of self-control that constitutes the problem.

The resonance between these proposals for reform and the law and order politics of punitive segregation is to be found in the rationale for sentence enhancement. These reforms are not specific to lesbian and gay demands, having a much longer history in other campaigns for the introduction of crimes of 'hate', particularly associated with the politics of race, ethnicity and civil rights (Jacobs and Potter 1998; Jenness and Broad 1997; Jenness and Grattet 2001). The importance of these demands for reform lies in the fact that they offer a standard set of arguments and an established orthodoxy of legitimate grounds for change. Lesbians and gays have deployed this orthodoxy for a different politics, to rationalise, re-value and legitimate their own particular demands for law reform.

The organising principle of this orthodoxy is that 'hate' or 'bias' crime is a *more* damaging and dangerous form of violence (Lawrence 1999), therefore demonstrating a moral claim through damage and injury.[2] Hate crime is said to be more damaging for the individual in various ways:[3] some have suggested that hate violence is frequently physically more extreme and more brutal (Iganski 1999; Levin 1999). Extra damage also takes a psychological form as it generates added trauma. One dimension of this is explained in terms of the particular nature of the act of violence, which is seen to have a strong impersonal dimension: the perpetrator acts on the basis of his perception of the victim's membership of a social category. The impersonal nature of this violence makes the crime 'very personal' and thereby more damaging in its effects (cf. ACPO 2000). Another aspect of the extraordinary impact of hate violence is explained by reference to its wider effect. In the first instance this is upon the immediate identity community. Some have characterised the nature of the threat as a form of 'terror' (Weinstein 1992), in which members of the community live in constant fear and isolation. It also has a wider impact as the perpetrator's perception of the victim's membership of a particular vilified group has a certain arbitrary quality. Therefore, a much wider group of persons are seen to be at risk of this form of violence as identity connections based on self-identification are made. Finally, the extraordinary nature of this violence is associated with damage to culture and respectable 'society' more generally, where the violence threatens to fracture the community and to threaten the very possibility of social order.

This orthodoxy of 'a more dangerous and damaging violence', Frederick Lawrence (1999) suggests, is informed by two main legitimating themes. The first is 'retribution'. The second is 'utilitarian'/'consequentialist'. Retribution explains and fashions these demands for enhanced punishment in terms of just deserts: 'an eye for an eye', 'that the punishment fit the crime', etc. Others have described punishment in this scheme of things as a form of 'debt' paid to the state/society, the 'creditor' (Solomon 1999). The utilitarian/consequentialist position is characterised by Lawrence as a set of themes that orientate punishment towards the promotion of the overall welfare of society and crime reduction. The argument that 'hate' violence is more damaging and therefore punishment must be more severe has a particular resonance with 'retribution'. At the same time utilitarian/consequentialist themes are also associated with enhanced punishment. They protect both individuals and society from the exceptional danger by way of extended incapacitation, which in turn is a symbol of the specific nature of that danger. As a symbol the new punishment functions at the level of moral education; purporting to give out a message to individuals and society that 'hate crime' is no longer tolerated and is now being taken seriously. Rehabilitation is also another possible objective associated with the utilitarian position.

While all these themes may be used to rationalise and legitimise the lesbian and gay demands for enhanced punishment, they also need to be situated within the wider contemporary context of law and order politics. Particular attention needs to be paid to their contemporary social and cultural resonances, as this will affect the manner of their incorporation into a system of purposes (Nietzsche 1956). Thus when refracted through the law and order politics of punitive segregation, the various themes that rationalise sentence enhancement will be subject to reinterpretation and rearrangement. Nietzsche suggests that in this process some of the meaning and purposes will be re-imagined, obscured or maybe lost. Thus, while the utilitarian/ consequentialist frame has the potential to legitimate and promote demands for rehabilitation, as much as promote longer and more severe incarceration, it is the latter aspects that will be taken to be the key rationale. In turn it is in this context that the retributive dimensions of lesbian and gay demands for state violence will have particular significance and influence.

Of importance here is the way sentence enhancement signifies homophobic violence as the *exceptional.* This also resonates with suggestions that there is an epidemic of violence. 'Epidemic' stands for novelty: the novelty of the appearance of homophobic violence as disorder and the novelty of an awareness of the scale of such violence. These novelties ignore a past of systematic homophobic violence legitimated both in and through the state institutions of safety and security (Perry 2001). 'Exceptional' also resonates with a perception, promoted by contemporary law and order politics, that violent crime is a growing problem and a sign of social crisis. It is particularly in this context that a sexual politics that exposes the ordinariness of homophobic violence resonates with the politics of punitive segregation.

Making an event exceptional is a technique of making a claim on the nation that relates to the wider contemporary restructuring of national personhood identified by Berlant (1997, 2000, 2001). Berlant shows how the exceptional and the traumatic have come to be the major methods for people in the US to tell their relationship to the state and thereby be entitled to state belonging and protection. Telling has to be novel and exceptional rather than mundane and everyday, it has to make an impact and it should be a transformative event (trauma should transport from one life to another through its power as exceptional). By eclipsing tales of everyday suffering and structural inequality, exceptional trauma enables a more powerful moral position to be taken and therefore a greater claim to be made. The trauma generated through violence is a powerful form of exceptional personhood, legitimating greater claims for retribution as the next section will show.

## Emotional attachments to violence

We want to linger a little longer over the demand for more severe punishments to focus attention upon the nature of the legitimation that is being produced here. First, we want to return to Murphy and Hampton's comments about the emotions associated with criminal law:

> Criminal law institutionalizes certain *feelings of anger, resentment and even hatred* that are typically directed towards wrong doers, especially if we are the victims of those wrong doers.
>
> (1988: 63; emphasis added)

In this quotation Murphy and Hampton point to certain emotions, 'anger', 'resentment', 'hate'. More specifically, they suggest that criminal law institutionalises these emotions. These emotions identified in relation to resort to state violence pose a particular challenge for a contemporary sexual politics of violence as they seem to promote that which the new laws seek to bring to an end. We want to explore the relationship between punishment and these emotions. In particular we want to further consider the emotions associated with the theme of 'retribution', which appears to be so central to a contemporary sexual politics that demands state violence.

In pursuit of this objective we turn first to the image of retribution as a relation of credit and debt. It is a relation the heart of what Shane Phelan (2001) has described as legal or 'negative' citizenship (p. 23). Here the state as the provider and guarantor of security takes the role of creditor to the citizen debtor. The original 'credit' takes the form of the state's provision of privileges, in particular safety and security. The citizen's debt is paid as individual obedience to the laws and institutions that produce and sustain this social order of safety and security. A violation of law by the citizen interrupts the satisfaction of the ongoing debt. Punishment is the means whereby the state calls in the debt and extracts the outstanding value. This relation of credit and debt offers an extended metaphor that makes punishment intelligible in particular ways: it provides a scheme of valorisation and it offers a way of making sense of the violence of the law as a phenomenon that is managed and administered. Furthermore, this extended metaphor makes punishment an economy that works with themes of equality, balance, harmony and stability (Solomon 1999).

A reflection by Nietzsche, on punishment as a relation of credit/debt, offers some other examples. He describes the outstanding debt and the process of its repayment in the following terms:

> Hence [the criminal] is not only stripped of his advantages as is only just, but drastically reminded what these advantages are worth. The rage of the defrauded creditor, the community, returns him to the wild and outlawed condition from which heretofore he had been protected. It rejects him, and henceforth every kind of hostility may vent itself upon

him. Punishment at this level of morality simply mimics the normal attitude toward a hated enemy who has been conquered and disarmed, who forfeits not only every right to protection but all mercy as well.

(Nietzsche 1956: Bk 2, IX, 203–4)

Here Nietzsche draws attention to various themes associated with retribution. In order to demonstrate the full value of the unpaid debt the debtor is purged from the domain of law and given an experience of the 'wild', as an outlaw. Retribution is connected here to purification. Once outsider, the one who has failed to obey the law is in the position of the 'enemy'. In this position as debtor he/she is not only outside law's order and security, but is also subject to the full unmediated force of law. A popular contemporary manifestation of this logic of punishment is to be found in references to various 'wars' on crime. As an enemy of the law (and the law-abiding citizen) the state's resort to the full force of law becomes a legitimate practice.

Of particular interest here is the range of emotions associated with this legitimate hostility. Nietzsche pinpoints one, hatred. Others associated with 'hostility' include anger, ill-will and malice. These echo the emotions identified by Murphy and Hampton. The connection between retribution and the criminal law provides a means whereby these emotions inform and infuse the law.

Nietzsche makes reference to other emotional ties: to the role of fear and terror in punishment. He also suggests that there are others that are more 'difficult', 'embarrassing' and 'underground'. 'Let us ask once more,' he suggests, 'in what sense could pain constitute repayments of a debt?' (p. 197). In reply, he concludes that the satisfaction of an outstanding debt connects pain to the creditor's 'supreme pleasure'. He explains:

In exchange for damage he had incurred, including his displeasure, the creditor received an extraordinary amount of pleasure; something he prized the more highly the more it disaccorded with his social rank.

(Nietzsche 1956: Bk 2, VI, 197)

Nietzsche offers an insight into a diverse range of emotions, some more commonly acknowledged than others, that may be generated and deployed in and through the legal practice of retribution. Some have particular resonance in the context of the histories of lesbians and gay men as objects of law's violence. Same-sex practices have long suffered the ignominy of being outlawed, characterised as impure (Mason 2001), as a threat to the state and thereby subjected to the full force of law's violence. The attempts to name homophobic violence as violence motivated by 'hate' echoes the past and present of these emotional attachments within a politics of heterosexuality. At the same time, we want to suggest, the creation of new criminal categories of 'hate' crime offers to reproduce them in the service of what many would call an emancipatory political project.

Nor does this exhaust the emotional ties produced in and through retribution. Solomon (1999) points to another emotion commonly associated with retribution: vengeance. He argues, 'emotion' in relation to law has negative connotations. Emotion is and continues to be understood as something that is antithetical to law and criminal justice. Emotion is not rational, it is associated with its opposite: the irrational.[4] This is the case not only in relation to vengeance, but also in relation to emotions generally, including 'hate', 'anger' and 'malice'. It is in this context that Solomon's critical analysis of the fate of vengeance as an emotion has wider significance. Using Solomon's work on vengeance we examine the fate of emotional attachments made in and through the law.

As an 'emotion', Solomon notes, vengeance is made an untempered, immediate, unruly, and an uncontrolled response to wrongdoing. In addition, we would add, 'emotion' also individualises, personalises and pathologises vengeance (Govier 2002). In contrast to this, punishment as a law-bound practice is celebrated as impersonal, tempered, measured, reasonable: an institution that is a rule-bound and reasoned response to wrong. Thus as an 'emotion' vengeance has no place in punishment through law. Vengeance, as a legitimate form of punishment, is disavowed. Solomon challenges this by arguing that, vengeance is 'both an intense emotion and a cool, calculating strategy' (p. 127). As such, vengeance is made in the image of law. We also add another dimension to his argument.

Vengeance brings together the emotional dimensions of law and law's violence. If we return to the meaning of vengeance via *The Oxford English Dictionary*, we find a definition of vengeance as punishment that involves the infliction of injury, hurt and harm. Vengeance is a characterisation of punishment that highlights the violence of punishment and thereby the violence of law. It is in this context that the fabrication of vengeance as emotion has particular significance. Emotion as a category of denigration, in its link with vengeance, works to disavow the place of vengeance/violence in punishment in particular and in law in general. Through emotion the injury and harm that constitute vengeance is made violence over against punishment made in the image of the reason of law. Thereby the violence of the law is disavowed and displaced on to vengeance as a degraded category (Sarat 2001). Solomon's analysis of vengeance as a cool and calculating strategy by which injury and harm may be inflicted offers to reconnect violence to law. More specifically, it makes that connection by making the violence of vengeance in the image of law: as rational violence, but also as moral.

One context in which the rationality of vengeance is made is through the link between retribution and vengeance. Through this link the credit/debt metaphor of retribution is connected to the idea of vengeance. The 're' of re-venge draws attention to the fact that vengeance is a response to and the return of, a prior act: a re-payment. This re-turn places vengeance in the frame of a potentially civilising economy of violence: just deserts. In turn just deserts connotes equality, balance, harmony and stability.

At the same time this economy of return is presented as a problematic dimension of revenge. Revenge may give rise to another return, which may escalate into further acts or revenge. This is a problem particularly associated with revenge as a practice of individuals. This brings us to another dimension of the rationalisation of vengeance in law.

In law, vengeance is a practice that takes place in the context of law's monopoly of violence (a feature of law's violence we highlighted in Chapter 2). Law's monopoly of violence ensures that the relation of vengeance to revenge is not a relation that leads to a spiral of escalating violence. In fact, law's monopoly of vengeance ensures that this cycle is brought to an early end. Girard's (1989) work on law's violence as a sacrificial economy offers one of the better-known examples of the capacity of law's monopoly of vengeance to break the cycle of individual revenge.

At the same time the institutionalisation of vengeance in and through the law as violence generates problematic effects: Austin Sarat (1997) identifies the victim's perceived loss of agency in and through these state practices of vengeance. Various initiatives, such as better police and prosecutorial relations with the victims, and the development of institutional settings within the criminal justice system for the victim to directly influence and inform the process, such as victim impact statements, are examples of attempts to address this state of affairs. In this way using violence as a resource to make a claim on the state (as we demonstrated in Chapter 1) becomes a way of gaining back the control that has been lost through violence itself.

It is in this context that the proximity of vengeance and retribution has particular significance. As an economy of credit to debt, and more specifically as a re-turn, vengeance is made in the image of a calculation: reason and resource. Thereby vengeance is civilised, legitimised and made into a moral prerogative. Linking retribution to vengeance provides a means whereby violence is reconnected to law. It is also a movement that makes law's violence into good violence.

It is at this point that we need to return to the other 'emotions' of 'hate', 'anger' and 'malice'. As emotions their place in law may be denied and disavowed. Solomon's analysis and our take, on the fate of vengeance as emotion and its rehabilitation, also have significance for these 'forbidden' emotions. The economy of retribution provides a means whereby their degraded status as emotions may be reinterpreted and overcome, rendered invisible. As dimensions of retribution they become civilised (they disappear) by being made in the image of reason and rationality: they take their place as a part of law's legitimacy. 'Choosing' to use these emotions as a resource becomes a matter of rational choice, a response to one's place (one's self) in front of law.

## Conclusion

In this chapter we have added a new dimension to the analysis of lesbian and gay demands for law's violence. In the law and order context these demands are associated with a politics of retribution and revenge. It is in this conjunction that a politics of sexual identity informed by a desire for recognition seems to be giving form to a 'politics of recrimination and rancour' which, in Wendy Brown's (1995a) critique seem to 'disdain freedom rather than practice it' (p. 202). Our particular concern has been to explore some of the emotional attachments to unfreedom, 'that can be discerned in contemporary political formations ostensibly concerned with emancipation' (Brown 1995a: xii).

It is in the guise of reason and civility that the lesbian and gay emotional attachments of hate, anger, malice and revenge, take shape through demands for access to state violence. At the same time it is also in this form that these emotional attachments disappear, being disavowed in the name of law as reason and moral right. That moral right may take various forms: through 'legal moralism'[5] lesbians and gays frame their argument for access to state violence by reference to popular sentiment. For example the current popular support for the prohibition of 'hate crime' to protect 'vulnerable' minorities through the law becomes an accepted moral position, a form of political rhetoric, to advocate the incorporation of sexual orientation into the category of 'hate crime'. 'Equality' offers a second set of moral arguments. Here equality is a free-standing value, not one that establishes its significance by reference to popular support. All citizens should have equal access to the resources of the institutions dedicated to safety and security. In turn, all minorities should be given equal status and therefore should be treated as the same in law (Thatchell 2002). Both legal moralism and equality offer civil means of connecting lesbian and gay politics to a logic that disavows the emotional attachments that have in the past been associated with legitimate oppression and social exclusion of those who have same-sex genital relations. Furthermore they offer to dignify the hate and malice that is connected to this sexual politics by naming it reason and justice.

We would suggest that it is through these connections that attempts to turn the state against itself are always/already informed by the virtues and values that lesbians and gay men are seeking to challenge.

Following on from Chapter 2, this chapter has also explicated the contradictory and paradoxical claims that are packed into the demand for law. We have demonstrated a troubling potential within contemporary sexual politics which aligns with the very emotions that it seeks to challenge and change. We seek to break the silence that attaches to these emotional investments that are made in the name of emancipation. In the last chapter it was the use of violence as a resource that was seen to be particularly problematic. In this chapter it is the use of 'choice' to be a good citizen (or good self) that presents us with problems when examining political claims. Responses to violence through vengeance become a means of restoring the supposed power and agency of the self that has been exposed to violence. The lesbian and gay demands based on punitive segregation, retribution and vengeance expose a desire for spatial and physical difference which position some cultures and the self as wrong and bad.

It is also worth pointing out how the demands for law mirror so many other forms of exclusion, in which the other is designated beyond the self, beyond redemption. These different demands and spatialisations by different groups create a struggle in front of the law, where only those with access to the right resources for being recognised and getting their claims heard can win. And in the telling of the stories of violence, through the techniques and production of 'hate crime' and trauma, a new form of personhood is produced which corresponds with the more general eclipsing of everyday violence. It is a move away from everyday homophobia to the incident, the event, that can be told in which the victim is able to make a relationship to the state that would be denied those for whom everyday suffering is less dramatic. It is of these wider dimensions of sexual politics that we need to be cognisant.

This chapter is a call to bring these investments into view so that the terms of a lesbian and gay commitment to hate, malice, vengeance can be discussed and if necessary affirmed. It is also a call for the consideration of alternatives.

In drawing attention to the emotional investments that are being made in and through a lesbian gay politics of law and order it is not our intention to dismiss the turn to 'hate' or 'bias' crimes on the basis that they will be ineffective or destructive of social cohesion. Nor is it our intention to suggest hate crime activism should be abandoned merely because it appears to generate a politics of revenge. Maybe if heterosexual violence is to be taken seriously as disorderly behaviour and its everyday operation is to come to an end then retribution and revenge has a part to play. Furthermore it may be necessary to invoke retribution and revenge in the context of the most intimate and banal acts (the minor incivilities) through which the heterosexual order comes into being. The experiences of lesbians and gay men offer countless examples of the importance of the smallest and the most intimate details of same-sex relations in the production of heterosexual order. The deployment of retribution and revenge for a heterosexual order is not limited to major wrongs (whatever they might be) but has been put into operation in the service of social order by way of an obsessive concern with minor incivilities attributed to those engaging in same-sex relations. We consider that it is problematic merely to criticise a well-established and legitimated use of law's violence merely because it is being used to give birth to a new social order.

Our objective is to provoke more debate on these issues. In disturbing the relationships between sexuality, state and violence that are being forged in the context of a lesbian and gay politics of violence and safety, we seek to draw attention to the complex and contradictory nature of the relationship. We hope that we have helped to contribute to a debate that will query the alliance that queers are making with law and order.

We now want to turn our attention to our third and final challenge to lesbian and gay demands for state violence. It is a challenge that arises out of changes in the crime control landscape which suggest the institutional limits and new institutional forms of crime control.

# 4 The limits of law and order
## Individual responsibility

### Introduction

Our third and final challenge to lesbian and gay demands for state violence again arises in the context of contemporary debates about the role of the state in the provision of internal security and safety. A feature of the current crime control agenda, Garland suggests, is the announcement that the capacity of the sovereign state to ensure safety and security, in the face of crime in general and violence in particular, is limited. The novelty of this official declaration indicates that crime control is being re-imagined. The sovereign state is no longer to be thought of as either the only, or the primary, provider of safety and security in response to violence (Garland 1996). Instead, the new institutional landscape of crime control is one of 'partnerships' and 'networks' of public and private institutions. A key dimension of this new model of crime control is private responsibility. The morally responsible individual (or self) is a key provider of safety and security in this new order of crime control.

This new landscape has particular significance for the lesbian and gay turn to the state as the key institutional provider of safety and security from violence. In general lesbian and gay politics of violence and safety work with an expectation that the state will or can provide effective security and safety. Garland's work suggests that this is problematic. We want to focus on one particular challenge that arises from this state of affairs. In exploring the issues raised we draw upon some of our data generated in the two research locations, Lancaster and Manchester.

For a prolonged period, due to state hostility, lesbians and gays have had primary responsibility for their own safety and security from homophobic violence. Now, a major dimension of the state's new and more positive response to lesbian and gay safety needs is to require that lesbians and gay men assume responsibility for their own security. There is considerable irony in this state of affairs. The role of the state seems to be to tell lesbians and gay men what they already know and practise; self-management of safety and security (Corteen 2002; Mason 2001). In this chapter we want to examine this particular dimension of the 'new' police response to lesbian and gay safety needs in more detail.

We begin by turning to the UK's *Guide to Identifying and Combating Hate Crime*.[1] It offers an example of the institutional challenges to be found in the contemporary landscape of crime control that frames the issues we want to address in this chapter. The *Guide* is the primary police text in the UK which sets out a model for police responses to hate crime, including homophobic violence. The subtitle of the *Guide* is 'Breaking the power of fear and hate'. Hate crime is generously defined in the guide in the following terms: 'a crime where the perpetrator's prejudice against any identifiable group of people is a factor in determining who is victimised' (ACPO 2000: 1). This includes, 'Any incident which is perceived to be homophobic by the victim or any other person' (p. 1). Following the definitions section, the *Guide* opens with 'The New Agenda' which begins with the following statement: 'Hate Crime is a most repugnant form of crime.' Together these definitions and statements appear to point to a new willingness by the police to recognise hate crime in general and homophobic violence in particular as a serious threat to order.

The *Guide* then turns our attention to the police response to this violence. It begins with the following remarks:

> *The police service alone cannot be effective in combating it.* The active support of partner agencies, group leaders, communities, witnesses and victims is essential to effective prevention and investigation.
>
> (ACPO 2000: 1; emphasis added)

This draws attention to the contemporary context in which lesbian and gay demands for state violence in response to homophobic violence are being made. Just as lesbian and gay activism succeeds in documenting the everyday reality of homophobic violence, and appears to change the police attitudes to lesbian and gay demands for the state services of safety and security, these demands are met with official declarations of the limits of policing.

The state institutions dedicated to the task of securing the safety associated with good order, we are now told, are incapable, on their own, of achieving internal security and safety. This public declaration of the limits of the sovereign state is connected to shifts in crime control: the promotion of private and multi-agency initiatives. Internal safety and security is now not so much a state monopoly but an activity undertaken by a complex network of organisations both public and private. In the US and the UK in particular, the neo-liberal folding back of the state, where markets intervene in areas previously occupied by the state, promotes the idea and practice of safety and security as a matter of consumption rather than a part of state-provided welfare. Individuals are now formally recognised as key players responsible for the provision of their own safety and security. The demand for law and the problems and the perils of pursuing the purportedly emancipatory political demand for the good violence of the state therefore have to be viewed within the context of this changing landscape of changing state and person relationships, and shifting responsibilities for internal safety and security. Our challenge is to question the assumptions about the role of the state that continue to inform the lesbian and gay politics of violence and safety.

## New limits and forms of crime control

Garland notes that over and against punitive segregation that emphasises the state's monopoly of violence, there is, in simultaneous operation, another very different landscape of crime control. Here the emergence of everyday crime is connected to a different set of responses. The 'everyday' of crime, Garland suggests, gives a, '. . . new focus . . . upon the supply of criminal opportunities and the existence of "criminogenic situations"' (p. 16). Attention centres not upon individuals but upon,

> the routines of interaction, environmental design and the structure of controls and incentives that are brought to bear upon them. The new policy advice is to concentrate on substituting prevention for cure, reducing the supply of opportunities, increasing situational and social controls, and modifying everyday routines.
>
> (Garland 2001: 16)

In institutional terms, far from having a monopoly over responses to crime the state now, Garland suggests, seeks to,

> spread out the crime control effort beyond the specialist state organizations [sic] that previously sought to monopolize it.
>
> (2001: 17)

Disorder and insecurity is now being addressed through state institutions set within a multi-agency network (Newburn 2001) which include other state institutions, such as local government, as well as institutions of civil society, such as voluntary and community organisations (Crawford 1997). In the tradition of neo-liberalism the diffusion of responsibility for safety and security extends to link private institutions to those of the state. These may take the form of the use of private security services to police order and the use of insurance schemes to provide a certain economic security as a way of managing the financial insecurity that flows from (property) crimes.[2]

Individuals are formally incorporated into this network via self-responsibility, which involves an official expectation (and corresponding political rhetoric) that promotes the perspective that individuals should take more responsibility for their personal safety and security. Hence, the state becomes a provider of *advice* to individuals on crime prevention and security management. This advice may also connect to other state, voluntary and private provision. The private consumption of security and safety services offers, perhaps, the most immediate experience of the limits of the state as a provider of safety and security. It demonstrates how the state supports the moral position of the law by legitimating the claims that are made – they must correspond with the advice that is given. But by not providing any means to resource the individual responsibility, state responsibility transfers to the private sector. The individual then has to make the 'choice' of taking up these private provisions. To not make the 'choice' is to show irresponsibility and bad judgement and a refusal to care for the self.

Garland (2001) describes the decline of the state monopoly of institutions of crime control and the development of a security network, as a 'responsibilization strategy' (p. 124). This security network of responsibilities is comprised of people and organisations that have been allocated a duty to participate in crime control practices. The role of the state becomes to activate these responsibilities through non-state organisations and actors. This network is also connected by accountability. A failure to satisfy the requirements of private and individual responsibility for safety and security may impact on a person's status as a good victim and citizen. In turn this may impact upon evaluations of that person's worth in terms of access to state provision of safety and security (Phelan 2001; Stanko 1999). We focus on the theme of individual responsibility within this landscape of crime control in order to explore and highlight some of the institutional limits and challenges that a lesbian and gay politics of violence and safety needs to address.

## Responsible citizenship

The emergence of lesbians and gay men who chose to be responsible individuals as key players in crime control has many interesting and contradictory dimensions. One dimension of this is suggested in Garland's observation that:

> For the first time since the formation of the modern criminal justice state, governments have begun to acknowledge a basic sociological truth: that the most important processes producing order and conformity are mainstream social processes, located within the institutions of civil society, not the uncertain threat of legal sanctions.
>
> (2001: 126)

We would agree that individual responsibility for safety and security is hardly a new reality. However, the lesbian and gay experience of this state of affairs suggests a need to approach Garland's observations with some caution. In the past (and we would argue also in the present) the burden of individual responsibility for personal safety and security has not fallen evenly on the shoulders of all individuals. For lesbians and gay men responsibility for safety and security arises from the fact that the state provision of safety and security has long been denied. In many instances, individual strategies of taking responsibility for safety were developed in response not only to the violence of private individuals but also in response to the violence, and the threat of violence, of the state. What differs is that in the past, individual lesbian and gay responsibility for safety and security was not so much associated with citizenship, but rather a mark of lesbian and gay oppression, and lesbian and gay exclusion from citizenship. There is considerable irony for lesbians and gay men in the suggestion that the practices that marked their exclusion in and through the infrastructure of criminal justice might now be a feature of their inclusion through the contemporary infrastructure of that same social institution of safety and security. Certainly some of the lesbian participants in our research focus groups were blatantly aware of the cynicism and spin behind 'new' crime control initiatives (Corteen 2002).

We want to examine one context in which the strategy of 'making responsible' is being generated in more detail: the formulation and dissemination of safety advice. We will briefly examine two examples of police safety advice taken from our two research locations.

The first example comes from Manchester. Published by the Greater Manchester Police, it takes the form of *A Guide to Personal Security* (MacKenzie 2000). As such it is not advice specific to lesbians and gay men; it is, as the guide explains, 'for everyone'. At the same time it includes a section dedicated to lesbian and gay security under the rubric of 'Gay and Lesbian Hate Crime'. First, let us focus on the security advice to lesbians and gay men.

It is brief. Advice takes the form of a direction to report gay and lesbian hate crime to the police or another agency. The lesbian and gay reader is also directed to 'Further reading and advice', where we find a short list of three organisations and contact numbers providing 'lesbian and gay advice/counselling'. In addition, the reader is directed to read the 'points raised under the racist incidents section'. However, the only advice here is a repetition of the direction to report the incident. Let us follow the police instructions and turn to the more general advice.

The guidance offered to 'everyone' is organised by various headings, including the following: attacks, on public transport, while walking alone at night, driving alone (including breakdowns), while sitting in your car in traffic, being followed on the street. In the home, the imagined perpetrators of violence are outsiders, described as nuisance callers, doorstep crooks, bogus workers and dealers. Common to all these locations and characterisations of insecurity and un-safety is an association between danger and perpetrators of violence who are unknown to the victim (frequently referred to as stranger danger). This is also a theme found in the context of the advice specific to lesbians and gays. Under the rubric, 'Gay and lesbian', the only location of danger mentioned is 'cruising grounds', which seems to exclude all reference to the security problems and safety needs of lesbians.

A second example of safety advice offered to lesbians and gay men comes from a leaflet about hate crime produced by the Lancashire police. It is entitled 'Action against hate crime'. It contains a section on 'safety talk', in which the police urge lesbians and gay men to: 'Be Streetwise, Don't be a Target'. Various aspects of the 'safety talk' are of interest. Danger is associated with particular (public) locations: 'clubs, pubs and cafes . . . badly lit streets, dense shrubbery, alleyways and hidden door ways . . .' The safety advice includes the following instructions: 'don't walk alone', 'project self confidence', 'leave with someone'. Again, the locations and advice are infused with the logic of stranger danger; a logic that has long been exposed by feminist research on crime control as being wrongly focused.[3]

It would be wrong to conclude that the locations pinpointed in these documents, or the focus on stranger danger, have no significance for lesbians and gay men. Various victim surveys, for example in the UK, Stonewall's *Queer Bashing* (Mason and Palmer 1996), a Scottish survey of gay men in Edinburgh (Morrison and Mackay 2000) and *Low Down* (GALOP 2001), a survey[4] of the experiences of black and ethnic minority lesbians and gay men, offer some support for the particular importance of stranger-danger and violence in public places. At the same time, there is evidence to suggest that significant danger takes other forms. For example, research produced by the Greater Manchester Lesbian and Gay Policing Initiative, 'Lesbians' experiences of violence and harassment' (GML & GPI 1999) indicates that 42 per cent of reported violence against lesbians took place away from the street: 18 per cent in the home, 17 per cent in the workplace, and 7 per cent in lesbian and gay venues. In turn, when perpetrators are known to the victim, 35.6 per cent were neighbours, 24 per cent work colleagues, 19 per cent family members, 14 per cent ex-partners, 5 per cent partners and 3 per cent friends (see also Valentine and Johnston 1995; Valentine 1998). Research on reports of homophobic violence to the police in London demonstrates that most perpetrators of homophobic violence are neighbours and family members (Metropolitan Police 2002).

When placed in this context, the lack of references to violence in and near the home and workplace (including schools and colleges), or the lack of mention of the danger posed by persons known to those who suffer the violence, has a rather different significance. Making invisible significant locations and relations of violence reproduces myths about the nature of the danger and safety lesbians and gay men experience.[5] At best, the police safety literature may merely tell gay men and lesbians what they already know and already practise. At worst, it produces strategies of becoming responsible that may work to perpetuate the vulnerability, insecurity and lack of safety of lesbians and gay men.

Another dimension of the safety advice is also significant. The authors of the Manchester security guide explain that the advice is intended to be, 'thought-provoking to get you to examine your lifestyle'. Various points are of interest here. Security (and insecurity) is formulated not so much a matter

of policing, but a question of 'lifestyle'. Security becomes a project of examination and evaluation of that 'lifestyle'. The guide goes on to explain the
terms of that examination, which involves 'crime risk' analysis. Crime risk
management has the objective of ensuring that an individual's 'lifestyle' is
crime free: 'just one crime is one too many'.

This example illustrates features of what Garland describes as the 'criminology of the self'. Crime control here becomes a 'problem of life' (Rose
1989), focusing not on the perpetrator of violence but on the possible victim,
on the choice that the victim makes and on the way they take responsibility
for the 'care of the self'.

Only one feature of gay and lesbian 'lifestyle' is singled out in the
examples of this literature referred to above. Cruising in a public place is *the*
'lifestyle' crime risk. From this, we can probably safely assume that this
lifestyle crime risk relates only to gay men. This seems to suggest either that
lesbian lifestyles are free of crime risk, which is clearly contradicted by
evidence drawn from research or victim surveys, or that the risks lesbians
face have yet to be translated into risks that are formally recognised and
codified. Another point is that the crime risks identified bear a remarkable
similarity to the signs of same-sex behaviour, which have in the past (and in
the present) marked gay men as deviant, dysfunctional and pathological
(Weeks 1981). Perhaps, the change, if any, is that they are now taken to be
factors that might precipitate exclusion by normalisation rather than criminalisation (Phelan 2001; Robson 1998). Furthermore, the safety literature of the
state appears to be perpetuating associations between particular sexualised
(and gendered) identities (inflected by class and race) and danger (Madriz
1997; Stanko 1988), leaving out of the picture the sexualised and gendered
behaviour of those who perform the violence (Stanko 1997).

In framing security and safety in terms of a 'lifestyle' that can be managed
and risks that can be reduced, the literature reproduces an assumption that
individuals, in general, and lesbians and gay men in particular, can *choose* to
be and can choose not to be a victim of homophobic violence. This is
problematic in various ways. It seems to directly contradict other messages in
police hate crime literature suggesting that it is the perpetrator's perception
of the sexuality of the object of his/her violence, rather than the sexual
orientation of the one assaulted or abused, that informs homophobic
incidents. Lifestyle management undertaken by the victim may be remote
from the causes and experience of violence. In turn lifestyle changes may
have little effect as lesbians and gay men have little or no control over a
perpetrator's assumptions and intentions. Gail Mason (2001) has also noted
a more general problem with the management of lesbian and gay sexuality.
She suggests that the 'imperative to manage one's homosexuality is . . . an
imperative to manage the unmanageable' (Mason 2001). This conclusion is
based upon her analysis of the trope of visibility, which, she suggests
(following Eve Sedgwick), is central to the politics of homosexuality (p. 81).
Visibility (being in or out of the closet) is, 'the "defining structure" for

lesbian and gay oppression in the twentieth century' (p. 81). The ambiguity of visibility (being both positive and negative – good and bad) generates both the imperative to manage and the impossibility of achievable management. When translated into the context of safety literature the imperative to manage becomes an imperative to responsible citizenship. To paraphrase Mason's earlier conclusions this 'imperative to responsibility is an imperative to achieve the unachievable'. This suggests that far from offering a form of security, this approach to safety may work to more firmly link the victim's management of safety to the violent event as one of its 'causes'.

It is particularly ironic that the skills developed as a survival strategy by those socially excluded in response to state hostility are now being fed back to them by the state and used to evaluate the victim's contribution to the violent event. No wonder the lesbian and gay participants in our research were so scathing. These practices of safety are being recycled to (re)produce social exclusion, now as formal state policy in the name of both protection and choice. Furthermore, the normalising dynamic of the safety literature carries in its wake new modes of blaming, by making a distinction between good victims and bad victims (Stanko 1999; Tomsen 2001). While some may welcome the appearance of this safety literature as evidence of the success of a politics of recognition and the incorporation of lesbians and gay men into legal or 'negative' citizenship in which citizens trade obedience to the laws in exchange for protection (Phelan 2001: 23), we would raise a note of caution. Our reading of that literature suggests that such recognition remains limited and in some respects severely flawed.

At best, the benefits of the turn to individual responsibility might be the codification of safety knowledge and expertise, that is already well-known and extensively practised. At worst, it reproduces myths and misinformation that represent long-standing institutional investments that misrepresent the reality of everyday violence, giving institutional credence to problematic ontological assumptions. While it would be premature to conclude that these problems are necessarily reproduced in all the institutional contexts that have emerged to manage this 'criminology of the self', the analysis offered here suggests there is a need for caution. Much more research needs to be done to examine the practices and effects of these different contexts. This is of particular significance because of the diffusion of crime control across a range of sites, through the new 'criminology of the self' orthodoxy of multi-agency and community partnerships.

A final aspect of the safety and security advice to which we want to draw attention relates to what Stanko and Curry (1997) have described as the 'self at risk'. 'Lifestyle' offers to produce identity in general, and lesbian and gay identity in particular, in terms of ontological vulnerability and ontological insecurity. Giddens' (1991) analysis of the emergence of 'ontological (in)security' offers some insights into this idea of the 'self at risk'. He suggests that the emergence of 'ontological (in)security' needs to be placed in the wider context of modernity, where loss of trust in professionals is a key dynamic. This assumes, of course, that trust was once invested in professionals, which for lesbians and gay men is problematic. However, this lesbian and gay ontological state needs to be placed in the specific context of the politics of crime control, which is a politics of trust. Following Garland, the emergence of the criminology of the self is connected to public declarations of the limits of a professionalised criminal justice system. The rise of the various institutions and practices associated with this 'criminology of the self' might be interpreted as a formal acceptance of a loss of trust in criminal justice professionals and attempts to re-establish trust, but this time by way of security networks and private responsibility.[6] It may be that the rest of society, once protected by and invested in the state (the white heterosexual middle-class), is now catching up with the exclusions which were long been experienced by other groups (the homosexual, the working-class, the raced). And this may be why the demands for law represent a particular white middle-class response. They emerge from a position of once-belonging, of once-ontological security, and it is that which is being eroded.

At the same time, Garland's work also offers a different analysis of contemporary responses to the loss of trust indicated by Giddens. The juxtaposition of punitive segregation and 'the criminology of the self' is of significance here. Demands for sentence enhancement offer evidence of renewed trust and confidence in state violence and state institutions of safety and security, whilst at the same time the official declaration that the police cannot realise safety and security institutionalises a certain limit to that trust. In turn, the safety literature deploys and institutionalises ontological insecurity in support of state-sponsored regimes of social order, promoting a moral position on choice which, as Strathern (1992) argues, in the terms of compulsory individuality, the individual has no choice but to chose. To not do so would be to occupy the position of irresponsibility in which no demands could be made on law.

## Conclusion

The declaration that frames this chapter, that the sovereign state has a limited capacity to realise the safety and security for individuals and the community, raises some challenges for lesbian and gay politics of violence and safety. At the same time it needs to be treated with some caution. What is the 'novelty' of this state of affairs?

The limit to the sovereign state is hardly a novel dimension of lesbian and gay experiences of state provision of safety and security from violence. For many, the limits of the state are well established. Victim surveys report that for many lesbians and gay men the day-to-day reality of their encounters with violence highlights the limited role of the sovereign state to provide safety and security. But, in this context the limit is seen as contingent, rather than a necessary or inevitable aspect of the state. This is evidenced in lesbian and gay responses to these reported limits. There is a renewed turn to the state and demand for reform, which centralises the state as the provider of safety and security.

One context in which these issues are being explored and assumptions about the importance of the state are being reproduced is in a debate about the 'under-reporting' of violence against lesbians and gay men. The police frequently point to 'under-reporting' as a limit upon their ability to take this violence more seriously. Victim surveys do consistently suggest that only a small percentage of incidents are reported to the police (see, for example, Greater Manchester Lesbian and Gay Policing Initiative (GML & GPI) 1999; Group 1999; Kuehnle 2001; Mason 1996; Morrison and Mackay 2000; National Coalition of Anti-Violence Programmes (NCAVP) 1999; Sandroussi 1995). Yet, these victim surveys also report that perceptions and expectations of prejudice continue to be key factors in limiting access to the operation of the institutions of the sovereign state, limiting their operation when finally called upon. Even in those jurisdictions where the law requires the composition of 'official' statistics, reports of homophobic incidents are less frequent than other 'hate crimes', such as racial and gender violence (Perry 2001). Official reports remain low even in locations where more positive relations with the police appear to be relatively well established.[7] In response to the practical limits of the sovereign state, both activists and the police have worked to improve reporting mechanisms through new direct systems and through third party (private) reporting schemes.

How are we to make sense of this state of affairs? What assumptions about the role of the state are produced in this context of an imperative to report? What significance does the limit of the sovereign state have in this expanded context?

One of the key factors here is the importance of the 'crime paradigm'. The crime paradigm informs the victim surveys that purport to document the 'gap' between 'community' and 'official' sources of information, giving rise to an assumption that the current limits of the state are problematic. The particular limits that 'produce' under-reporting are assumed to be contingent upon a particular politics of gender and sexuality (Phelan 2001), rather than structural (a part of the current crime control landscape). As the limits of the sovereign state appear as changeable, the security role can generally be enhanced.

There is also a second assumption, suggesting that those who have suffered harms arising out of violence will want to define either the incident or the injuries as 'criminal'. In turn, once so defined, it presupposes that individuals will necessarily turn to the protective institutional mechanisms traditionally associated with 'crime', the state institutions of policing and criminal justice more generally (Bumiller 1987). While 'third party' reporting mechanisms, which facilitate reporting to a wider range of state and private institutions, evidence some recognition of the limits of the sovereign state to provide safety and security, as a response to under-reporting to the police, their ultimate objective is to assist the police. As such, they retain an assumption of the importance of the state as a provider of safety and security. The question of what can the police do in response is usually left out of the frame. This chapter suggests that a major response is not to turn attention on to the police but to turn attention back to the individual.

In turning back to the individual much is forgotten. The long tradition of lesbian and gay responsibility for safety and security tends to be ignored. Our own research data (Corteen 2002) and the work of other scholars (Mason 2001) offer numerous examples of the skill and expertise of lesbians and gay men in this respect. 'Under-reporting' needs to appear in the context of effective management of safety, not the failure of safety management. As Gail Mason (2001) notes, lesbians and gay men do not experience their practices and expertise as safety managers just in terms of an imposition imposed by and serving the interests of others and more specifically those who might oppress us. For lesbians and gay men safety management is also a question of caring for one's own self (p. 93). It is also about controlling and taking charge. It is about compliance *and* defiance. To reduce self-management to 'under-reporting' and expectations of prejudice is to devalue and to ignore much of lesbian and gay experience. It also fails to take seriously what we might learn about the existing specific policing needs of lesbians and gay men.

Current understandings of under-reporting must be challenged. Under-reporting is evidence of a lesbian and gay solution to violence management. Bumiller's work on women's management of violence points to the limits of the crime paradigm in making sense of violence and safety, suggesting it may be only be one (relatively insignificant) way of framing and responding to violence and the threat of violence. The crime paradigm may well be an exceptional (and final) way of making sense of, first, either the injury or the required response to help an individual manage incidents of violence, or second, the threat of violence, when all else fails, pointing to the urgency to address policing issues, but also of the need to be sensitive to the context. Little research exists on the context in which lesbians and gay men resort to the state services of safety and security. Much more research is needed to understand how and when law and criminal justice paradigms come into play in lesbian and gay attempts to make sense of violence and safety management; it is in this context that their failure is most acute.

It is perhaps in this context of safety management that the 'novelty' of the declaration of the limits of the sovereign state needs to be taken seriously. The problem we draw attention to here is the way the crime paradigm reproduces assumptions about the role of the state that need to be challenged. This paradigm is woefully out of line with the *realpolitik* of crime control and criminal justice.

Nor is this a problem that is specific to the contexts of under-reporting or safety advice. It points to a challenge that has wide spread significance and is applicable to all engagements with the institutions of policing and criminal justice system more generally.

There is much research that highlights the limits of policing in those contexts, where the police profess to perform the sovereign state's function as provider and guarantor of internal safety and security. The emerging body of work on recent reforms relating to the introduction of 'hate' and 'bias' crime is of particular importance here. It draws attention to many problem areas that limit the impact and effectiveness of those reforms. For example, hate crime research highlights the impact of particular gate-keepers in the naming of violence as 'hate' or 'bias' crime (Bell 2002; Boyd *et al.* 1996; Rosga 2001). Some have noted the way that police resistance to the idea that 'hate' motivated violence is a significant feature of their immediate society is a key factor that works against the criminalisation of violence categorised by way of 'hate' or 'bias' (Boyd *et al.* 1996). The police face many conflicting challenges in the management of the whole process of responding to violence: ensuring immediate security of the victim, pursuing the perpetrator and the investigation. The ambiguities and complexities of the events offer significant opportunities to disavow 'hate' or 'bias' (Bell 2002; Jacobs and Potter 1998). The various formulas used to criminalise 'hate' and 'bias' violence provide varying degrees of opportunity to limit the applicability of offences to particular acts of violence (Lawrence 1999; Jacobs and Potter 1998). In various ways these factors, this research suggests, may work to limit the possibility of naming the event as an instance of 'hate' or 'bias' and limit the pursuit of perpetrators, and frustrate attempt to punish wrong-doers. Work that focuses in particular on the criminalisation of homophobic hate in the wake of 'hate crime' reforms is still in the early stages of development. As a result there is less data on the institutional limits to lesbian and gay demands for state violence. At the same time there is sufficient evidence to suggest that there are and will continue to be many institutional limits. For example, much existing research on lesbian and gay experiences of these institutions shows that they continue to be homophobic.

The aspects of crime control we have explored in this chapter are not separate from the continued importance of the sovereign state as provider of internal safety and security, but connected to it. A focus upon the institutions and politics of punitive segregation that fails to address key aspects of the private, market-driven security network that is now providing safety and security will impose severe limits on the potential of any sexual politics to turn the state against itself. In this chapter we offer a reading of some of the limits of the turn to state support for and state demands of individual responsibility.

It is with these limits in mind that we now turn to examine in depth the private and individual acts of safety and security production and management that have been, and continue to be, so significant to lesbian and gay safety. In the chapters that follow, drawing upon our empirical data, we pursue an analysis of four dimensions of contemporary lesbian and gay politics and practices of safety and security. First, we explore the uses and limits of the rhetoric and politics of property, which has particular significance in the context of claims for recognition. The rhetoric and politics of property within the western liberal democratic tradition is intimately connected to claims upon the state for improved safety and security. As such, sensibilities and practices that in the first instance are to be associated with individuals, the private sphere and civil society, are not remote from claims made against the state. We then turn to examine other intelligibilities which inform and give shape and meaning to practices of safety and security. In Chapter 6 we explore comfort, which, we argue, is an affect associated with home, offering an exploration of the ways in which comfort works as a politics and rhetoric of belonging. This chapter offers a challenge to much existing scholarship on safety talk, drawing attention to the importance of belonging in the generation of experiences and practices of safety and security. At the same time we note that comfort is a politics and a rhetoric that is fraught with problems. By examining these problems, we explore how they are resolved on a day-to-day basis. We then turn to two further strategies used to manage safety and security, exploring these through debates about cosmopolitanism in Chapter 7 and through the uses of estrangement in the fabrication of safety and security in Chapter 8.

# 5 The rhetoric and politics of property

## Introduction

Property talk, we want to argue, is a pervasive feature of the everyday safety talk of lesbians and gay men. Property talk is to be found in common terms that indicate possession and belonging such as 'my' and 'mine', 'our' or 'ours'. Danielle, a key informant interviewee (KII) from Manchester,[1] provides an example of the use of everyday property talk in an observation about Manchester's gay Village. She explained:

> If heterosexuals come here then they need to be aware of what it is about and be friendly towards *our* needs and what we're about, and remember and respect. They're here on *our* invitation in a way because it is *our* space.
>
> (Danielle, KII, Man., 1999; emphasis added)

Her use of 'our' in this instance produces a particular range of meanings and effects. It conjoins lesbian and gay as subject(s) to an object, in this instance a particular 'place', 'the Village'. Danielle's observation also draws attention to the way in which this relation of subject(s) to object is also a relation between subjects. In this instance it is characterised as a relation both between lesbians and gays as subjects and between those subjects and heterosexuals (as subjects). It connects lesbian and gay subjects to the object in particular ways. 'The Village' is perceived as a possession and a place of belonging that gives shape and location to particular needs; identified with that space. As an inter-relation between subjects the subject/object relation is made a matter of representation, recognition, memory and control, coming together as a requirement that the lesbian and gay needs invested in the object are acknowledged, respected, complied with, preserved.

Property talk also has another dimension. Nick Blomley (1997) has noted that, 'To talk of property in legal and political terms is to talk of order' (p. 286). We would add that property talk, as talk of order, is also talk of safety and security. Likewise to talk of order and safety is also to talk of disorder, the loss of safety and the lack of security. Danielle's property talk offers an illustration. 'Our needs' refers to a particular order, which constitutes the safety and security that is at stake. 'Our space' is the location of that order of safety and security, talk of the disorder and the threat to that order which, in this instance, takes the form of heterosexuals and the location of the insecurity that flows therefrom. This talk of order/disorder is talk of the limits of the sphere of control, the borders.

Everyday property talk as safety talk relates to the nature of the investments in the object, control and the limits and boundaries of that control, where the distinction between order and disorder is most vividly experienced.

Our objective in this chapter is to offer an analysis of the rhetoric of property and the politics of property in order to consider its significance in the generation of everyday lesbian and gay experiences of safety and security (Sarat and Kearns 1993).

## The rhetoric and politics of property

The rhetoric of property has significant political purchase . . . the modern flexibility of the concept enables it to be deployed in a multitude of ways . . . The successful characterisation of a thing as an object of property, a process which takes place in everyday language, in law, and in political discourse, can be an immense strategic value both in engineering and retarding social change.

(Davies and Naffine 2001: 39)

In this extract Davies and Naffine suggest that the rhetoric and politics of property has both great political significance and limits. They draw attention to the fact that in some instances these political claims and assertions may also have important legal consequences.[2] Jennifer Nedelsky's (1991) work offers a valuable general insight into the importance of property talk in the formation of the political and legal landscapes of western liberal democracies. Property relations, she argues, have been associated with the, 'basic human goods, in particular liberty and security.' Boundaries and borders are not only central to this notion of property, but they are also key metaphors through which we make sense of freedom; freedom from more powerful individuals and freedom from the state. They are also central to the characterisation of the function of the state: the protection of property interests. Property, Nedelsky maintains, 'is a right that requires collective recognition and enforcement' (p. 165). The rhetoric of property is thus intimately connected to access to state violence. Mark Neocleous (2000) focuses particular attention on the relation between the rhetoric of property and the state institution of the police. Police and the political economy of property are intimately connected: they are, 'two sides of the same coin' (p. 57). The history of the police as a security project, he concludes, is a history of private property. The rhetoric of property not only gives form to political claims but in turn those political claims are given institutional juridical significance (Turner 2000), be it in the form of civil rights or more recently victims rights and human rights (Brown 1995b; Douzinas 2000).

Boundaries also play a key role in joining sexual politics to the rhetoric and politics of property. The boundary is a central metaphor in the discourses of the sexual politics of freedom. Boundaries are at the heart of privacy, which has been the dominant strategic response to the state's intervention, particularly, in genital relations between men (Lauristen and Thorstad 1974; Weeks 1981). Within the dominant tradition of sexual politics, which has given particular priority to men, property has been deployed as a powerful way of making sense of individuality, sexual freedom, safety, security, and sexual rights of citizenship and human rights as limits (Nedelsky 1991). Our focus on the rhetoric and politics of property may offer insights into the ways in which property informs the politics of sexuality, violence and safety and thereby structures the political and legal claims of sexual citizenship.

In pursuing an analysis of the uses of property talk in the context of sexual identity we turn to the work of Margaret Radin. We draw upon some of the insights she developed in her exploration of the distinction between two types of property relation: personal and fungible property. This distinction provides a vehicle through which we explore the symbolic meanings of property. For Radin (1993) personal property is property 'bound up with a person'. This is in contrast with 'fungible property', described as property, 'held purely instrumentally' (p. 37). Radin explains this 'instrumentality' as, 'holding an object that is perfectly replaceable with other goods of equal market value' (p. 37). In the idea of 'personal property' Radin explores the way property talk forges a link between the subject and the object, between identity and property, with significant political and legal effects in western liberal democracies. We draw upon the personal/fungible distinction to analyse the connection between identity, possession and belonging that is to be found in our research data. Our objective is to explore the political and strategic significance of this conjunction.

We need to approach Radin's work with some caution. A key concern informing Radin's focus on personal property is to challenge one of the characteristics of property, the right to break the subject/object connection, more commonly known as alienation. Alienation has attracted most critical concern in the context of self-ownership. In this context alienation is associated with the transformation of the self into just another commodity. Examples include slavery, prostitution, or the sale of body parts (Davies and Naffine 2001). Jeanne Schroeder (1998) draws attention to the way in which making property personal in order to protect interests, investments and persons is problematic. Reinforcing the relation between subject and object may protect the subject from the dangers of the market but it also offers to separate the subject from other subjects (Nedelsky 1991). But property is not just a relation between subject and object but also a relation *between* persons in respect of an object. To ignore or displace this as a central dimension of property is to misunderstand or misrepresent a fundamental aspect of relations of property. To reinforce and thereby reduce the relation of property to the relation of subject/object is problematic in at least two senses. First, it ignores the importance of property in the generation of inter-relationships (communities) in the formation of the subject. Second, it fails to take seriously the role of inter-relationships at the heart of both the problem of safety and security of the subject and its very possibility. An idea of personal property that places the subject outwith institutions of exchange may threaten to place the individual outside the experience of community, which is made through processes of inter-relations with others. We approach Radin's work with these caveats in mind, using her idea of personal property as a tool to understand how the particular formation and investment in the object works in the generation of identity. Our resort to the idea of personal property explores how investment in the object works to produce the mundane sexual politics of safety and danger, of security and insecurity.

Mindful of the suggestion made by Davies and Naffine (2001) that the rhetoric of property may not only have immense strategic value but may also have significant political limits, we pursue an analysis of those limits in examples drawn from the research data. Our first reflections focus on propriety. We offer an examination of limits that may arise in the use of 'gay' as a definition that (in)forms the property of the object. Our second reflection examines the politics of property as a gendered politics. Feminist work has long exposed the way that gender informs and structures limits to the politics of property. In crude terms men are subjects of property and women are objects of property, things to be possessed, objects to be exchanged between men (Irigaray 1993; Pateman 1988; Rubin 1975; Schroeder 1998). Women have long struggled to gain access to and control of property. In exploring the impact of gender through the research data we examine lesbian experiences and uses of the rhetoric and politics of property.

Last, but not least, we turn to the impact of location on the property talk of lesbians and gay men. In the first instance the talk of property we are concerned with here might be associated with particular geographical origins: the West and more specifically liberal democracies. However, beyond this there is little that formally indicates that these ideas differ in proximate locations. Our two research locations were less than 50 miles apart. Yet much seems to separate Manchester's gay Village from Lancaster. Manchester's gay Village has been described as 'a European gay Mecca' in campaigning group Healthy Gay Manchester's publicity (1998). It has a high concentration of gay (mainly gay male) businesses and organisations. It is also a gay space that has a certain sustainability and a durability. In contrast Lancaster has few designated gay and lesbian spaces; at the time we gathered our data they were transitory rather than durable (once a week, once a month, in winter but not in the summer) venues and events. They were partial, mainly described as 'mixed venues' by their owners and organisers, small in number, largely invisible and of questionable sustainability. Our concern here is to examine the difference, if any, location makes on resort to and the impact of property talk. In practice resort to the rhetoric and politics of property may have different significance and effects in different, albeit temporally and spatially proximate, locations. We explore these issues through the Lancaster data. This data offers something of a contrast in terms of the sexual use and effects of property. Thereafter we return to the Manchester data and offer a re-reading of some of the data with location in mind. This provides an opportunity to explore and challenge the totalising assumptions of place.

We begin our exploration of the rhetoric and politics of property with extracts taken from the interviews with key informants in Manchester. The focus of these observations is safety and danger in the gay Village. More specifically, they appear in the context of what turned out to be a pervasive theme peculiar to the Manchester key informant and focus group data: the 'straight invasion' of the gay Village, a theme with many dimensions. For example 'straight invasion', as a threat to order and safety has both spatial and temporal dimensions. Sometimes it was represented as a threat associated with particular places, gay bars, the main streets and the central bus station. At other times it took the form of a more general threat, to the gay Village as a whole. It also had a temporal dimension: a threat particularly associated with the weekend, especially Friday and Saturday evenings. In Chapter 8 we examine this theme through the politics of estrangement. In this chapter we focus on the role of the rhetoric and politics of property in the formation of 'straight invasion' as danger and disorder.

## Intelligibilities of property

Our first objective is to draw out some of the key themes of property which make up an intelligibility of property (Laplanche 1988). This intelligibility works to make sense and non sense of sexual politics as property relations.

Let us begin with an extract from an interview with 'Norman',[3] a gay man with business interests in Manchester's 'gay Village'. Norman explained:

> I've bought gay clubs and I open gay clubs and I'm keeping them gay clubs, as gay as I can keep them. And nobody's gonna shove me any other way. I want gay . . . no straights. I think you should shoot . . . all [straights], they do your head in.
>
> (Norman, KII, Man., 1998)

Norman's observation in the first instance may sound extreme. His observation contains many features of the classical liberal idea of property. The eighteenth-century English legal scholar Blackstone (1979) described these features in the following terms: 'the sole and despotic dominion which one man claims and exercises over the external things of the world, in total exclusion of the right of any other individual in the universe' (p. 2).

Norman's comments illustrate some of the key characteristics associated with this idea of property as 'sole and despotic dominion'. The first is *exclusive possession.* This informs his comments that he will not allow anyone to interfere with his decision to buy, open and run a gay bar, 'nobody's gonna shove me any other way . . . I think you should shoot them all'. Another is *use.* This is expressed by way of his determination to 'run them gay . . . [keep] them gay'. In the first instance another attribute associated with the classical liberal idea of property, *alienation*, appears to be absent. However, further reflection shows that it does inform Norman's comments. Alienation is expressed in his observation, 'I've bought gay clubs . . .'. That which is bought may also be sold, alienated. Exclusive possession, use and alienation have been described as the 'liberal triad' of (neo)conservative property rights (Radin 1993).[4]

The juxtaposition of 'gay' and 'club', in Norman's observation, draws attention to another aspect of 'property': *propriety.* As propriety the property relation is concerned with the object's particular characteristic, quality or its mode of being which might be described as its nature or its essence or its *order* (the proper, the respectable) (Davies 1994, 1998, 1999; Naffine 1998). Propriety is also connected to use, which is concerned with the realisation and preservation of those qualities, attributes and the good order of the thing. Norman deploys propriety in his nomination of the place as a 'gay club'. It is the focus of his determination to maintain the thing. It is central to his experience of the thing under threat and in need of protection: 'I bought a gay club, it's gonna stay a gay club and no straights. I think you should shoot them all' Propriety seems to have particular importance in Norman's concerns about order and disorder, safety and insecurity.

Together these ideas of property take the form of a claim which is not only a claim to secure, preserve and alienate, but also a claim to secure, preserve and alienate *the very nature of the thing.* The claim also takes the shape of entitlement. Entitlement is both a reference to 'title', the claim to property (possession, use, alienation), and a reference to propriety: 'title' as superscription or designation that names the nature of the thing, in this instance 'gay'.

Finally, talk of propriety, use and exclusion is also talk of limits: of *borders* and *boundaries.* For Norman the boundary has particular characteristics. It is a location associated with the immediate threat to good order and its preservation. It is also the locus of the practice of *exclusion*, of that which is a threat to good order: 'straights'.

In some respects it is trite to note the importance of the attributes of property for Norman. Over the last 20 years he has operated and had legal ownership of several businesses in 'the Village': a taxi company, clubs and bars. Property talk is not only pervasive in the world of business and commerce but in many instances this property talk is officially recognised and subject (if necessary) to state enforcement. In this context property talk is also law talk: talk of legal rights and duties, capacities and responsibilities.

But there is a need for some caution here. Norman's 'sole despotic dominion' is not absolute, despite his characterisation of it in these terms. It is subject to external limit and restraint. For example his use of the place as a bar is regulated through licensing laws which control the use of the space for the consumption of alcohol. Certainly in the past, and we would add in the present, the nomination of property as gay was not something that might be given legal recognition or protection. It was, and in many instances remains, more likely to attract attention and intervention by the police and local authorities in their efforts to control the use of the space. However, this does not render the nomination insignificant. As we have already noted the rhetoric and politics of property cannot be reduced to legal ownership. Propriety also has political significance.

We now want to return to Danielle's observations that appeared at the very beginning of this chapter, in order to re-examine them in terms of the themes of property we have drawn out of Norman's comments. Her observations provide an example of the resort to the rhetoric and politics of property in a different context: before and beyond the official recognition of property relations as legal relations (Bower 1994). Danielle explained:

> If heterosexuals come here then they need to be aware of what it is about and be friendly towards our needs and what we're about, and remember and respect. They're here on our invitation in a way because it is our space.
>
> (Danielle, KII, Man., 1999)

The themes of property play a key role in her comments. For example, her observation that heterosexuals are 'here on our invitation' is informed by ideas of exclusive possession, control (the capacity to regulate access and to exclude), boundaries and boundary maintenance. Her suggestion that heterosexuals, 'need to be aware of our needs and what we are about' speaks of the nature of the place, its propriety, its order and the control of use. As we noted earlier, of particular significance here is the repeated resort to 'our' ('our invitation', 'our space'). Danielle's qualification of her use of 'our invitation', by the phrase 'in a way', indicates her awareness that she deploys property as a metaphor, framing property as a matter of politics rather than, in the first instance, as a matter of law and legality. Ownership is used not only in terms of individual property, but in the context of a claim of collective possession and belonging, one that incorporates the speaker.

An extract from an interview with 'Sue' the ex-organiser and continuing member of the South Manchester lesbian social group, illustrates another dimension to the use of the rhetoric and politics of property. She explains:

> Because too many straight people are . . . in the Village at the weekend . . . for the [gay] men who traditionally go out, it obviously seems to

affect them because their own private space is being invaded in their eyes.

(Sue, KII, Man., 1998)

Of interest here is the way she uses the language of property in relation to the Village. Sue characterises the Village, its bars and clubs (places and institutions of civil society), the public space of the streets that criss-cross that place, as the private space of gay men: 'their own private space'. It is a phrase that resonates with the associations of possession, belonging, and ownership and conjoins them to the Village. Here the rhetoric of property generates ideas of ownership of the locations that represent the group. In turn, individual ownership is also a symbol of the collective investments and interests in the location.

Having set out some of the key dimensions of this intelligibility of property and demonstrated their legal and political significance we now want to focus attention on two particular aspects of the intelligibility of property. Both have particular importance. The first is propriety. In particular we want to examine the characterisation of 'property' as 'gay' and to explore the role of propriety in the generation of the relationship between property and safety. The second theme is borders. Borders and boundaries not only locate propriety but do so in terms of its limit. As a limit the border locates the experience of both order and that order under threat.

## Proprietorial investments: personal/fungible

Margaret Radin's (1993) work on the distinction between property as personal and property as fungible offers a useful tool through which to analyse the effects of 'gay' as a matter of propriety. Personal property, for Radin, is property 'bound up with a person'. This is in contrast with 'fungible property', that is described as property 'held purely instrumentally' (p. 37). Radin explains this 'instrumentality' as 'holding an object that is perfectly replaceable with other goods of equal market value' (p. 37). Norman's comments again offer a useful point of departure in exploring these dimensions of property in the everyday property talk of lesbians and gay men. In the first instance the property relation that informs Norman's observation could be understood as a relation of fungible property: of subject (Norman) to object (a club), where that object is perfectly replaceable by another object (another club, or another business) of equal value. However, Norman evidences a rather different investment in the property. Norman's property relation involves an investment which gives the property a particular symbolic significance: 'gay club'. Its importance is evidenced in his insistence on the maintenance of its particular propriety, 'gay': 'I've bought gay clubs and I open gay clubs and I'm keeping them gay clubs, as gay as I can keep them.' This investment has another dimension. Here the property relation is made a relation of sexual identity. Through an identity investment property and person are intimately connected. Following Radin we would suggest that Norman's relations to the club takes the form of a set of property relations that are 'bound up with a person'. As such the club is, in this instance, figured by Norman, in Radin's terms, as personal property rather than fungible property.[5]

Further evidence of the intimacy between the rhetoric and politics of property and sexualised identity is to be found in the research data on discussions about other bars in the 'gay Village'. The personal/fungible dichotomy informs a range of evaluations about bars made by research participants. Distinctions are drawn between gay bars (with lesbian and gay owners) and bars owned by 'big firms' (which in some instances were managed and run with lesbian and gay staff). It also informs evaluations of gay bars and lesbian and gay events.

In general gay bars are characterised as personal property, in contrast to the 'big firm' bars that are represented as fungible property. This distinction is symbolised in various ways. For example, the fungible quality of 'big bars' is identified by Norman by ownership. The owners are called 'shareholders'. A key quality of the shareholder is that their relation to the business is purely a financial one: of profit (and loss). Here the instrumentality of the object (the bar) is reflected in its limited purpose: to produce profit. This reduction gives the bar as a property relation an abstract quality. Abstraction also informs the characterisation of the customers of these bars. 'Big firm' bars, Rose explains, are 'not interested if [the customers] are gay or straight or anything, all they want is to fill the place' (Rose, KII, Man., 1998). The indifference towards customers makes customers a sign of the instrumentality of the relations of property expressed in the phrase 'big bars'.

Profit is also another context in which the personal/fungible distinction is put to use. In the context of 'big bars' profit has negative associations. In this context, the financial exchange that is represented as profit is experienced as *a loss* of value to both the individual and the community. In sharp contrast is the profit made from gay bars. Again, in crude terms, this is profit (from personal property) that has a positive value. It is an exchange that circulates *between* persons. It is experienced as movement of value that ultimately remains or at best adds value, producing an experience of community. The movement of this exchange emphasises 'between' and 'proximity' in contrast to a movement away and distance associated with the negative profit of fungible property (big bars). Positive profit is associated with value to the community, the gay community. Its associations with an individual and collective sexual identity appear to displace negative attributes of profit that are aligned with the instrumentality of property. As positive profit the movement of value binds the community: as negative profit value flows away from the 'community' and fractures the 'community'.

In general the person/fungible distinction is a distinction between being in place and being out of place. The figuration of commercial relations (the bar) as personal property produces the relations/place as a location of belonging, of being in place. Following Nedelsky (1991) and Neocleous (2000), this formulation of property relations also connotes that place is a location that is more likely to be associated with freedom, security and safety.

In contrast, the figuration of commercial relations (a bar) using the rhetoric of fungible property, promotes that place as the location of an experience of being out of place. This informs an experience of relative insecurity, and pending danger.

The shift from personal to fungible is a common theme in our data. It figures the invasion theme. Invasion is signified through a shift in property relations in the Village from personal to fungible relations of property. Invasion is the representation of a shift from a rhetoric and politics of property that reports a movement from order and safety to disorder and insecurity.

Before we leave the personal/fungible distinction we want to sound a note of caution, which has particular significance in terms of understanding experiences of safety and security, danger and insecurity. The 'fungible' quality attributed to 'big firms' may also be experienced in terms of the personal. They need to be understood as a relation. Rose illustrates this in the following observation;

> I mean if I was going into a straight place I wouldn't dream of sitting with my arms around a girlfriend or kissing her in front of anybody.
>
> (Rose, KII, Man., 1998)

The experience of the potentially more abstract category, 'customers', (and one could add shareholders and profit), of the 'big firm' bars is shown here to be an already personalised, sexualised experience of heterosexuality (Valentine 1993). Thus the fungible qualities of a particular thing may also be read as giving a personal dimension to an other, which in this instance takes the form of heterosexuality: the personal is not separate and apart from the fungible but imminent in it. The relation between the negative (fungibility) and the positive (personal) is contingent.

How are we to make sense of the personal/fungible distinction and its distribution? First, the concept of bars as personal property, in contrast to bars as fungible property, draws attention to the symbolic importance of property relations in contrast to thinking of property purely in terms of the economic (Knopp 1994) or more abstract symbolic relations (Forest 1995). Our data suggests that the personal/fungible is intimate and unstable. Both in the case of Norman, as the owner of the gay club, and in wider discussions about the 'big firm bars' as a vehicle for heterosexual invasion, the economic and symbolic are closely connected. The fungible/personal relation as an either/or situation needs to be treated with caution. More attention needs to be paid to who is making the claims and the particular claims that are made. This will enable a more nuanced reading of the politics of property. In our data the personal/fungible distinction of property relations is perhaps best understood in terms of struggle, tactic, strategy (de Certeau 1984).

The talk of 'straight invasion' in the Manchester data (a matter we explore in more detail in Chapter 8) gives the rhetoric and politics of property talk a particular focus: border and boundaries, their violation and the techniques used to sustain and maintain them. Boundaries bring the themes of exclusive possession, use and control, alienation, propriety and entitlement into stark relief and emphasise their geographical connotations. They also foreground the connections between safety and danger, security and insecurity. Our Mancunian key informant and focus group transcripts are full of references to boundaries. In the next section we first want to examine techniques of boundary formation as techniques of safety and security. We then turn to the question of the location of boundaries in order to challenge some assumptions about borders and boundaries, safety and danger.

## Border practices: the everyday management of safety

Our examples illustrate practices of marking not only the boundaries of particular bars and events but also the boundaries of the Village. Manchester key informants offer many examples of techniques of boundary formation. One common technique is the employment of official border guards, doormen or bouncers. They can be found at the threshold of premises. They also appear elsewhere. Rose describes the way in which her bar staff function as boundary keepers by the way they, 'walk around all the time'. Ruth notes that staff use particular techniques to police the boundary of the bar: 'A lot of them are doing it obliquely, they might say, "you're not a regular", that sort of thing.' Lynn describes a less formal, but rather more spectacular instance of a border guard:

> This drag artist'll go around in a limousine . . . with a megaphone, shouting to people in the streets, 'You are now entering a lesbian and gay zone!' . . . He did it for two nights before the police turned up and told him to shut up . . . There was a group of them – about half a dozen of them – that did it.
>
> (Lynn, KII, Man., 1998)

In these examples boundary-marking and boundary maintenance in addition to making the limits of a place, involves mechanisms of surveillance and evaluation (Moran and McGhee 1998) with various degrees of formality and informality.

Our data contains evidence of many other techniques of boundary formation. The 'gay' of 'the Village' has been symbolically marked through creative vandalism that continually erases the 'C' and the 'S' from Canal Street. More official activities such as street banners and wall posters of a local HIV/ AIDS organisation, Healthy Gay Manchester, and billboards advertising the Manchester Mardi Gras festival have further contributed to the gay signification of the locality. On special occasions, such as the Manchester lesbian and gay Mardi Gras events in late August, a temporary fence is erected to enclose several streets where the lesbian and gay venues and events are concentrated. Another more routine technique found in bars and clubs takes the form of a demand for a formal confession of identity, 'I'm queer,' followed by a demand for proof as a precondition of passage across the imagined threshold. Less frequently this is followed by an oath, 'I agree to abide by the [bar's] rules and only fetch in my gay friends'. Another mechanism that gives the experience of a boundary is the use of a token of membership or identification that must be displayed prior to entry. This might take the form of a VIP card or a key ring without which access is denied. In 1998 the Manchester Mardi Gras festival policed the boundaries of the event by way of a passport which took the form of a plastic bracelet: 'a pledge band'. Secured on the wrist of the participant, the band ensured passage across the boundaries of the temporarily enclosed Village. The pledge band and thereby the boundary was explicitly connected to safety and the person. The organisers of the event explained that the pledge band would 'guarantee' that boundaries worked, making the Mardi Gras a 'lesbian and gay' event. It would be a 'safe, friendly, and a secure environment'.[6]

A different range of techniques of boundary marking are illustrated in the following extract by John, the marketing manager of Metz, a bar in the Village. The bar, John explained, had been in the Village since 1993. When asked to describe the bar he explained that it was 'gay to the core'. More specifically:

> It was designed to be a place for gay men and women and their atti-tudinally correct friends, to coin a phrase, where they are treated with greater respect . . .

He continued:

> Our position, incidentally it's on the front of our menus, is 'don't discriminate, integrate'. That is a message in fact to both sides of the community. I mean its saying to gay men and women, 'Let's not live in an enclave which we've had to for political reasons for long enough, let's integrate'. You've got to integrate with gay men and women because you're in their space.
>
> (John, KII, Man., 1999)

John's comments are of interest in various ways.[7] '[G]ay to the core' suggests a strong and pervasive personal link between the owners, operators and the business: the bar as personal property. '[I]ntegrate don't discriminate' is described elsewhere in the interview as the bar's brand. The brand makes explicit the theme (propriety) as a property in itself. (The brand is in legal terms a form of intellectual property.) John offers many examples of the way the particular brand appears as a pervasive feature in and across the space. While it is only formally marked on each menu card, John suggests that it informs the wider aesthetics of the place, from the menus to the music policy and the choice of design of the tables.[8] The boundary of the place, making it distinct, separating out this bar from all others, is stamped on and through the different media.

Finally our data draws attention to the importance of the body as marked by and marking boundaries. Through ways of dancing, ways of looking, modes and topics of speech, the body is marked by the boundary and signifies boundary violation. As Bourdieu (1987) notes, bodily dispositions always exist to mark distinctions; they are the most intimate of symbolic markers and the most difficult to disguise. Not only does property's boundary mark the body but, as McNay (2000) suggests, bodily dispositions are experienced as the property of the person. Here property produces the very experience of the self: as something that is owned through embodiment and perceived as an asset, attribute, attitude, limit. In both respects property is experienced in and through the mobile, moving body. The body is the means for generating experiences of entitlement to social spaces through distinction.

## Border practices: locating safety and danger

Before leaving the issue of borders and boundaries we want to draw out a feature of the data on borders, data which challenges assumptions about their location. During the course of an interview with two workers from the Sikh gay men's helpline based in Manchester, we asked for their opinions on safety in the Village. In response, Ali singled out two locations where safety was at risk (which in this instance took the form of dangers associated with sex workers and pimps). Danger, Ali explained, was located, 'behind the Village' and 'just outside the Village' (Ali, KII, Man., 1998). These phrases characterise the boundary as the location of danger as an outer edge that is fixed and geographically remote. This is perhaps the most common understanding of the location of boundaries and the geography of danger. An example of this in other work on gay space is to be found in Myslick's (1996) study of Columbus Circle in Washington DC. Myslick locates homophobic violence on this 'outer edge'. However, our key informants suggest that this common understanding is problematic. The boundary (and danger) is geographically more complex.

For example Terry, a gay men's worker with the Manchester City Council, problematises any simple notion of the geographical specificity of boundaries. While on the one hand they are clear, at the same time, he explained, they are 'a bit fuzzy' (Terry, KII, Man., 1999). Another respondent, Lynn, offers an insight into the 'fuzzy' nature of these boundaries. She comments that the boundary is also to be found, 'in the middle you know, in between, not even just like down by the side . . . It tends to be all over' (Lynn, KII, Man., 1998). Lynn's insight draws attention to the way in which the boundary as location of danger, might not have a privileged geographical location. In all of the examples above the boundary is an edge. In some it is represented as a geographically fixed relation of periphery to centre. In others it is more mobile and multiple. John's explanation of the markings used in Metz is one instance of this. It is on each chair and table. It is on each menu card and in the music policy. The mobility and multiplicity of the edge draws attention to the way the border and boundary as the edge is metaphorical rather than literal (Smith and Katz 1983; Smith 1993). Borders and boundaries are (re)made in the experiences of safety and danger which are multiple and mobile. Their location is as varied and as ubiquitous as the location of the experience of safety and danger. In turn, boundary-making and marking is a constant, universal, mobile process.

## The limits of property I: 'gay', 'lesbian'

We now turn our attention to explore some of the limits of the rhetoric and politics of property. First we focus on limits generated by propriety in the nomination of the thing as 'gay' or 'lesbian'. Our concern is not so much with the way the nomination of the thing generates associations of possession and belonging, but rather to focus on the ways and contexts in which 'gay' or 'lesbian' fails to personify and personalise the property relation and thereby limits personal investment in property talk. These limits are of interest not only in the way they point to limits on the generation of the relation between subject and object but also in the way they draw attention to the limit of relationships between persons in respect of the thing exchanged. The limits to the process of exchange raise issues about the limits of property as a medium through which experiences of community are formed and circumscribed.

The limits of 'gay' propriety appear in different forms. One context in which it emerged was the changes which our lesbian and gay focus group participants suggested to improve safety. Many were concerned with the limits of propriety as evidenced at the boundaries of particular places and in the practices of boundary keepers (Corteen *et al.* 2000). Various proposals related to ways of reinforcing the particular propriety of gay and lesbian locations and events. Some were concerned with the need to improve the management of boundary keepers: to limit their violence and to better target their boundary-keeping activities to ensure attention focused on those who threatened the safety and security of the place, rather than against the gays and lesbians who seek access to the space as safer space. Special training for door staff was recommended. The objective here was to generate skills relating to policing of homophobic violence.

Some proposals focused upon promoting safety through the reinforcement of the propriety of the place. One popular suggestion was that the gender and sexuality of door staff should echo the gender and sexual propriety of the place. Another was that venues and events should display clear markers to signify the event/place as lesbian and gay.

For others the nomination of the place by reference to sexuality may in itself be a limit on resort to property as a rhetoric and politics of sexual belonging. Dennis, the owner of a 'mixed bar' in Lancaster, offers perhaps the most extreme example of this: 'if you've got the label "it's a gay bar" a lot of people will stay away from it if they're "closets"' (Dennis, KII, Lan., 1999).

Another context in which the limitations of propriety is to be found is in the distinctions and expressed preferences for particular gay and lesbian bars and events. These preferences are informed by a multitude of criteria. They may relate to music policy, interior decoration, the sexuality of the owner, manger, bar staff and bar users, as well as perceptions and experiences of safety. They draw attention to the ways in which 'gay' and 'lesbian' are complex proprietorial terms informed by economic, social, cultural and aesthetic factors. These factors not only separate straight from gay but also separate gays and lesbians as well as gay men from lesbians. Terry, the gay men's officer with the Manchester City Council, captured some of the factors that might be refracted through the prism of proprietorial relations in the following observation:

> The Village is most attractive to . . . 20–40-year-old white able-bodied lesbians and gay men with some money to spend.
>
> (Terry, KII, Man., 1999)

Terry's comment draws attention to ways in which relations of property might institutionalise violent hierarchies not only of homo and hetero but also of age, race, disability and social and economic class (Hubbard 2000; Sibley 1998). He also draws attention to the ways in which the equation of gay male visibility with consumption may limit the expression of differences within and between gay males and between lesbians (see Warner 1993, and specifically on Manchester, see Whittle 1994). Sue, the ex-organiser and continuing member of a lesbian social group, provides an illustration in the following terms:

> Young people who are out and about will probably have a different view because they'll see the Village in a different way and they're probably sort of, you know, skewed one way. But I think it's because we spend most of our time in our private spaces . . . young people, because of their age, are probably more in public spaces than they are in their private space.
>
> (Sue, KII, Man., 1999)

Here Sue notes how age may pattern access to property as a rhetoric and politics of belonging. The contrast between private and public space is a contrast between a strong property relation (private space) and in this instance public space, where property interests are at their most fragile and difficult to establish. At the same time, Sue's comments draw attention to the ways in which the lack of proprietorial claims on public space make it a space that those without property, in this instance young people, occupy, albeit problematically.[9]

While the deployment of property may be implicated in the generation of intellegibilities that promote awareness of social exclusion and provide a vehicle for legitimated cultural investment of belonging and participation, at the same time they are also problematic. The rhetoric and politics of property may ground belonging and participation on further social exclusion (Wilson 1991a). So we need to be circumspect about resort to the rhetoric and politics of property and to be sensitive to how they impact upon movement, circulation and participation. We need to develop our understanding of who benefits from their use. We now turn our attention to one particular ground of exclusion that has been produced though property relations, namely gender, and to consider its significance in the context of lesbian and gay uses of property talk.

## The limits of property II: gender

Feminist scholars have long drawn attention to the way the rhetoric and politics of property is also a rhetoric and politics of gender. We begin with some of the key themes explored in this work. The subject of property is man/masculine. Woman/femininity is positioned as the thing, the object, and not the subject of property (Irigaray 1985; Pateman 1988; Rubin 1975; and Schroeder 1998).[10] In this order of property woman/femininity, as object, is that which is possessed in contrast to the male/masculine as the one that possesses. In terms of property as relationships between persons in respect of an object, woman/femininity is that which is exchanged in contrast to the male/masculine as the gender position of the subject who exchanges (Irigaray 1985; Rubin 1975). Some have drawn attention to the impact of the rhetoric and politics of gender in other property contexts such as borders and boundaries: as the masculine, borders separate, isolate and individualise. They are impenetrable, representing absolute security, defence and control. In contrast, as a feminised limit, borders are characterised as penetrable, porous, incomplete, a site of vulnerability, insecurity, lack of and loss of control. They are also the point of interconnection rather than separation (Massey 1994; Rose 1993). These metaphors of gender boundaries produce a violent hierarchy of masculine/positive and feminine/negative.

It would be wrong to conclude that in some contexts neither straight nor lesbian women can take up the position of the masculine subject within this gendered economy of property relations. At the same time in some contexts it remains impossible. In all, it remains problematic, as shown in data provided by our lesbian key informants and focus group participants.

Earlier we noted the use of use of the rhetoric and politics of property by two of our lesbian key informants. Sue suggested that gay men are particularly affected by the presence of straights in the Village at the weekend. She explained, 'for the [gay] men who traditionally go out, it obviously seems to affect them because their own private space is being invaded in their eyes' (Sue, KII, Man., 1998). The rhetoric of property is associated with gay men. Lesbians are noticeable by their absence, even in a context, 'the invasion of the straights', that also has significance for lesbians in the Village. This absence may be explained in various ways. At least in good part this reflects the fact that the Village is predominantly a gay male space. Sue framed her comments by reference to the relative absence of lesbians from the Village, 'You see it doesn't bother me . . . I'm not there' and '. . . there weren't many women out . . .'. Her comments may also reflect the gendered dimension of property relations: the subject of property is always already male/masculine. The gendered use of the rhetoric of property in this instance may also reflect the difficulties women face in making and establishing proprietorial claims in the Village using the rhetoric and politics of property.

There is some support for this in a comment made by Ruth, the Manchester City Council lesbian officer. She explained:

> If lesbians want a lesbian-only space they have to say 'this is women only' whereas men just kind of create their male space. There's a tradition of not saying 'this is a men's space' but it just becomes one because women go in and they don't feel comfortable. I can think for instance about the Rembrandt, never having had a written policy that says 'men only', though there's certain anecdotal evidence to say that there's a bouncer policy on certain nights. . . . Whereas if women try and make women-only space, it has to be a rule because men will try to get in. I can think of Follies for instance, the trouble they sometimes have keeping it a women-only space, but men come to the door and they'll get frustrated that they can't get in, even though there are a lot of women in there.
>
> (Ruth, KII, Man., 1999)

Her comment that 'men just create their own space' draws attention to one of the ways in which gender works through property and entitlement, producing different experiences and possibilities of belonging. Ruth's comments suggest that property has greater political significance and fewer limits for men than for women and lesbians in particular. Men assume property claims. This appears to be the point of departure against which women must constantly work; already existing entitlements must be constantly (re)established.

Ruth highlights a dimension of this. The proprietorial capacities of men are invisible, represented as 'natural'. Over against this scheme of things women's claims, and in particular lesbians' resort to property relations, are 'unnatural', at best problematic, and at worst impossible to establish or maintain. In turn more effort is required to mark lesbian space as 'women-only space'. Finally, Ruth points to the absence of proprietorial validity associated with 'lesbian'. In response lesbian space has to be marked as 'women's space'.

The interview with Rose offers further insights into the relation between lesbian identity and the rhetoric and politics of property. Rose, with her partner, has been running a business in 'the Village' for over 11 years, and has lived in Manchester for over twice that length of time. She explained her decision to open a bar by reference to the history of lesbian and gay space in Manchester and in particular to the impact of the feminist movement on spaces shared by lesbians and gay men:

> [It] caused a load of trouble with the gay lads because all at once they [the women] were slagging them off and they didn't get on and [the women] wanted their own space, so I opened this little bar.

Describing the business as Manchester's 'first women-only bar', she continues:

> I opened it as an exclusive restaurant with a dance floor in the back. I was trying to attract like these business women that haven't come out, that can't come out because of their jobs, like lawyers . . . But it just didn't work out because you find that women come out at the weekend. There's not many of them come out in the week because they've got more responsibility than gay lads . . . It's [different] now because women get as much [as men] . . . It just didn't take off as that, so I made it into a disco, took all the tables out and made it into a disco club.
>
> (Rose, KII, Man., 1999)

After abandoning the restaurant project she turned the premises into a club. Thereafter, she explained, it developed into a women-only (lesbian) space incrementally. Monthly events developed into weekly events, every Saturday. Otherwise the venue hosted 'mixed' commercial events such as 'Homo-electric'. It was also used as a venue for mixed 'community events' such as the Manchester lesbian and gay police liaison meetings, attended predominantly by gay men.

Various factors seem to inform Rose's experiences of property in general and her attempts to invest the business with a particular propriety, 'women's space' and 'lesbian space'.[11] First, is the importance of economics. The economic position of women/lesbians makes it more difficult to sustain a business as women/lesbian-only. As others have noted, this is not to suggest that lesbians have no interest in consumption or the strategic use of the politics of consumption. For example, Gluckman and Reed note:

> The hunger for visibility and acknowledgment – not to mention for a long list of specific products and services – is a strong one for gay men *and* lesbians.
>
> (1997: xv; emphasis added)

At the same time, Clarke (1991) notes how lesbians have rarely been addressed as consumers. They have not been targeted as a specific group because, she argues, they are not profitable; not identifiable, accessible or measurable. Nor, as noted by Adler and Brenner (1992), may they want to territorialise their visibility through commercial investment in the same way as gay men. Our research showed a significant 'community' of professional-occupation lesbians in a suburb outside of central Manchester. It is known locally as the 'social work suburb' and has access to 'good schools' and good health services. For strategic reasons lesbian resort to the rhetoric and politics of property may be focused upon these institutions and services rather than in the context of bar occupation and ownership. Rose draws attention to this in her reference to family responsibilities. Proprietal claims arise in different contexts and locations.

Together these factors make more problematic the idea of the bar as sustainable women's/lesbian space. At the same time Rose has been able to sustain the bar over a considerable period. In part her ability to have and keep the business going is due to economics, 'not paying a lot of rent'. This reflects the previously marginal status of the area that is now the Village. It also reflects the geographically remote position of Rose's bar within the Village.[12] It is distanced from the main concentration of gay bars on Canal Street. The bar and business has also been sustained through the multiple use and multiple significations attributed to the place. It is women-only *and* a mixed space for lesbians and gay men. The contingent and multiple propriety of place raises some interesting questions in terms of propriety and the nature of the 'personal'. The bar as personal property demands that the personal have more than one configuration.

## The limits of property III: location

So far we have focused attention on the use of property talk in Manchester's gay Village. We have examined some of the uses of property rhetoric and location. We have noted some limits on its use. However, there is little to suggest that the use of this rhetoric and politics of place and belonging is limited to this particular location. On the face of it, certainly within the wider parameters of locations that might be characterised as western neo-liberal democracies, there seem to be few location-specific features to property talk. At least resort to the rhetoric and politics of property would appear to be free of this limitation. In this section we want to reflect upon the impact of location on the use of the rhetoric and politics of property.

In the first instance much separates the two research locations, Manchester's gay Village and Lancaster, as lesbian and gay spaces. As already mentioned, the gay Village has been described as 'a European gay Mecca' (Healthy Gay Manchester 1998). It has a high concentration particularly of gay businesses and organisations. Covering an area of little more than three blocks, it con-tains nearly 40 bars, clubs, restaurants and shops, including 'the country's first gay-centric consumer emporium' as well as numerous gay and lesbian community organisations, help lines and support services. It is also a gay space that has a certain durability. Lancaster barely registers on the lesbian and gay map of the north-west of England, let alone the bigger map of lesbian and gay Europe. Its gay and lesbian spaces are partial (mainly described as 'mixed venues' by their owners and organisers), small in number, largely invisible and of questionable sustainability. At the same time little separates the two locations. They are barely 50 miles apart. They are linked by multiple communication systems. So, what difference does location make? How does lesbian and gay property talk differ, if at all, in these two locations?

We turn first to Lancaster and begin with the experience of Marge, the lesbian organiser of WILD, a monthly women's disco in Lancaster. It is an event that has considerable durability, being in operation for over 10 years in various locations in Lancaster. In talking about the event, Marge, in some instances, resorts to a rhetoric of property. For example, 'our' is a significant signifier when she talks of WILD in terms of 'our group' and 'our money'; property talk is used in relation to things that are relatively intangible, 'group' and 'money', in contrast to the particular tangibility of place.

Marge explained that WILD was started as a 'women-only' event because:

> We were fed up with the mixed stuff because whenever there's a mixed thing going on, you always find that it's 90 per cent men 'cos women won't turn up to them but they'll turn up to women-only things.
>
> (Marge, KII, Lan., 1998)

With regard to the problems of finding a location for the event she went on to explain that, 'Its not really a case of where we can choose to put these [events] on. There isn't a choice.' Various factors inform this lack of choice. Economic capital was one important factor limiting access. However, Marge goes on to explain that money is not the only factor limiting choice. Others include problems with the size and decoration of venues. Another factor is the support, the 'backing', of the venue's owner/licensee.

Marge's observations offer some points of connection with the lesbian experiences of property reported earlier in the context of Manchester. For example Marge reported difficulties of maintaining the space as a women-only space. The nomination of the event as a 'women's disco' echoes sentiments about the gender of property articulated by Rose's experience in Manchester. The impact of economics upon property is another. All of these suggest that, as gendered talk, property talk may be similar, imposing similar limits, in different locations.

Lesbian focus group discussions suggest that there are other points of similarity between limits on property talk in Manchester and Lancaster. The resort to 'lesbian' and 'gay' as a property may impose limits in both locations. For example in discussions about WILD members of the lesbian focus group offered many reasons why they did not attend these events. WILD was 'too smokey', 'too cliquey'. The perceived style of the majority of lesbian women who attend was also raised as an issue. As one member of the group explained, 'it's not really my type of scene to put it politely'. In response to a request for more information members of the group described the disco as 'the Mullet show . . . it's just full of Mullets'. Karen, acting as the facilitator, asked for further clarification, 'What's a mullet?' In response one group member explained: 'For me a Mullet is like a 1960s feminist, checked shirt, like really rough, drinking.' Another member of the group added: 'For me the music is not my type of thing either.' Here investments by way of propriety are made not only by reference to economics but by reference to a wider range of cultural factors. Particular attention needs to be paid to the specific form and combination of these cultural factors in order to examine the impact of location upon the nature and mode of property investments and its limits.

While economics may connect experiences of gendered property talk in different locations, there is a need for caution in considering the impact of economics on access to the rhetoric and politics of property. An issue highlighted by Marge is the importance of other modes of value and investment. For example, she explains:

> I have to find volunteers to do it and it's incredibly difficult and it riles me sometimes, it really annoys me sometimes, but I can't get any help. All these women want to come along, they complain about the music, they complain about this, they complain about that, but no one's prepared to sort of pull their finger out for, you know, an hour once a month to give me a hand . . . I got so annoyed with it last summer that I cancelled two WILDs . . . They weren't coming, for one. They weren't turning up because they were saying it was boring or whatever, they weren't coming along, and they were complaining about the music and I thought fine, you don't like it, tough I'm not doing it any more and I didn't do any more until, the first one was the October one last year . . . It was absolutely heaving, absolutely heaving. They were craving for it and they turned up and said, 'Oh, we've missed it'. I was like 'Right! Fine! OK! Give me a hand', and you know what? No one gave me a hand.
>
> (Marge, KII, Lan., 1998)

Here the sustainability of the event is not limited to access to economic capital but takes the form of non-commercial investments, in particular, labour, in the form of participation. While economic capital, 'the pink pound' may facilitate access to places it would be wrong to conclude that economic capital is the only value that is necessary for the establishment of tangible locations of property talk.

Other property owners might be interested in providing locations in order to gain access to these other modes of capital. Marge's observations suggest that a lesbian event may incorporate different forms of value. One of the reasons Marge gives for the bar owner's willingness to offer the space for the WILD disco is that there is 'no trouble' at lesbian events. Here good order is a positive value, which may facilitate access, particularly in conjunction with the 'pink pound'. Again, this is not an experience peculiar to the location of Lancaster.

Interviews conducted with gay men who own and run businesses in Lancaster offer another context in which we might explore the impact of location on access to and use of property talk. We interviewed the gay owners of two businesses in Lancaster. One business consisted of a bar/canal boat tour operation (The Navigation). The other was a cafe/restaurant (No. 6 Café). Lesbians and gay men frequented both. The owners of both, respectively 'Dennis' (The Navigation) and 'Richard' and 'Freddie' (No. 6) described their businesses as 'mixed'. (Neither is now a 'mixed' venue. The bar has closed and the café is no longer gay-owned or run. A gay bar opened in the town shortly after the data gathering phase of the research was completed.)

Dennis explained his resort to propriety of 'good order' in the following terms:

> We run boat trips from here as well and we get all our visitors in the summer, all the families. It can't be labelled [a gay bar]. You couldn't paint [the bar] pink because it would just kill it. It would just die . . . You put a big advert in the paper in Lancaster saying 'we are a gay bar', you just wouldn't get any customers. You'd get your windows broken for that . . . One or two have tried before but it's never worked. Not just to aim at that market. You'd have to have an entrance discreetly positioned somewhere . . . It wouldn't be obvious how they were getting in.
>
> (Dennis, KII, Lan., 1998)

In part, the nomination of the business as 'mixed' reflects the sexual assumptions associated with these different businesses, respectively the canal tour business (heterosexual) and bar (heterosexual/lesbian/gay). The balance between these two aspects of the business has particular significance. Dennis explains the sexual investment in the place by reference to both violence and economics. Painting the bar pink would 'kill' the straight business. It would also expose the lesbian and gay business to straight violence. In this instance violence and the threat of violence undermine the economic viability of the business. Others explained the economics of Dennis' nomination and operation of the 'mixed' business in somewhat different terms:

> It's a place that's gay when it's quiet . . . it's the sort of place that tends to be more gay in the winter when it's quieter. [The owner] has been known to sort of tell people to leave if they're sort of, you know, getting

a bit loud or anything, he'll tell them to leave because he's got, you know, straight people in the bar.

(Richard, KII, Lan., 1998)

Freddie commented by way of illustration that, 'he once banned a friend of mine because he was a bit camp'. The different interpretations given to the significance of economics is of particular interest. In the opening observation economics is used to indicate the unviability of property talk for sexual investment. The second comment suggests something rather different. Market distinctions between straight and lesbian and gay may work *together* to promote economic viability and thereby multiply proprietorial investments.

Other distinctions were also used by Dennis to explain the nomination. In particular he drew a distinction between a gay bar as a 'meat market' in contrast with his bar business, which he described as 'a meeting place' for 'nice', 'sensible' people. Manchester and Blackpool, he suggested, offered the former if needed, pointing to the need for a nuanced reading of the multiple cultural factors that inform the sexual investments that might be made in and through property talk.

Richard and Freddie, the owners of the café/restaurant business also offered economics as a major rationale for the nomination of the business as 'mixed'. The economic basis of the nomination was explained in various ways. Richard suggested that the economic viability of a 'gay' business in Lancaster was problematic. The market is too small: 'there's not enough trade' (Richard, KII, Lan., 1998). The gay population in particular was also described as 'too fickle', explained in terms of the proximity of gay venues in Manchester and Blackpool and the mobility of gay men. When asked about the significance of violence they reported neither direct violence nor threats of violence. Some competitors had made derogatory comments about their sexuality but others had reported this state of affairs to them. They put these comments down to business jealousy and a mark of the success of their business.

There is also a need for caution here as other research data suggests that the resort to 'mixed' doesn't necessarily preclude the use of the rhetoric and politics of property in these locations. For example, in the survey of users of lesbian and gay spaces in Lancaster, the canal-side bar The Navigation was named as the most popular venue by lesbian and gay respondents. Focus group data produced evidence of a wide range of perceptions of and investments in these two spaces.

While in the first instance the experiences documented and described here point to a distinction between the uses of property in the two locations, they also describe certain connections. Economics offers both a medium that connects the experiences of property talk in the two locations and makes some connection between the experience of lesbian business owners in Manchester and the experience of the gay business owners in Lancaster. At the same time it divides the experiences of property in the two locations. The use of gay as a proprietorial feature of gay-run business in Lancaster seems to be different from that of gay men in Manchester.

The experience of these gay business owners does suggest that location may have an impact on property talk of gay men. It is a limitation that works through economics. The economic factors of a particular location are connected to the wider economic landscape. Furthermore, the economic needs to be placed within the wider context of other social and cultural factors that frame the sexual use of property talk.

Finally, in our reflection on location we return to Manchester. Our concern here is to put some of the points made in the sections on the limits of propriety and the gender of property into the context of location. As a location, the analysis of the use of lesbian and gay propriety draws attention to the fact that the Village is neither a singular nor a uniform experience of the rhetoric and politics of property. It is made up of multiple and sometimes contradictory experiences and investments that have both positive and negative aspects to them. For example, while we suggested that lesbians as women experience property differently and, more specifically, experience the limits of the rhetoric and politics of property differently, in certain circumstances property is a resource that is available not only to gay men but also to lesbians. For instance during the course of an observation on violence and safety in the Village, Rose explained that while she always walked around the Village on her own, and experienced little anxiety, this was not the case for all people:

> I've seen [straights] shout to the other girls what are together, you know, linking one another, and more to the lads, you know these effeminate looking lads, they really pick on them. You know, I've seen them, I've seen them throw bottles and I've heard them shout after them. And really it is *our* village.
>
> (Rose, KII, Man., 1999; emphasis added)

Our previous analysis of the limits that arise by way of the nomination of the space as gay suggests that the property talk of young gay men or Asian lesbians will be different from that of other lesbians and gay men. These different experiences of the space are brought together in an expression of property in the Village, 'our Village' that includes both lesbians and gay men. The proprietorial claims offer to erase the complexity of the place in the constitution of its singularity as 'our Village'.

## Conclusion

This chapter offers another dimension to the study of lesbian and gay safety by examining property as a rhetoric of a sexual politics of violence and safety. Property is a way of talking about the individual and the collective as issues of freedom, liberty, claims of rights, and rights as limits. Resort to property as metaphor escapes the reduction of this talk to claims that are already officially recognised in laws and political institutions more generally. 'Talk of property' provides a vehicle through which to 'talk of order', a mode of investment in place as an order of belonging, generating this order of belonging in particular ways. Through property this order is produced by limits which provide an experience of order, safety and security in particular ways, bringing opposites into close proximity; order and disorder, safety and danger, security and insecurity. Simultaneously, it produces their separation; property as order is safety not danger, security not insecurity.

Property talk is not necessarily a rhetoric or a politics reducible to a particular status quo, be it defined by way of economic position or specific social status. As a rhetoric for a politics property is de-essentialised and dislocated (Bammer 1992). We have explored the ways in which property talk seems to offer an intelligibility that connects the agency of individuals and the activism of social groups to which they belong with the policies and institutions that seek to shape social relations (Gould 1988).

We draw attention to the dangers of examining the rhetoric and politics of property in isolation from other social and cultural factors such as economics and gender which mediate the strategic resort to property as a politics of belonging. While ideas of property may be implicated in the generation of intelligibilities that promote awareness of social exclusion and provide a valued cultural investment through which participation might be staged, at the same time they are also problematic. Not only might they ground participation on further social exclusion but also, in addition, they might facilitate the misrecognition of the nature and form of the social and cultural factors of violence that they seek to work against. So we need to be circumspect about resort to ideas of boundary and property and how they impact upon movement, circulation and participation, and to develop our understanding of who benefits from their use, a matter we return to in Chapter 8. We offer a preliminary analysis here of the pragmatics of property, propriety and entitlement.

This chapter provides some evidence of the pragmatics of property in particular spaces by different people: property and economic capital investments, those based on institutionalising sub-cultural capital, those generated through imaginary belongings, those based on generating social networks (social capital). Investments are not just economic – although usually material – but are a measure of how our bodies can move through space; they are about time, energy, commitment and conditions of possibility. Property works as a vehicle for these different investments.

In the western capitalist neo-liberal tradition the rhetoric and politics of property is a rhetoric and politics of citizenship. The pragmatics of property draws attention to the problematic nature of citizenship. At worst intimate citizenship becomes just another location for the inscription of established social hierarchies in a new guise (Berlant 1997). At best the conflation between belonging, location and citizenship produce the possibility of social and civic inclusion only at the micro level; on almost a bar-by-bar and street-by-street basis. In producing 'the Village' as the locus of gay citizenship, other sexualised spaces and sexual subjects can only be, in the first instance, its other and thereby excluded. On a wider scale civic developments in the context of one locale and one state organisation, in this instance one police authority, appear to have limited impact on adjacent authorities. During the time of the research the 'Bolton 7' were being criminalised for engaging in consensual sex with other men in private (Moran 2002). Also in contrast to Manchester, local government in Lancaster failed to address lesbian and gay issues because, they argued, nobody had ever suggested they should:

> Well I just don't think they've been raised as a priority. No group has raised the issues as priority. Nobody's raised issues, you know and presented them as being a crisis or an issue. You see we have, for example, an ethnic member of the committee who frequently raises racist issues and we will respond to that.
>
> (Ruth, KII, Lan., 1998)

Intelligibilities of property, our data suggests, may in some instances challenge social exclusion and create forms of civic recognition and promote participation. However, these are not indifferent to other social structures that produce and valorise different subjects in different ways, thereby generating and securing social elites. There is a need for further cross-analysis between the different 'high risk' groups that are being studied here. The impact of gender on this intelligibility suggests that we need to avoid assumptions that people occupy only one homogeneous category at a time. An individual may experience moments of belonging, entitlement and exclusion simultaneously. We need to 'think through' different categories and attempt to bring together an analysis of how the different categories (such as women, men, gay, straight, working-class, black, etc.) impact upon each other, constituting and disrupting each other in specific contexts. Property and propriety, we argue, is a start to thinking through these issues.

Property talk offers one mode of intelligibility through which investments in place are made sense of in terms of order and disorder, safety and danger, security and insecurity. But it is not the only intelligibility at work in the practices that produce these experiences. We now want to turn to another way of making sense of safety and danger which operates simultaneously with the intelligibility of property: comfort. Their separation can only be explained by reference to the practical difficulties of analysing their simultaneous connection and operation. So with property firmly in mind we now turn out attention to comfort.

# 6 Comfort and the location of safety – home

## Introduction

We begin our exploration of comfort with three snapshots. The first comes from the second meeting in a series of six focus group discussions with gay men in Lancaster. Paul, acting as facilitator, used the 'kissing test' to begin a group discussion of the spatial dimension of actions which had been identified in other focus group discussions as 'dangerous'. He posed the following question: 'So what can and can't you do and where? What about kissing another man?' Phil replied in the following terms:

> I suppose I'd be comfortable kissing another man at my home or in their house or . . . possibly in a gay pub. I wouldn't feel comfortable at all kissing someone in the street or anything like that, because you would always have in the back of your mind, 'Are there any scallies coming to beat your head in?' And you're sort of encouraging [violence].
>
> L (Lancaster), gmfg (gay male focus group), 2)[1]

Phil's response offers a catalogue of locations organised in a hierarchy of safety and danger. The key term he uses to characterise safety is comfortable. This use of comfort to name the experience of safety in response to danger was something of a surprise for us. It was not a term that we anticipated, rather expecting terms such as 'safe', 'secure'. In general the data suggests that these terms are not as significant as we expected: comfort and comfortable were much more common. Our objective in this chapter is to examine the meaning and uses of comfort in the generation of experiences of safety and danger, security and insecurity.

This first snapshot is of interest in another way. Phil's catalogue of experiences of safety and danger is a list of different *locations*. The first in Phil's list is home. Home, as Mary Douglas (1991) has noted, is '. . . a kind of space . . . It is always a localizable idea' (pp. 288–9). The term home makes comfort a matter of location. In addition Phil's catalogue of experiences of comfort indicates that the location of safety is not limited to one place. From its initial connection with home comfort is also associated with a series of other locations: the other person's house, a gay pub, the street. This suggests that the spatial significance of comfort is complex and significant in the characterisation of a wide range of locations as safe.

This catalogue of locations of comfort poses a puzzle that we will unravel in this chapter. In the first instance comfort seems to be closely associated with the private and the domestic. In its subsequent uses comfort is attributed to the spaces of civil society, public spaces. The private *and* public significance of comfort makes it appear to be ambiguous and contradictory. We examine these dimensions of comfort. We begin with the spatial relation between comfort and home. Thereafter we explore the significance of this association in the production of other locations of safety and security. In undertaking this task we draw out the ambiguities and contradictions of comfort and analyse their significance, use and management.

Phil's comments raise another issue, the relation between comfort and safety. In our first snapshot comfort is set against the threat of violence, which offers to shatter safety and security: having your head 'beaten in'. Our second snapshot taken from an exchange in one of the lesbian group meetings in Lancaster also highlights this relationship between comfort and safety.

In response to a question about the comfort/safety relationship the group's initial discussion pointed to differences between the two terms. Safety/unsafety was explained in terms of being 'mugged', 'beaten' or 'hit'. In contrast, Bev, one of the group members, explains 'uncomfortable' in the following terms: 'Some people can make you feel uncomfortable by not even saying anything . . . Just by their body language'. Here, the distinction between unsafe and uncomfortable rests upon the presence or absence of immediate physical violence. In contrast the behaviour that is associated with being uncomfortable is more wide ranging. Comfort appears to be used to name a more diffuse form of threat and a wider spectrum of insecurity.

Others in the group emphasised the connection between safety and comfort. Paula explained: 'The reason it is uncomfortable is because it doesn't feel safe.' Here 'safety' and 'comfort' are intimately connected. Paula's observation suggests that comfort is *always* about safety. Keri offered another perspective on the relationship:

> I think, sometimes, they inter-link. If you are uncomfortable it compromises your safety as well. A man walking behind you is uncomfortable but it also compromises my safety because he could attack me.
>
> (L, lfg (lesbian focus group), 2)

Keri's comment suggests that comfort diffuses experiences of safety and danger. Thus, comfort is a term associated with a much wider continuum of experiences of danger and safety which also refers to the wide continuum of violence and the threats of violence. Both Paula's and Keri's comments suggest that comfort is a necessary aspect of safety and that the language of comfort plays a central role in the characterisation of safety and security.

Comfort is therefore always at the heart of safety and security. At times, the terms safety and security may be used to describe particularly intense experiences of threats to comfort; loss of comfort is not limited to those experiences. It is a term that refers to a much wider range of experiences of danger, insecurity and loss of safety.

This brings us to our third opening snapshot. It is made up of insights drawn from three studies of violence against lesbians and gay men. The first is a study of 'male gay-hate related homicides' (Mouzos 2000). The study found that the majority of incidents of homicide (62 per cent) occurred in the victim's home. The second study, by the Greater Manchester Lesbian and Gay Policing Initiative, 'Lesbians' Experiences of Violence and Harassment', found that lesbians 'experience a high incidence of crime and harassment either in their home, workplace or neighbourhood and it is perpetrated by neighbours, family and work colleagues' (1999: 6). The third study, 'Understanding and Responding to Hate Crime' (Metropolitan Police 2002) was conducted by a team of researchers working with London's Metropolitan Police and suggests that over 50 per cent of incidents of homophobic violence reported to the police occur in and near the home. In over 70 per cent of reported instances of violence the victim knew the alleged perpetrator.

All of these studies problematise the reduction of home to comfort and thereby safety, highlighting a major problem with comfort and bringing into sharp relief a key dimension of the ambiguous and contradictory nature of comfort as a located experience of safety. Far from being a localisable idea of safety and security, for many home is a location where we might be most vulnerable and unsafe. It is a location where we are most likely to experience violence in its most extreme forms. This suggests that any analysis of the relation between comfort and home needs to be vigilant against a will to forget the proximity of comfort and danger that is made apparent in the well-established relation between violence and the home. More specifically it needs to be undertaken with the knowledge that home offers multiple and contradictory experiences of safety and danger. The challenge is to sustain an analysis that brings out these ambiguities and contradictions.

With these points in mind we pursue our objectives drawing upon research data that are to be found in lesbian and gay focus group discussions undertaken in Lancaster and Manchester. We begin with an examination of the many meanings associated with 'comfort' and home, draw out their ambiguities and contradictions, exploring the ways in which these ambiguities and contradictions are managed. Examples of the use of comfort to characterise experiences of safety in both private and public locations are considered. We then turn our attention to lesbian and gay scholarship on identity, space and violence, in order to examine the significance of home and 'comfort' in this scholarship and, second, to outline our own contribution to this work. Finally, we reflect upon the critical contribution that the lesbian and gay data on home and 'comfort' makes to policy debates and practical initiatives addressing violence, danger and safety.

## Comfort and the politics of home

We begin our exploration and analysis of the focus group data by consider-ing the relationship between comfort and home. An extract from Carl, one of the gay men in the Manchester focus group, offers the following insight into the relationship between home and 'comfort'. Carl explained:

> I think the expression 'to feel at home' is to feel comfortable. There's nothing that compares to being at my own house. I just lie there in front of the TV and have my scruffy jumper on. That is home to me. It's not being at home, it's not living at home but just to feel at home. It's just being comfortable.
>
> (M (Manchester), gmfg, 5)

Echoing ideas found in the first snapshot that opens this chapter, Carl's comments suggest that 'comfort' is not merely one amongst many attributes of the spatial term home but also a feeling that is the very essence of that location. This is reinforced with the suggestion that 'nothing compares'. Comfort and home are one and the same. Comfort, Carl suggests, is a synonym for home. *Home is comfort as an experience of location.* When placed in the context of our second opening snapshot this can be developed further. *Home is comfort as a located experience of safety and security.*

Nor is comfort merely just another experience of safety and security; Carl's reflections suggest that comfort is a term that articulates a very particular experience of safety as location, 'nothing . . . compares'. The designation of a safety experience as one of comfort is perhaps the expression of the ultimate state of safety. As Sheila, one of the Lancaster lesbian group said, 'I think the ideal space is just everywhere really, you've got to be comfortable wherever you are' (L, lfg, 1). Comfort is therefore an imaginary and an essence, an attribute of 'ideal space'.

Carl's comments indicate another dimension of 'comfort'. The phrases 'to feel at home', 'to feel comfortable' draw attention to the way in which the spatial experience of safety is an affect. Furthermore, these 'feelings' have an ontological dimension (cf. Bachelard 1963; Cooper 1994; Forty 1986; George 1999). Comfort, as Carl notes, is an experience of 'just being'. It is an expression of ontological security.

The ontological dimension of comfort/home is connoted in various ways by members of the focus groups. Simon, from the Manchester gay men's focus group, explained that home is 'where the heart is'. When asked to explain further, he added, 'it's about where you feel most comfortable, it's about personal freedom' (M, gmfg, 5). 'Heart' has many connotations here. It indicates that the comfort/home conjunction is a way of expressing an idea of safety at the core of experiences of 'the self'. The use of 'heart' also reinforces the emotional dimensions of comfort and home. The heart is emotion in contrast to the mind, which connotes reason. 'Personal freedom' is another phrase that has ontological resonance. It suggests an absence of restraints which limit the realisation 'of the self'. For Carl this takes the form of lying in front of the TV, and wearing a scruffy jumper.

Many comments by other group members emphasise comfort as an experience associated with the 'true self'. Andy, one of our Lancaster gay focus group participants, notes: 'I think my home is a gay space as well . . . I live with my partner and . . . I can be a complete wally there, and just be myself, which is good' (L, gmfg, 1). For this gay man home is the location of a particular experience of security. It is a space free from judgement; a location where his 'self' may appear free of heterosexual surveillance. This enables it to be named gay space. 'The self' and the space merge via sexuality.

Fran, one of the Lancaster lesbian group members, explained, 'If you are genuinely happy and at home with yourself then you will be that wherever you go . . .' (L, lfg, 2). Of interest here is the phrase 'at home with yourself'. It captures the particular conjunction of location and ontology. The preposition 'at' draws attention to the importance of home as a social position, produced in a very specific context; 'with yourself'. The preposition 'with' suggests home as a place with the quality of proximity, intimacy, nearness, connection to 'self'.

The focus group data contain many other positive associations connected to comfort/home. One example is to be found in a contribution made by Fran: some people, she explains,

> don't want information, they don't want to go . . . to discos and they
> don't want to go to all these women's groups, they just want to sit at
> home, have a pint, have a spliff, you know what I mean, watch the telly
> or something.
>
> (L, lfg, 1)

Ed, one of the Lancaster gay men, explained, '[sitting] at home watching TV [is] easier and it's as rewarding' as a visit to local gay youth group or the monthly gay disco. The positive references to home in these two extracts set the positive qualities associated with home against negative attributes associated with the public realm of civil society, which in these examples, is connected to feminist, lesbian and gay community activities. These extracts draw attention to the way in which both male and female participants deploy home as retreat, sanctuary, respite, haven, in contrast with the stresses and struggles attributed to civil society and the public realm. Home connotes stability and harmony and a particular sense of peace or certainty with its specific rewards.

The spatialisation of positive and negative attributes to respectively private and public locations found in these examples, however, cannot be reduced to the particular experience of being a lesbian or gay man in Lancaster, a small and in many ways parochial and provincial place with few formal lesbian and gay spaces. Ian, from the Manchester gay men's group, makes similar associations in the following comment:

[A gay friend] hates The New Union [one of Manchester's most popular gay bars] 'cos he says it is too rowdy and noisy . . . I suppose he doesn't hate it but I just find it is very hard to get him to come out. You know, to even go for a drink say once a month. I suppose in a way he probably does hate it. He doesn't like being there. As soon as he gets there, he wants to go home.

(M, gmfg, 1)

The examples of attributes set out above do not exhaust the positive associations connected to comfort/home. One of our Lancaster lesbians associated home with 'real joy'. Other participants have explained it in different ways: the private ('not public') as the place of relaxation and the locus of being at ease.

How are we to make sense of these many meanings? How does comfort/home work in the context of this complexity? We suggest that comfort and its spatial synonym, home, are points of connection and condensation producing many chains of association often by metaphor and metonym. In their connection and combination they produce, inflect, re-focus and shift the meaning of comfort and home in a variety of ways.

Before we leave the many positive associations connected to comfort/home, we want to draw attention to one more dimension of these experiences. We want to return to Carl's comments about 'lying in front of the TV', and 'wearing a scruffy jumper'. He concludes, 'That is home to me.' Let us also return to Fran's comments on being at home. She drew attention to the way having 'a pint', 'a spliff', 'watching TV' were also connected to comfort. These comments draw attention to a key feature of comfort. They are not only signs of 'comfort' but, more importantly, they draw attention to the way comfort is about particular cultural practices. These practices of 'comfort' have a metonymic relation to home; each particular practice provides a fragment of the whole of the experience, of comfort/home. As such, they are practices that produce the emotional experience of retreat, sanctuary and being in place that amalgamate in the experience of a particular location as safety and security, as being 'comfortable'.

## The other side of home

So far our exposition paints a rather one-sided and nostalgic picture of home. Little supports our opening comment that comfort and home offer ambiguous and contradictory experiences: this we now explore.

Reflecting upon her childhood experience of home, Gill, one of the Lancaster lesbian group, explained:

We were kicked out of the house when we came home from school and we didn't go back until half past ten at night. You know that's how I was brought up.

(L, lfg, 1)

In this instance, far from being experienced as the location of being, onto-logical security or sanctuary or retreat, home is characterised by exclusion. Another member of the group talked of the vulnerability of being at home. Fay's comments illustrate an aspect of this vulnerability. They arise in the context of a contrast between her experience of living in the paternal home in her home town and that of living as a student in a home 'of choice':

> I got involved with a group in Lancaster, they were mainly students from the University. The big thing ten years ago was we were all going to come out. We were all going to stand up and be counted . . . They were saying to me 'you've got to stand up and be counted'. I was the one who lived here. My family, my parents, were in Lancaster. I said to them 'It is okay for you. You are a student. You are here. You can do what you want and then you can go away. You can go home to where you belong and it means nothing to anybody because you are not going to hurt your family and friends.' They said to me 'We will help you to come out. We will do it for you.' I had to say, 'You can't do this. My career, my family everything is on the line.' You can do it as a student because you are in a strange town, your family aren't here. Most of your friends aren't here or the friends that you care about. Your not going to work here, so it makes it easier.
>
> (L, lfg, 2)

Here vulnerability is generated by the home being a location of exposure by surveillance, scrutiny and policing. Michael, a student who participated in the Lancaster gay group provides a different but related perspective on the experience of home as a home of choice. He explained:

> With most of my friends at University [my sexuality] is not an issue. Since about week 2 they've always thought I was gay, so it didn't surprise them. They'll ask me about who I fancy and I'll tell them just like I would if I was straight. But back home I have my parents, they don't understand.
>
> (L, gmfg, 4)

Both Fay and Michael problematise the home as the located experience of ontological sanctuary and security. The home, as the parental home, is a site of anxiety and insecurity, where the sexual self is experienced as a self that is invisible, absent and a 'self at risk'. Home is comfort under threat and or the absence of comfort. The negative aspects of home are made apparent through contrast with the home of choice. More specifically, in these examples the parental home is the 'straight home'. For Fran and Michael the parental home as a sexualised location is marked by the sexual home that is elsewhere.

Fay's comments also draw attention to home as a place of surveillance where there is little or no privacy, where you are 'known'. Home in this context is stripped of its associations with privacy and the private as a location of withdrawal, retreat and anonymity, where practices 'mean nothing to anybody'. The experience of home as the location of an intense experience of surveillance was described by Peter, one of the Mancunian gay men, in the following terms:

> as a place where you are criticised, and abused, and condemned and judged and offended.
>
> (M, gmfg, 5)

The dichotomy between the parental home and the home of choice draws attention to what Lefebvre (1991) describes as the genitality of home. Lefebvre suggests that the (hetero)genitality of home works to link home to nature and the natural. In turn this is implicated in the idea of home as the guarantor of meaning. In the context of the lesbians and gay men the straight home as nature is an experience of the homo in the home and the homo-home as the unnatural, artifice, a second-order home. The genitality of home is one attribute of home that makes home ambiguous: as an experience of both being in place and being out of place; of security and insecurity; of withdrawal and exposure; of being one's 'self' whilst out of place.

While these examples draw attention to the negative features of home, they also expose the need for caution. This relates to the way the negative of home is produced in relation to the positive of home. More specifically, the negative is related to the parental home by the positive being attributed to the home of choice. This threatens to reduce these different locations to nothing more than the respectively positive and negative attributes of home. Thereby the contradictory experience of each location of home is threatened with erasure. The data reveal many instances where, for example, the positive home of choice also provides many experiences of the negative associations of home. For example, Justine, a lesbian mother from the Manchester group, explains that the home of choice can also be experienced as a location of surveillance, exposure and vulnerability. Justine's experiences are associated with her role as a mother in which the home as a permeable space is produced in relation to her children. Home for Justine was associated with the surveillance and the normative gaze of school officials, children's friends and neighbours.

Our attempts to expose the negative aspects of home resonate with much feminist scholarship. This work has documented the myriad ways in which women's experience of home has been one of confinement, containment, exploitation and exclusion. Feminist work has paid particular attention to the way home as security and safety has strong class dimensions. In addition home has particular associations with right-wing politics, within a reactionary politics of nostalgia, in which a sentimental domesticity is evoked

(Bammer 1992; Irigaray 1993). Others have critically examined the ways in which metaphors of home, as sanctuary and security, have informed feminist scholarship and progressive politics more generally. In particular, they have examined the way feminism and feminist practice has understood home, as sanctuary, security, refuge, and thereby (re)produced home as silence, violence, hierarchy and exclusion (de Lauretis 1990; Honnig 1994; Martin and Mohanty 1986).

Feminist criminologists working on gender, violence and fear of violence have also been keen to work against the associations between home, security and safety, for good reasons. A central concern has been to expose 'the myth of the safe home' (Stanko 1988, 1995, 1998), documenting the many ways in which home as safety misrepresents the reality of the everyday nature of violence in women's lives (Stanko 1990). Much official 'safety talk' reproduces the association between gendered violence and the public realm, thereby putting women's most common experience of violence (in the home) out of the frame (Pain 1997; Valentine 1989; Valentine 1992), perpetuating the idea that the major threat to women's safety is the random violence of strangers in public places (Saraga 1996). Much work has been done and much still remains to be done to demonstrate that the home is the primary location of violence against women. In general this work suggests that home as comfort, safety and security appears to be implicated in the perpetuation of perceptions, policing policies and practices that sustain and promote gender violence, rather than realising safety for those who experience violence.

Our analysis of the lesbian and gay experiences of violence must meet the warnings and concerns articulated in this feminist literature. There is much potential to facilitate the reproduction of the 'myth of the safe home' in a lesbian and gay context. Lesbian and gay work on home as safety and security needs to proceed with caution in order to avoid the further perpetuation of the 'myth of the safe home' and all the problems associated with it.

At the same time we want to argue that there are problems with the feminist responses to the myth of the safe home and offer a preliminary note of caution. We would agree with Mason (2002) that there are dangers in proceeding on the basis that the nature and experience of heterosexist violence and lesbian and gay experiences of safety is the same as experiences of violence against women. However, this does not necessarily lead to the conclusion that the feminist challenges to home and comfort as safety and security need not be taken seriously in a lesbian and gay context. We have already noted how some of the survey evidence highlights the significance of homophobic violence in and near the home. Likewise in Chapter 3 we noted the way existing official safety literature misrepresents the dangers and the safety needs of lesbians and gay men.

We also want to raise another problem with the feminist attempts to expose the myth of the safe home. Much of that scholarship brings the dangers of home back into the frame of understanding but, in doing so, the safety of home is erased from the picture. In short, these analyses of home often reproduce a logic of either/or (either the safe home or the home of danger) which perpetuates the very one-dimensional understanding of home that feminist scholarship seeks to challenge.

Our lesbian and gay data suggest this is a problem, erasing the ambivalence of home. This is particularly ironic in the context of feminist criticism that exposes the tendency to impoverish the experience of home. In the name of adding a forgotten dimension of home there is a potential to produce new gaps and silences that limit our understanding. The challenges that ambiguity raises for research on comfort and home need to be taken more seriously. Particular attention needs to be paid to the way the logic of either/or is deployed to manage (and erase) ambiguity.

## The ambiguity of home

Far from presenting home in terms of a sentimental or nostalgic place, the lesbian and gay experiences above suggest that comfort and home offer lesbians and gay men complex and contradictory experiences of safety *and* insecurity. The extracts also point to the close proximity of these contradictory attributes. The ambiguous quality of comfort and home is captured by Eric Hobsbawm (1991) in his observation that home is *both* 'essentially private . . . [and] . . . essentially public' (p. 67). How are we to make sense of this?

Freud, in his essay on 'The Uncanny', offers a useful insight:

> We are reminded that the word *heimlich* [homely] is not unambiguous but belongs to two sets of ideas which without being contradictory, are yet very different . . .
>
> (1985: 345)[2]

He continues:

> Heimlich is a word the meaning of which develops in the direction of ambivalence, until it finally coincides with its opposite, unheimlich. Unheimlich is . . . a subspecies of heimlich.
>
> (1985: 346)

Applying these insights to our data suggests that home is comfort *and* discomfort, safety *and* danger, the quintessential ontological experience of security and the location of the most destructive insecurity that challenges the very possibility of 'being myself'. Home is deeply ontologically ambiguous.

Carole Vance suggests that the logic of either/or is one way in which that ambivalence is managed and thereby denied. She reveals how the logic of either/or is used to manage the ambivalence of sexuality in much feminist work:

Sexuality is simultaneously a domain of restriction, repression, and danger as well as a domain of exploration, pleasure, and agency. To focus only on pleasure and gratification ignores the patriarchal structure in which women act, yet to speak only of violence and oppression ignores women's experience with sexual agency and choice and unwittingly increases the sexual terror and despair in which women live.

(1984: 1)

Vance's observations resonate with our concerns about scholarship on home. She suggests there are many problems with the application of the logic of either/or. This logic is at play when critiques of home as safety only offer the home as violence, as the appropriate 'correction' to the prevailing myth. In an ironic twist the either/or logic that promotes home as danger also promotes home as safety. What threatens to get lost in the application of this either/or logic in feminist scholarship on violence against women is women's experiences of violence and practices of safety. Similarly, to apply a logic of either/or to the lesbian and gay experience of violence and safety produced by home would be to impoverish, misrepresent and misunderstand the location and the experience of home.

Home is *both* danger and safety. Our focus group data provide much support for this. In the first instance, the data seem to tell us little about how these apparently opposite aspects of home are managed. When the point was directly raised in the Manchester gay men's group, the only response evoked suggested that holding these different perspectives on the idea of home was 'not a personal statement'. This explanation distanced the speaker from the apparently contradictory associations of home he had deployed earlier in the discussion. Dissociation, we would suggest, is one way of managing the ambiguous and contradictory experiences of comfort and home.

Another way of managing these contradictions is in the distinctions drawn between homes, for example, between the parental home and the home of choice. Here, different aspects of home are managed through attempts to distribute particular characteristics to particular sites of home: home of choice as good home: parental home as bad home. This works through a relation of either/or: the dangers of the parental home or the safety of the home of choice; either the safety of the gay bar or the danger of the family home; either the safety of the home or the danger of the street. In the context of lesbian and gay experiences of violence and safety, the imposition of a logic of either/or and a failure to take ambiguity seriously threatens to misunderstand and misrepresent its complexity and to ignore the experience of violence and safety. The rejection of home on the basis that it is a reactionary category and the failure to recognise the importance of home for progressive debates on safety and security may perpetuate the subordinate position that home, emotion and femininity has within our culture.

## Home: beyond the domestic and the private

One of the ambiguities we have already noted is reported by Hobsbawm (1991) in his observation that home is both 'essentially private . . . [and] . . . essentially public' (p. 67). We now explore this in more detail. Many of the associations outlined above work with the assumption that home is the domestic and the private. This might suggest that home has no significance in the context of the civil and the public realm other than as a location that is elsewhere. However, the focus group data do not support such a conclusion.

We illustrate this with three extracts. The first is a comment made by Pete, a gay man in the Lancaster group. It was made in response to a question about the use of gay spaces. Pete explained: 'Starting with my home life, I was working, well sort of working on a YTS scheme [a government employment programme] and I met someone . . .'. The second illustration is an observation by Daniel who was another member of the same group. Talking about being gay in Lancaster, where there are few lesbian and gay events and venues, he explained: 'So you make yourself in the city, make yourself at home – who you are.' The final extract comes from a gay male Mancunian group discussion. Carl explained, 'I think the expression to feel at home is to feel comfortable. You just feel comfortable in "the Village".'

These three extracts have a feature in common. They offer illustrations of the use of home and comfort to talk about locations and experiences *outside* the domestic/private realm. In the first, Pete uses home to talk of his experiences outside the domestic sphere in the world of work and training and in context of the wider geographies of Morecambe, his 'home town'. In the second Daniel uses home to refer to experiences of life in the city: 'at home in the city'. In both, home is a location and experience associated with civil society and the public realm.

In the third extract home, and its attribute comfort, is used by Carl to describe his experience of Manchester's gay Village. When asked for more detail Peter, a member of same focus group, explains the experience of 'being at home in the Village' in the following terms:

> I was thinking about 'at home' in a pub in terms of the Village. I was thinking about a kind of absence of threat, an absence of judgement and the anxiety that somebody's going to disapprove, or that somebody's going to come across and be aggressive or whatever it is.
>
> (M, gmfg, 5)

In this instance home and its many associations are used to name the experience of safety and security *as* a lack of insecurity in civil society.

These extracts suggest that comfort and home are not to be thought of as just affects and specific locational experiences that are limited to private or domestic space. Rather, they illustrate the way in which home and its attribute comfort have a much wider spatial significance. Many different sites, domestic or private, civil and public places, can be experienced as sites of comfort: as home; home as metaphor.

One question that needs to be considered is the relationship between the domestic and private experience of home and the experience of home as a characteristic and imagined location of civil and public society. The data presented so far might suggest a particular relation between home and civil/public space: home, as domestic/private, as a prior and autonomous experience; home, as a civil/public experience, as secondary and dependent. However, the lesbian and gay reports of home and comfort indicate that such a conclusion is problematic.

This is illustrated in the following extract from the fifth Manchester gay male focus group. Simon explains:

> Saturday evening was always dinner at [friends' houses] or they would come to us . . . we could all sort of do exactly what we wanted to. There was never going to be the question of getting beaten up or having to spend an inordinate amount of money to enjoy yourself. [It's] far easier, far far better at home. There was the whole ritual of cooking a meal . . . You can choose your own music . . . A mini Village at home.
>
> (M, gmfg, 5)

Here Simon describes his experience of home by reference to a range of domestic/familial practices: interactions with a partner, with friends, cooking, entertaining. These are characterised as practices not only of relaxation, economic prudence, but also of safety. In the first instance these are set up in contrast to the civil/public space of the village, which is represented as the antithesis of home and a place lacking in comfort: a place where the possibility of violence is located.

However, the reference to 'a mini Village at home' problematises this relation. Here, the homely attributes and experiences of the domestic are characterised in terms of meanings and practices of home associated with a civil/public space, the gay Village. Rather than there being a single register of meaning here, of home as domestic practices of safety, security, authenticity and so on, we would suggest that there is a double register of meaning: a 'double hermeneutic' (Giddens 1990). The meanings and practices generated in the context of home as domestic space inform the idea of the Village (as (un)homely) and the homely meanings and practices of the civil/public realm, the Village, such as the music of the gay Village (as home), inform the practices and experiences of the domestic as the location of home.

The uses of home as metaphor not only separate home from the domestic and the private, but also raise another challenge. Home is no longer singular, reducible to and fixed in one location: it is 'de-essentialised'. Home, as metaphor, has 'an indeterminate referential quality' (Bammer 1992).

This has significance for feminist work on the 'myth of the safe home' which tends to reduce home to an idea and set of practices associated with a particular place. And in so doing it ignores the metaphorical deployment of home, failing to recognise that home is an indeterminate space, threatening to (re)essentialise the notion of home and its many attributes such as 'safety'. Thereby, it impoverishes our understanding of the nature, experience and significance of home and safety.

It also may leave progressive scholarship with no academic language or analysis to account for safety (Stanko 1988). Furthermore, it may also impoverish our understanding of the relation between fear and the private/ domestic, and fear and safety talk in the public realm. In this context, a recognition of the indeterminate referential quality of home suggests that fear ascribed to the public realm is not remote from the domestic experience of home and fear and violence within the home, but an expression of it. By acknowledging the metaphorical significance of home, the supposed 'gap' between perceptions of fear and the threat of violence in the public realm is transformed into the proximity between fear of violence in public realm and violence in the home.

## Home beyond the private

How might we explain the dominance of the correlation between home and the domestic and the private? The tendency to collapse home into the domestic can be explained by the characteristics attributed to home, which have much in common with the features attributed to the private, both its positive associations: refuge, sanctuary, security, safety, ontological authenticity and its negative associations: silence and secrets, isolation, confinement, invisibility, alienation and ontological insecurity.

Eve Kosovsky Sedgwick (1990) draws attention to the current cultural importance of the topologies of the private and the public. The public/ private binary, she suggests, does phenomenal cultural work in western liberal democratic societies, through an extensive metonymic chain of associations condensed within the public/private binary. Such is its range of meanings, she argues, that it threatens to make it difficult not only to differentiate it from, but also to imagine, alternative metaphors.

Likewise, historians of the private (Aries 1989), and of home (Rybczynski 1988) problematise the reduction of home to the private, drawing attention to the contingency of the relationship between the private, the domestic and the home, by demonstrating the ways in which the private emerged as the quality of a place and a set of practices and attributes associated with particular locations within the home. They map the ways in which the relationship between the private and the home differ, both over time and at any one point in time. Social class is significant here; while privacy of and within the home does not have its origins in the middle-class home, historians suggest that it is in that context that the relation between private and home comes to assume particular importance (Betsky 1997; Rybczynski 1988). This historical work problematises any tendency to reduce home to the private.

The uneasy relationship between the private and home and the private and the domestic is also memorialised in the ambivalence of the private: as both individual and communal. Within the domestic sphere the private retains the trace of this ambivalence. The private may be a characteristic of the whole house (as a communal space) and a characteristic of a part of the house, such as a bedroom, bathroom or toilet, where it is associated with the individual. In turn, this ambivalence might be read as a reminder of the way in which the private stands as the whole or as the part: as both an essential and a contingent characteristic of home.

Another instance of the spatial ambivalence of private is to be found in the relation between private and public. On the one hand, the private is a withdrawal from a particular communal context, the public, which stands for some formal institutional communal context, say an office or more particularly the state. As that which is against the state, the private is the collective and communal of civil society. This private is remote from the domestic. On the other hand, at the same time the private is also the domestic, the familial, understood as the individual over and against the collective/communal understood as civil and/or state society.

This reflection on the relation between the public/private relation and home is significant in the context of our data on home in various ways. While there is considerable overlap between the attributes of the private and the attributes of home, there is a need to treat the private/home relation with caution. In particular, there is a need to take account of private as metonym of home, as well as a synonym of home. Home is simultaneously both the private and *more than* the private. This has particular significance in the context of the use of home as a metaphor. Home as metaphor puts into play the ambivalence of the private as individual and as communal (civil) society. In addition, as a poetics of public space, home is more than a reference to the communal/collective as private society. Home offers an alternative metaphor.

## Home and comfort in lesbian and gay scholarship

The data analysis offered above suggests that home is a key spatial metaphor of safety and danger for lesbians and gay men. In this section we want to situate our analysis of comfort and home in the context of existing lesbian and gay scholarship. Of particular significance is work that focuses upon spatial concepts of belonging.

Spatial themes are an important feature of lesbian and gay scholarship. 'Neighbourhood', 'community' and 'nation' have all attracted much scholarly attention (Adler and Brenner 1992; Bell and Valentine 1995; Berlant 1997; Bouthillette 1997; Castells and Murphy 1982; Cooper 1998; Stychin 1998). However, work that directly focuses upon home is rare. While references to home are to be found in various contexts, such as oral histories (Cant 1993), literary theory (Jagose 1994) and work on class politics (Raffo 1997), when home does appear, in the main, it is a term that is quickly passed over. The spatial theme that has dominated much lesbian and gay work and which is closest to home and comfort is the private.

Within that body of work the private has been both celebrated and criticised. Its multiple positive and negative associations have been excavated and evaluated. The private has been characterised as refuge, haven, sanctuary, security, and as the locus of ontological authenticity. These positive attributes of the private have been offered in juxtaposition to the negative attributes of the public: a location of hostility, violence, danger, often, as we noted in Chapter 2, taking the form of state violence (Lauristen and Thorstad 1974; Moran 1996).

More recently, the negative associations of the private have been emphasised. The 'closet' has come to symbolise the negative attributes of the private. Here, the private takes the form of terrifying silences and weighty secrets. It is a place of complete isolation and crushing confinement that perpetuates and secures violent exclusion. It is a place associated with invisibility, alienation and 'ontological insecurity'. Against this is 'coming out' which symbolises the public. Here the positive of the public is celebrated and advocated (Gross 1992; Mohr 1992): the public is a place of 'salvational certainty' in contrast to an equivocal privacy (Sedgwick 1990), figured as the site of ultimate ontological transformation, the location of ontological fulfilment, in contrast to the private where the 'true self' will remain, at worst, impossible, and at best, partially realised.

Lesbian scholarship has challenged the either/or logic that seems to inform much of this work, drawing attention to the ambivalence of both the public and the private (Jagose 1994; Wilson 1991b). For lesbians the private is not so much the locus of a sanctuary from state violence against same-sex relations but the very site of interpersonal (state-condoned) and State violence. While the use of criminal law against same-sex relations between women is of less significance due to the relative absence of criminal prohibitions (Majury 1994; Mason 1995; but see Robson 1992, 1995), much state action against lesbians has focused upon lesbians as wives and mothers within the private realm. While, in the first instance, this might suggest the public is a more viable locus of sanctuary and security, particularly for lesbian women, such a conclusion is problematic (Mason 1997a). In Chapter 4 our analysis of the rhetoric and politics of property offers further evidence in support of the conclusion found in this body of work, that lesbian access to the public and civil society needs to be understood in the wider social, cultural and economic context, which (re)produces the public as masculine and the private as feminine and continues to limit women's access to the public (Gluckman and Reed 1997).

Our analysis of comfort and home exposes some of the limits of this scholarship. While some of the positive and negative affects and locational aspects of comfort and home may resonate with those reported and analysed in and through the private/public, our analysis suggests that comfort and home are not reducible to the private, or the distinction between private and public. The metaphorical uses of home and comfort challenge any tendency within lesbian and gay scholarship to think of spatial themes as determinate or essential locations, pointing instead to their indeterminate referential quality.

Furthermore, comfort and home offer a spatial trope that has been neglected in lesbian and gay scholarship. It also offers a challenge to the lesbian and gay scholarship that has been uncritical of the central role of the private/public distinction within contemporary sexual politics. It offers to disrupt the colonising and totalising effects of the private/public distinction, which threatens to subsume other spatial regimes within the private/public order. Our analysis of comfort and home suggests that lesbians and gay men resort to a different, wider and more complex repertoire of spatial tropes than is suggested by the public/private distinction, in imagining the locations and practices of belonging. The data set out above suggest that to reduce these to a private/public distinction will result in a failure to take account of their specific features, the specific experiences they represent, and the specific needs they inform.

We now want to turn to work that more directly addresses the location of home and the experiences of comfort. Home is a feature of some recent work by Dunne (1997) and Carrington (1999), and by a team of scholars working on lesbian and gay families (Heaphy 1999; Weeks 1999, 2001). This research offers the beginning of a scholarly engagement with the idea of home in the context of lesbian and gay family relations. However, it suffers from various limitations. Home is not the specific focus of this work, being reduced to domestic relationships of couples and to the private realm.

A limited amount of work escapes these limits. We want to engage here with three examples. Valentine and Johnston (1995) and Rothenberg (1995) consider home in the context of lesbianism; Betsky (1997) analyses home in a predominantly gay male context, and we want to consider Holliday's (1999) essay 'The comfort of identity' which represents a rare attempt to study lesbian and gay use of the rhetoric and politics of comfort.

Valentine and Johnston's (1995) point of departure is the significance of home in the practices of day-to-day lesbian lives and networking. Whilst recognising the private as one aspect of home they do not reduce home to the private, even where home is understood as security and sanctuary. Their study is significant in the way it brings together both the positive associations of home, as sanctuary, security, authenticity, origins, and the negative, as the place of surveillance and exposure, hierarchy, insecurity, violence and exclusion. These negative attributes of home are drawn out in the specific context of home as a (hetero)sexual space. With respect to sexuality in general, and lesbian sexuality in particular, home is experienced as a place of surveillance, visibility and denial. For lesbians within the heterosexual home, being at home is being out of place. At the same time, for reasons that reflect the economic, social and cultural position of women, Johnston and Valentine draw attention to the importance of domestic space for lesbians, pointing to domestic space as the location of wider lesbian social networks that are central to the production of lesbian identity. More specifically, domestic space as home is implicated in producing an experience of a wider community as home. In the move from domestic to civil society, lesbian practices deploy and transform those associations of security and sanctuary that are part of home.

But there is also a note of caution in their analysis. At the same time that home is produced and celebrated, Johnston and Valentine draw attention to the ways in which the positive associations of home are always contingent. This is highlighted not only in their distribution in various zones within the house (the bedroom in contrast to the parlour), but also evidenced in the potential to 'dedyke' the home when particular, potentially hostile, visitors call.

In Betsky (1997) work on 'queer space' home emerges as a motif within a different context, that of architecture, interior design and aesthetics more generally. The theme of domestic space is, in the first instance, understood as 'the closet' rather than the home. The closet has a host of negative associations; it is the place that marks the fact that there is no place in the world for lesbian and gay sexuality. In the contrast between the 'hearth' and the 'closet', as metonyms of home, Betsky draws a contrast between the hetero- and homonormative home. The 'home as hearth' represents home as the place where the (hetero) family gathers to, 'affirm itself as a unit in the glow of the fire' (p. 17). The 'home as closet' represents the homo-home as a dark and secret place. At the same time for Betsky 'the closet' is not reducible to the negative of the heteronormative home. It is also to be understood as a container that stores and houses the building blocks, the masks, through which the world, as artifice, is created. Here Betsky draws attention to the ambivalence of the closet. As the 'ultimate interior', it is both the place most distant from the world and the place where the world begins; where, lesbian and gay identity is both denied *and* born (p. 16).

Like Johnston and Valentine, Betsky draws attention to the importance of interior decoration as representational practices of the self. However, he goes further than Johnston and Valentine in this respect. First, he draws attention to the challenges that gay men's preoccupation within domestic interiors create for a gender-normative distribution of spatial preoccupations, which offer a challenge to the correlation between the feminine with the private and domestic interiors and the masculine with the public and with architecture, with the public aesthetics of space. Second, he argues that gay men, who as men are not confined to the home in the same way as women, produce a different aesthetic. Betsky suggests gay men, as men, were able to take the aesthetic assumptions and practices they developed within the 'home as closet' into the public world. Thereby they reconfigured and blurred the boundary between the aesthetics and practices of the public and those of the domestic space of home. These aesthetic practices include fantastical transformations, collecting, posing, resort to masks, the centrality of artifice and the importance of surface.

The main focus of Holliday's (1999) essay is the rhetoric and politics of comfort (and discomfort) in the spatial performance of lesbian and gay identities, providing an examination of the uses of clothing in the production of comfort. Her study pinpoints both the importance of comfort and its spatial dimension, home. Comfort, she concludes, is the 'primary motivation' in the choice of clothing, the 'ideal' to which her research participants subscribe.

She documents the ontological significance of comfort and records some of its positive associations in this context: its association with the 'true (natural) self' (p. 481), relaxation, retreat, greater control and a safe haven. She also plots some of the negative associations connected to the spatial dimensions of comfort, home: surveillance, discipline.

There is also, for Holliday, another dimension to the negative associations of comfort and home. These appear when her analysis shifts to a different register of the negative. Holliday suggests that the space of which the research respondents are least critical is home. She explains this in the following manner. Comfort, she suggests, is individual and individualising rather than social and politicising. She characterises it as social and personal atrophy, rather than a practice or a location of critical or political engagement and change. It is these political dimensions and effects which cause Holliday most concern.

Various themes here are similar to the work of Johnston and Valentine and Betsky. First, ambivalence and contingency are the attributes of home for lesbians and gay men. Second, home is understood as a resource. Third, home is important in the creation 'of the self', not only as an individual, but also as a member of a community. Finally, all their work points to the significance of home in the (re)production of lesbian and gay representational (symbolic) space that cannot be reduced to the home as a domestic or private space. Yet, whilst Holliday's work shares some of these features she is more pessimistic about the political significance of comfort.

In response to the work of Valentine and Johnston (1995) and Betsky we would suggest that there is a need to proceed with some caution. One problem arises in the juxtaposition of the two studies of Johnston and Valentine and Betsky. The former explores lesbian spatial practices with particular emphasis upon the domestic sphere whilst the latter emphasises the significance of men in the public sphere. The problem relates to the way the specific focus of each study tends to juxtapose and reproduce particular relations between gender and space.

It is a juxtaposition that has wide-ranging spatial connotations, for instance, Iris Marion Young (1990) draws attention to the long-standing association between gender and spatial relations. Starting with Heidegger's (1997) essay 'Building, Dwelling, Thinking', she explores the distinction between building and preservation which she identifies as a gender distinction between the masculine and the feminine. Building and preservation is also a distinction between production and conservation, between the public and the private, of nurture and nature, value and lack of value, labour and lack of labour, of identity and non-identity.

The domestic context of Johnstone and Valentine's study tends to reproduce the predominant association of women, home, domestic/private space, albeit in the context of an argument that seeks to point to the capacity of lesbian women to transform that space into a civil and quasi public space. Betsky's focus on architecture and the professional role of interior designer situates the homely practices of gay men in the context of a relation between men and the public realm of paid work. The juxtaposition of these two studies threatens to reproduce the gendered distribution of negative (female practices of home) and positive (male practices of home) and a gendered distribution of absence of value (re-production, unpaid labour) and value (production, paid labour). In the distinction between these two studies there is a danger that they reinforce the gender distinction that represents lesbian women's home-making labour as conservation and preservation in contrast to the man's home-making as labour, production, creation, building. One solution to this problem offered by Young lies in her attempt to problematise the distinction between production and conservation. A key element of this distinction is temporality – of novelty in contrast to repetition – a present–future orientation in contrast to a past–present focus. Young's contribution is to draw attention to the productive and creative features of repetition and to the future projection of repetition. In short, the dichotomy between building and conservation is a false dichotomy. Young's analysis offers an opportunity to re-read the two studies of Johnstone and Valentine and Betsky in ways that avoid the reproduction of the problematic gender/space relation.

Our analysis of our focus group data offers an instance of work that may transcend this problematic by drawing on the everyday use of home and 'comfort' as a set of practices that produce the experience of safety and security, danger and insecurity; a concern therefore with male and female practices of 'conservation'. Offering new data about the uses of home by (gay) men, the data suggests that home and comfort cannot be reduced or limited in significance to the location of the private or domestic. Home as metaphor de-essentialises that imagined location and thereby problematises the reduction of home *as a resource* particular to, and limited to, the private and the domestic. The data suggests that as a resource used to make sense of safety and unsafety, security and insecurity, home and comfort are intelligibilities and practices that have significance in the private and domestic context *and* in the civil and public realm. Furthermore, their significance and use cannot be understood in terms of a crude male/female dichotomy, rather, they offer an intelligibility and a set of practices though which women as well as men produce and experience their gendered and sexualised 'selves' in the civil and public realm, as well as in the domestic and private sphere. Home as metaphor is a contingent location and experience: it has to be constantly created by practices of home which in our data take the form of practices of 'comfort'. Preservation and conservation now appear not so much as making manifest that which lies beneath or at the heart of the place called home, but as citational practices which create the very experience of location as home.

Our concerns about Holliday's study of comfort have a different focus. In many respects our analysis supports many of her findings about the rhetoric of comfort, especially on the ambivalence of comfort and home. But it is in the context of ambivalence that our work begins to depart from Holliday's.

As Holliday shifts from an analysis of the rhetoric of comfort to a focus on the politics of comfort her work begins to lose sight of the ambivalence of comfort and home, threatening to reduce comfort and home to nothing more than the negative: home, Holliday concludes, is the space of which the research respondents are least critical. The analysis we offer above suggests that this may be a problematic conclusion as there is much evidence in the data already presented, and in the section that follows, to suggest that lesbians and gay men are very critical of home.

The negative attributes Holliday finds associated with the 'gay scene' in contrast to the positive associations connected to home as domestic space do not support her conclusions about the experiences of home. These are that research respondents are uncritical of home, or that home is a less political experience; or that home is a socially remote spatial experience of being and belonging. First, Holliday seems to forget all too quickly the way in which home is a location that is far from fixed. The 'scene', our research shows is as much a location of home and comfort as is private and domestic space. The social and cultural struggles that saturate the 'scene' are directly concerned with comfort and home as key aspects of the experiences of civil society and public space as locations of belonging. The ambivalence of home is a feature of its use, wherever deployed. The management and negotiation of home's ambivalence demands an acute awareness of the contemporary social and cultural values and a constant critical and political engagement with, and evaluation of, them. Holliday's denial of this is infused by a logic of either/or, which, as we have noted above, is one way of managing ambivalence. It is particularly problematic here, first, because it reproduces the either/or of home that the data itself challenges. Second, it erases key aspects of home and comfort; its social, cultural and political dimensions. These criticisms should not detract from the importance of Holliday's intervention. But they do point to the difficulties that need to be addressed in an encounter with the difficult and slippery politics of comfort.

## Taking home seriously: practical and policy reflections

Finally, we shift attention to focus on some of the practical and policy issues that flow from the analysis offered so far, beginning with an extract from one of our key informants, 'Terry', a gay men's worker for the Manchester City

Council. We use this extract to illustrate the significance of home in the context of practical attempts to create safer public spaces. We also use it to offer an instance of the analytical significance of comfort and home for a critique of policy and practice. Finally, we point to some of the problems with strategies of home.

The following comments were made in the context of a reflection on the Manchester City Council's interventions in 'the gay Village':

> I think the council's initiatives, in improving street lighting and improving the cleaning and taking down of fly posters . . . we take down fly posters which make the area look bad – that's all about . . . environmental improvement . . . If you have safety, cleanliness and environmental improvement all tied together, people feel good about themselves . . . We would hope to encourage pride and self confidence as opposed to all the self oppression that can be implied by having to occupy a dirty, unkempt, uncared for, dangerous, slovenly space.
>
> (Terry, KII, Man., 1999)

Various things are of interest in this extract. Environmental improvements are presented here as practices through which lesbians and gay men, 'feel good about themselves', gain 'confidence' and 'pride'. This explicitly connects local government environmental hygiene policies and practices to ontology. It also joins these themes to questions of safety and security. Terry's comments highlight the connection between public hygiene and public security (Neocleous 2000). The task of cleaning dirt from the streets, Neocleous suggests, is also about cleaning moral filth and social dirt. The safe and secure city in this scheme of things is not only physically clean but also socially clean. Thus in response to danger, which, in this instance, takes the form of 'homophobia, discrimination, prejudice and anti-lesbian and gay violence' environmental intervention will bring this disorder to an end. Of interest here is the relation between the practices and objectives of 'environmental improvements', ontology, and the rhetoric, practices and politics of comfort and home.

The fifth gay men's focus group in Manchester provided an opportunity to explore these relations. We asked our participants whether the environmental strategies of public hygiene, suggested by Terry, would make them feel more comfortable in the Village. Stewart did not think that it would. He explained:

> Well to me everyone's got different opinions and you can't satisfy everyone. I might like one thing, you might like one thing but we're both gay. When you've got different opinions you're never going to have a right or wrong answer.

In response to a further question, 'Would neater, tidier, cleaner streets make you feel more comfortable?' Stewart added:

No, because the streets would have to be cleaned twenty-four hours a day. You're never going to satisfy somebody twenty-four hours a day . . . Everyone's got a different perspective on how they want it to be kept clean. Me and [my partner] are always arguing about the cleaning [laughter] . . . I've got one way of cleaning which is underneath and he's got one which is on top.

Carl commented:

I'd hate to walk down a completely steam-cleaned Canal Street . . . a few cigarette butts . . . papers and . . . boxes! That's all right . . . That's what makes it feel homely.

(all extracts from M, gmfg, 5)

These extracts draw attention to some of the problems arising out of the connection between safety, ontology and the policies and practices of environmental management. The differences between research participants raise a major challenge to a politics and practice of environmental design that works with a singular idea of the hygienic subject in mind, suggesting that there is no easy relation between ontology and the policies and practices of public comfort. It also suggests that this impoverished ontology is a problematic basis for intervention to promote safer space. In the first instance environmental interventions are as likely to disrupt a sense of belonging and be a source of discomfort and insecurity and a site of conflict, as they are likely to promote a sense of security, confidence and comfort.

Mary Douglas (1991) suggests that home provides an 'orientation' in the world. If the homely dimensions of environmental interventions are to be successful as strategies that might promote belonging, then much work will need to be done to produce subjects who all respond to these impoverished 'directions of existence'. In the alternative a more complex idea of home and a wider range of practices of home may be required if environmental interventions are to facilitate belonging, their avowed objective.

But this is not to suggest that the research participants were wholly negative about environmental improvements. The gay men's group expressed their enthusiasm and support of environmental changes. One environmental technique of comfort that attracted widespread support was 'lighting'. In the first instance this is not dissimilar to the long campaigning by feminists to prioritise lighting in making safer spaces. It arose in an intervention by Gary where he drew a comparison between the portrait of the gay Village to be found in the award-winning TV drama *Queer as Folk* and his day-to-day experience of the Village. He explained:

If you are talking about warm fluffy feelings [in *Queer as Folk*] the street [Canal Street] was decked out . . . was all brushed up neat and there were really nice lights and it did actually look quite nice. Although it doesn't feel like it's my living room it did feel kind of nice and homely. You think, 'oh! Isn't that great!' I suppose that kind of brings it a bit closer, which is maybe coming in line about keeping it tidier, better lighting type situation.

(M, gmfg, 5)

In *Queer as Folk*, the street lighting of Canal Street takes the form of strings of lights and torches. This is in contrast with the current street lighting of Canal Street, which uses standard small sodium street lights. Gary's comments draw attention to a departure from previous feminist concerns with street lighting; his concern is not with lighting as a way of promoting safety and security by way of visibility and surveillance. His comments emphasise the connection between safety and security and lighting as a matter not just of safety, but also of aesthetics. This is not to suggest that these different ways of thinking about safety and security are necessarily unconnected. However, it does suggest that safety and security as a matter of comfort and of home-making may challenge the ways safety initiatives are imagined. It may also challenge existing concepts and practices of environmental improvements. This raises a question about the values that inform the aesthetic choices that make up the public practices of home-making. Terry's comments suggest that the current aesthetics of environmental design have a specific focus and agenda (hygiene, surveillance) that may be very remote from the values expressed in the fabrication of Canal Street as a place in the drama, *Queer as Folk*. Rather than being dismissed by reference to the distinction between reality and fantasy, fact and fiction, we would suggest that the gap between the two points to the need for a much more rigorous and extensive debate about the aesthetics and thereby nature of safety and security.

At best Terry's comments reduce the aesthetics of comfort to an aesthetics of (total) visibility, hygiene and purity. Terry's focus is on exposure, surveillance and regulation, drawing attention to the continuing importance of what Elizabeth Wilson (1991b) describes as 'a paternalistic form of planning' (p. 152). In turn, Terry offers an excellent example of the way official policies and practices of comfort reproduce the ambivalence of comfort and home. Making a place safe and secure may also make the experience of that space an experience of confinement, restraint, containment and subject to an oppressive and soporific form of control. Furthermore the purification of space offers to produce a radical separation of clean space (order) from dirt (disorder). In separating out the dirt the improved space is produced in the shadow of the ever-present threat of its return. This safety may not produce the desired renewed and increased use of the space, but may promote its further abandonment as fear of disorder becomes a feature of the perpetual demand for safety and security (Neocleous 2000).

Ambivalence poses a major challenge for policy-makers and practitioners who seek to intervene in the environment to promote comfort. We suggest that two key issues need to be addressed. The first is the values that inform the aesthetic choices, which produce the fabric of home. The second is the management of the ambivalence of home. The two need to be addressed simultaneously as they are intimately connected.

Terry's observations offer an insight into how these two features of environmental intervention come together in current practices. Dirt is a concept that plays a key role in the management of ambivalence. The extended reflection on the role of dirt in the formation of experiences of order by Mary Douglas (1966) is useful here, drawing attention to the way distinctions that generate purity (such as clean/dirty), inform the aesthetics and practical decisions of environmental interventions, whose primary concern is exclusion of dirt and disorder. If applied to lesbian and gay space, safety and security would be produced by the evacuation of dirt, the disorderly and the unruly. As a regime of exclusion, practices of environmental regulation take the form of a project of social hygiene. They manage the production of safe space as a purified space.

One context in which we have already noted some of the effects of this project of purification is in relation to the operation of violent hierarchies of gender, class, age, race and ethnicity in the generation of the Village. When refracted through the prism of dirt and purity, the negative terms of gender (female), race (black), ethnicity (Pakistani), age (youth), class (yobs) become matter out of place. In the context of Terry's observations these categories of exclusion are given shape by reference to problems of social hygiene, environmental improvements, the aesthetics and practices of comfort. In the first, and final instance, these practices, offered in the name of producing safer space for lesbians and gay men, produce danger as something that is always elsewhere. When it appears in the Village it takes the form of a person out of place. We will return to this in Chapter 8 when we explore the uses of estrangement in the production of safer space.

Nor ought we to forget that we first noted the operation of these distinctions in our analysis of the rhetoric and politics of property in Chapter 5, where we described the role of the rhetoric and politics of property in the generation of exclusions. Talk of propriety and of property is also talk of limits, of *borders* and *boundaries*. Boundaries and borders are not only central to the notion of property but, as we noted in that chapter, they are also key metaphors through which we make sense of freedom; freedom from more powerful individuals and freedom from the state. As a limit the border locates the experience of both order (cleanliness) and that order under threat (dirt). Borders are also central to the characterisation of the function of the state: the protection of property interests; the promotion of social hygiene.

Boundaries work to both generate the experience of ambivalence, bringing inside and outside together, and they offer to bring ambivalence to an end, separating inside from outside. As such, safety and security, as matters of environmental improvements and social hygiene, are about the establishment and policing of boundaries and borders.

While in the last chapter we noted the importance of the rhetoric and politics of property in the generation of those borders, this chapter adds another dimension to that picture. Comfort is another rhetoric and politics through which those boundaries and borders come into being. Comfort provides another repertoire of meaning through which those boundaries might generate experiences of belonging.

The extract from our interview with Terry, the council worker, offers an example of the production of boundaries of comfort by way of policies and practices of environmental hygiene. While the boundary connects comfort (safety) and discomfort (danger), the practices of social hygiene seek to deny this ambivalence through the production of comfort/home as multiple different locations. The positive and negative of comfort/home are differentially distributed. Thus the Village, as the locus of security, authenticity, comfort, is produced through the displacement of danger and discomfort, insecurity and danger as that which lies elsewhere.

Our concerns then are twofold. First, when put in the context of feminist critiques of home the spatial division of safety and danger are, we suggest, positively dangerous. It is an approach that (re)produces the myth of the safe home in the context of the gay Village. This suggests that environmental strategies that separate safety and danger might make it more difficult to address violence, fear of violence and safety in the Village. Our research maintains that for lesbian and gay safety this is a very dangerous myth that needs to be challenged if safety is to be a possibility (see Young 1997; hooks 1990; Mohanty 1992). Second, our focus group data and the particular responses to the hygiene strategies, outlined above, show that this division is neither achievable, sustainable, nor desirable. Finally, the environmental policies and practices of safety, represented in Terry's comments, institutionalise a certain paranoia (Wilson 1991), appearing to perpetuate an idea of home as a place of exclusion (which has been a major theme within recent feminist critiques of home (de Lauretis 1990; Honnig 1994; Martin and Mohanty 1986). Environmental politics, practices of safety also perpetuate the idea that home is nothing more than exclusion.

## Conclusion

Comfort and home offered us many challenges and surprises, disrupting assumptions and expectations about the nature of the experience of safety, but providing a window into a related, but significantly distinctive, way of imagining and thereby experiencing safety that has widespread significance. Perhaps one of the greatest challenges is concerned with the spatial aspects of comfort. Comfort and home challenge assumptions that the private and the domestic are imagined and lived as distinct from the civil and public. Far from being limited to domestic and private spaces and locations comfort and home have a much wider significance as points of reference central to experiences of being in place, of belonging, ontology. Comfort and home are ways of imagining place and practices of location intimately associated with safety and security. Feelings of safety and security are about experiences of being in and out of place. These feelings are pertinent to an understanding of lesbian and gay experiences of public spaces and places of civil society, in particular pubs, bars and clubs, as they are to our experiences of private, domestic and intimate spaces.

The ambivalence of home in general and the ambivalence of the lesbian and gay experiences of home raise particular problems, exposing and challenging the pervasive logic of either/or in the politics of home. Our work adds to the chorus of scholars who have already warned of the dangers of this logic in the production and reproduction of the myth of the safe home. We also hope that we have amplified the need for vigilance, and the need to explore ambivalence. It is both naive and wrong to suggest that the ambivalence of comfort and home render them politically bankrupt for a politics of safety and security. The challenge is to take ambivalence seriously. The focus of political engagement needs to be concerned with the management of ambivalence and its effects.

The data on home and comfort that we have set out and explored in this chapter provides a vehicle through which to rethink the relation between violence, fear of violence and safety. A key task that lies ahead is not to abandon the idea of home, nor to reduce it to a new impoverished myth of the unsafe home, but to complicate the issue of home.

We finish this chapter with a final demand for a more complex understanding of comfort and home. We need to re-engage with the diverse meanings of home and comfort. The reduction of comfort to consolation, ease, warmth and cosiness is problematic. The history of the idea of comfort draws attention to the problem of reducing comfort to the attributes of consolation, physical and mental relief that appear to gain importance with the emergence of bourgeois sentimental domesticity in the nineteenth century. Comfort has other more politically dynamic, uplifting and ambitious connotations; it is also a term that signifies strength and support, incitement to aid and the encouragement of physical, material and emotional well-being. Again, our suggestion is not that these associations exclude all others, rather that we do not ignore their rhetorical and political significance.

# 7   Cosmopolitan safety

## Introduction

We now turn our attention to another rhetoric and politics of spaces of danger and safety: cosmopolitanism. A couple of snapshots taken from conversations in the Lancaster gay and lesbian focus groups will help highlight some of the key issues we want to explore. We begin with a comment made by Ed, one of the gay men in the Lancaster focus group. 'Cosmopolitan', he explained, 'is fine by me. But anything local . . . isn't.' He continued, '[P]laces that are very local are risky but something with a cosmopolitan feel to it is fine' (L, gmfg, 2). Here the distinction between cosmopolitan and local is a contrast between safety and danger respectively. When asked to define cosmopolitan Ed explained it in the following terms, 'Just people of different types, more than one type of person'. The danger associated with the local is illustrated in the following extract: Steve, in the same group, describes an experience of danger in a pub in Skirton, an area that borders on the western edge of Lancaster City Centre. Ed described Skirton as 'totally local'. So what is the nature of the danger and insecurity associated with the local? Steve explained:

> I've never been so petrified in my life. It was the Red Cross [a pub] in Skirton just by the bridge. I walked in and the whole place went completely quiet. Everyone was staring at the door. I had my brolly with me, and my record bag. I had a cap on. I'd been strutting around [with friends] and I strutted right in there. It went quiet. I just stood there. I was looking at the floor all the time we were in there. I just wanted to get out as fast as I could. I looked round and there were like slash marks in the chairs.
>
> (L, gmfg, 2)

Steve's comments draw attention to various dimensions of the experience of the local as danger and insecurity. It is experienced as a moment of transgression in a particular place produced by way of reading sights and sounds within that environment and the reactions of others in that place

(McGhee 2001). A key characteristic of the local as a specific environment is its particular homogeneity. Visibility and evaluation are key dimension of the local as an experience of being out of place, of not belonging. Surveillance by others separates out, it exposes and makes vulnerable. Steve offers a catalogue of signs that differentiate him from the rest, who represent the singular and uniform, over and against his experience of himself as different. Steve's experience is produced by way of a reading of particular items of clothing (brolly, bag, cap) and bodily gestures (strutting, ways of looking). These are read as signs that differentiate and thereby render him out of place. Insecurity and danger are associated with the experience of not belonging. Signs of the pending violent reaction to this perceived disorder take the form of slashed seats.

In the exchange between Ed and Steve the local, as danger, is an experience that is produced by way of a hierarchy. The negative (unsafe) of the local as a singularity and homogeneity is presented against the positive (safe) of the cosmopolitan as difference and the multiple. In the local the experience of self, as difference, is an experience of being and belonging out of place: of not-belonging. It is in relation to this idea of homogeneity as danger and insecurity that the cosmopolitan as the plural and the multiple is made an order of belonging: safety and security.

Our second snapshot again comes from the Lancaster data. It is an exchange taken from the first lesbian focus group discussion. The term cosmopolitan appeared in the context of a discussion in which the participants talked about their experiences of living in Lancaster. Gill offered the following:

> My experience of Lancaster is that it is incredibly small. It's not got past being a small town and yet presents itself as a city. It isn't a city. It's a small town with a small town mentality and a small town approach to problems.
>
> (L, lfg, 1)

Of interest here is the distinction between small town and city. What do these terms connote? The answer lies in the following comment. Echoing her suggestion that Lancaster was represented as a city when in fact it is just a small town, Gill explained: 'Lancaster thinks it's cosmopolitan but it isn't.' Here the contrast between small town and city is a contrast between the non-cosmopolitan (the local) and the cosmopolitan, This experience of Lancaster, she explained, was contrary to expectations expressed by friends who were enthusiastic about her move to Lancaster. How was the cosmopolitan of Lancaster imagined by Gill's friends? Gill explained, 'They said, "You'll have a great time in Lancaster. Loads of lesbians in Lancaster. Great place!"' Here, the cosmopolitan is associated with a strong lesbian presence. In turn it is the lack of visibility of lesbians, and more generally Gill's experience of the passivity and invisibility of women in Lancaster, which signify for her the small town nature of place. Nor was this connection between lesbian visibility and the cosmopolitan peculiar to Gill and her friends. Another member of the group, Trica, used it to challenge the suggestion that there is a necessary correlation between the size of the place and cosmopolitanism. She explained that, in her opinion, Ulverston, a small market town some 30 miles north-west of Lancaster, is much more cosmopolitan. She continued, 'There's quite a lot of gay women in Ulverston and it's much more cosmopolitan than Lancaster.' In turn she offered an explanation in support of Gill's experience of Lancaster as a small non-cosmopolitan place. Lancaster, she suggested is, 'very parochial because a lot of people here were brought up here. They've lived here all their lives. Whereas in other places, like Ulverston, people come from all over' (L, lfg, 1).

This exchange makes the same correlation between danger and the local, and safety and the cosmopolitan already identified in the first snapshot, adding new dimensions of how lesbians (and one could add gay men) are a sign of difference central to this idea of cosmopolitan. The visible presence of lesbians is the mark of a cosmopolitan place, which in turn is a place of safety. Second, this exchange highlights the significance of the contrast between fixity and mobility in the constitution of the local in contrast to the cosmopolitan. Finally, this exchange warns us to be cautious about the way we imagine the cosmopolitan. It is a rhetoric and politics that is as much about the small, the intimate and the particular as it is about the large. This raises a question about the relation between the local and the cosmopolitan.

Gill's comments about the attributes associated with a small town also draw attention to a connection between our previous analysis of home and the cosmopolitan. The negative of the local is characterised by various terms: immobility, stability, sameness. These have a familiar ring to them. In the last chapter they appeared as negative attributes associated with home. Likewise, the negative attributes of the local highlighted by Ed and Steve, of surveillance, exposure, vulnerability, are also associated with home. Their appearance in the context of a contrast between the local and the cosmopolitan raises various issues. In general it suggests that the rhetoric of home and the rhetoric through which the distinction between the local and the cosmopolitan are imagined are not necessarily distinct. In the exchanges reported here, the characteristics of home don't refer to domestic space, but to civil and public space: of 'home town'. Of particular interest is the way in which cosmopolitan is made in opposition to this negative, home. This is far from unique to our data. Others have also noted (Dikec 2002; Nava 2002) that cosmopolitan is an imaginary that appears as a place over and against this negative manifestation of home.

However, we would disagree with those who suggest that the cosmopolitan is 'not being home' (Dikec 2002). We need to bring the lessons we learned from the last chapter into this new context. To imagine or advocate a move away from the negative home to another place constituted by reference to positive attributes cannot be reduced to a process of leaving home or read as the absence of home. To be away from home may merely signify being in another home which may, as we noted earlier, be characterised as the home of choice (the positive home over against the negative home). There is a need to avoid any simple opposition between home and cosmopolitan. Cosmopolitan with its multiple associations (global, mobile, multiple and so on) may be a term for a home that is a displacement of another home, which is produced as an elsewhere (e.g. Rouse 1995). The cosmopolitan/local distinction is *both* a different rhetoric and politics of being and belonging from that associated with home *and* a rhetoric and politics through which another home as the location of belonging may be imagined.

Cosmopolitan, like home, is 'a kind of space . . . It is always a localizable idea' (Douglas 1991). As such, cosmopolitan is another spatial term that makes danger and safety a matter of location. Our point of departure and analysis is everyday cosmopolitanism as a parochial rhetoric and politics of representation and belonging (Nava 2002). Beck (2002) calls this a 'rooted cosmopolitanism' which rejects the dominant opposition between the global and the local. As Beck (2002) and others (Markwell 2002; Robertson 1992; Sassen 2000) have noted, the cosmopolitan – local and the global – local are not distinctions that refer to or constitute separate spheres that never contaminate each other (Grewel and Kaplan 2001). We want to examine how both are at work simultaneously in the constitution of specific locations and places. Thus our study is in contrast to much of the work on cosmo- politanism, which emphasises the connection between cosmopolitan and the global in opposition to the local. Our approach seeks to challenge this bald opposition. Our focus is on the manifestation and operation of cosmopoli- tan as a rhetoric and politics of place in our two research locations: Lancaster and Manchester. A key objective in this chapter is to focus attention upon and examine the uses of cosmopolitan and the political and social effects of the globalising, universalising and totalising connotations of cosmopolitanism in these two different but proximate locations (Rofel 1999).

The opening snapshots offer some preliminary examples of the way the cosmopolitan–local binary is a distinction and a conjunction that has significance in the fabrication of lesbian and gay safety and security as everyday responses to violence. Visibility and invisibility are key features of the local and the cosmopolitan as locations of danger and safety. The local as danger is an environment that appears to be characterised as a visibility produced by a restricted economy of signs of belonging. In sharp contrast the visibility associated with a safe cosmopolitan environment is an invisibility produced through a multiplicity of signs of belonging. Another characteris- ation of this invisibility is that it is an effect of a plurality of differences, which produces indifference. Through multiplicity you blend in; you go unnoticed, unmarked.

The local, cosmopolitan distinction may have particular importance within the context of a sexual politics that gives a particular priority to the theme of visibility (Mason 2001). Sedgwick (1990) has suggested that visibility is the 'defining structure' for lesbian and gay oppression and, we would add, recognition in the twentieth century.

Our overarching concern is with cosmopolitan as a term used to name a different and alternative social order of safety and security. We want to explore the attributes associated with this order of safety and security, its uses and its limits. We want to examine the nature and use of the cosmopolitan imagination in the formal policies, at least in Manchester, relating to the generation and promotion of sustainable gay and lesbian safer space. We also want to examine its significance in business policies and marketing strategies relating to Manchester's gay Village. Of particular interest is the uses of lesbian (and we would add gay men) as a sign of cosmopolitanism.

Before turning to the empirical data we want to set our study within the context of some of the recent scholarship on cosmopolitanism. This work clusters around two basic oppositions. The first position is one that advocates the positive features of cosmopolitanism, represented in the work of Cheah (1998) and Beck (2000), who argue that cosmopolitanism has the potential to 'better express or embody genuine universalism' (Cheah 1998). Beck (2000) also argues that cosmopolitanism is the way in which we can learn how to imagine, define and analyse post-national, transnational and political communities, in an epoch which he describes as the second stage of modernism. The second contrasting position taken by Brennan (1997) and Zizek (1997) advocates a much more critical approach. Brennan suggests that cosmopolitanism reproduces the dominant order, rather than offering an alternative to it, and Zizek pursues a similar argument using US multiculturalism[1] as the example of global-capitalist cosmopolitanism. In this context, he argues, multiculturalism involves a patronising Eurocentric distance and/or respect for local cultures without roots in one's own particular culture. More specifically, US multiculturalism is a disavowed, inverted, self-referential form of racism, a racism with a distance. It respects the Other's identity, conceiving the Other as a self-enclosed 'authentic' community towards which the multiculturalist maintains a distance rendered possible by their privileged universal position. Multiculturalism, he argues, is a cosmopolitanism that can only ever be incorporating within parameters that are set by the cultural logic of the dominant order, which for Zizek, in this instance, is Eurocentic and informed by global capitalism. The arguments of Brennan and Zizek suggest that cosmopolitanism needs to be approached with caution. As an idea of an alternative order of safety and social security their work suggests that cosmopolitanism may not only re-inscribe the dominant (racist and heterosexist) order but also, more specifically, reproduce social exclusions by way of a person's access to resources.

Three themes within scholarship on cosmopolitanism are of interest here. The first is the spatial politics of the relation between the local and the cosmopolitan distinction. In this context our analysis differs from the orthodoxy of scholarship on cosmopolitan. In much writing on the cosmopolitan it is 'nation' that signifies singularity and limitation (the local). This is in contrast to the wholeness, universality, totality and plurality that are associated with the cosmopolitan. Cosmopolitanism is here post and contra nation. In the first instance our concern is not the nation but the local in contrast to the cosmopolitan. This different spatial distinction offers to enrich the analysis, taking the debates about cosmopolitanism out of the frame of interstate politics. A second theme focuses upon the significance of consumption in the fabrication of cosmopolitanism. The third and final emphasis is concerned with the cosmopolitanism and the formation of subjectivity.

These themes inform the most frequently used definitions and discoveries of cosmopolitanism. To be cosmopolitan one has to be able to appropriate, distinguish and claim to know the other and one has to generate authority from this knowing. Ulf Hannerz maintains that:

> Cosmopolitanism is first of all an orientation, a willingness to engage with the Other. It entails an intellectual and aesthetic openness toward divergent cultural experiences, a search for contrasts rather than uniformity. To become acquainted with more cultures is to turn into an aficionado, to view them as artworks. At the same time, however, cosmopolitanism can be a matter of competence, and competence of both a generalised and a more specialised kind. There is the aspect of a state of readiness; an ability to make one's way into other cultures, through listening, looking, intuiting, and reflecting.
>
> (1996: 103)

This is reminiscent of Bourdieu's (1986) analysis of the formation of distinctions, which notes the importance of knowledge and disposition in the formation of social class. To turn the intellectual gaze into a form of knowledge and competence for one's own enhancement is precisely how cosmopolitanism as a disposition is generated by the ability to move through the cultures of others, turning them into objects of distanced contemplation for oneself. The cosmopolitan comes to know himself through travelling through the cultures of others.

The two opposite strands of scholarship on cosmopolitanism and the common themes and key definitions within the work outlined above raises, for us, a series of questions that we will address by an analysis of our research data through the remainder of this chapter. These questions include the following: who can take up the position of the cosmopolitan? What factors facilitate the adoption of a cosmopolitan position? What factors limit its use? What are the effects of cosmopolitanism? More specifically, what are the everyday practices of cosmopolitanism? What practices might be rendered more difficult or impossible? We pursue all these questions with a very specific focus in mind: violence and safety. Our objective is to interrogate and evaluate the role and significance of cosmopolitanism for safety from homophobic violence.

## The uses of cosmopolitan

As a starting point we return to the focus group data to examine the meaning of 'cosmopolitan'. The contrast between the local and the cosmopolitan has many connotations. It is not our intention here to outline them all. We begin with some preliminary points. The local–cosmopolitan distinction is relational. It is a distinction that connotes a spatial relation between the part and the whole. This may be deployed in many different spatial contexts. In the example that opens this chapter the local–cosmopolitan relation is made in the image of contrast between the neighbourhood pub and the city. The most common manifestation of the distinction in scholarly literature on cosmopolitanism is the nation as local in contrast to the cosmopolitan as global. In all of these instances where the local is uniformity and singularity the cosmopolitan, be it the whole, the 'globe', the 'world' or the 'universe', is a unity that can incorporate the multiple.

Metaphor and metonym produce the many different meanings generated through this distinction. One chain of contrasts is the cosmopolitan as autonomy, maturity, freedom from prejudices, which is set against the uniformity and the tyranny of conformity that flows from the homogeneity associated with the local (Nava 2002). In this scheme of things the local (pub, neighbourhood, town, nation), invariably symbolises an emptiness and an impoverishment in contrast to the plenty associated with the cosmopolitan whole (city, supra-nation, global). How do these associations of meaning inform the imaginary of the local–cosmopolitan distinction in general and in particular as a relation of violence and safety, danger and security?

We turn first to our Lancaster data. We begin by setting the scene. As the extracts at the beginning of the chapter demonstrate, for some, Lancaster is quintessentially an experience of the local, 'a small town with a small town mentality'. As such it is imagined as a place of danger and insecurity. Other research participants present a different picture. Ed, a member of the Lancaster gay men's group, suggested that Lancaster is:

> On the verge of being cosmopolitan without going the whole hog. It has a mixture of people, a very broad mixture of people . . . even though, you don't think of it as being that mixed. I was born on Dale Street and our neighbours were Asian, Polish, Irish, quite a mixture, so it was cosmopolitan in that respect, but at the same time it does not have the sophistication that usually goes hand-in-hand with the cosmopolitan thing. It aspires to it.
>
> (L, gmfg, 4)

Various aspects of this comment about Lancaster as a place on the 'verge of being cosmopolitan' are of interest. The first is the reference to Dale Street. The second is the reference to 'sophistication'. Dale Street is, almost literally, the only street in Lancaster that provides the domestic location for the city's small permanent racial and ethnic minority community.[2] Lancaster is predominantly a white community. The yet-to-be-realised quality of cosmopolitanism in Lancaster might be a reference to this limited geographical presence of the racial and ethnic other.

This limitation is also signified in another way. The spatial limit is indicated by reference to competence: to the lack of sophistication associated with Lancastrian cosmopolitanism. In this context sophistication connotes skill, practices and experiences of being worldly-wise, having developed particular knowledges and skills. In this extract they are linked to interactions with racial and ethnic minorities, echoing some of the key characteristics of cosmopolitanism identified by Hannerz (1996) above. The questionable nature of Lancaster's cosmopolitanism is perhaps both a reference to the spatial confines of these minority groups relative to the wider city and also to the way this spatial limitation restricts the interaction by the dominant group with these minorities in the town. The speaker's characterisation of his own cosmopolitanism is connoted by his place of birth, 'I was born on Dale Street', suggesting he was born cosmopolitan. Temporal and spatial proximity authorises the knowledge and legitimates the skills that make the speaker worldly-wise in relation to the racial and ethnic minorities in Lancaster. Over against this, the questionable sophistication of Lancaster suggests limited spatial and temporal opportunities to become acquainted with more cultures and thereby few chances to become knowledgeable. Lancaster must remain on the 'verge' of cosmopolitanism.

But there is a need for caution here as the comment on the lack of sophistication is made in the specific context of racial and ethnic communities. However, the characterisation of Lancaster as 'cosmopolitan' is, our data suggests, not limited to being produced by way of the racial and/or ethnic other. It also arises in the context of another group of outsiders: 'students'. Students, as a category, not only relates to the current student population, but also to those who came to the city to study and stayed. (We should add here that in the UK it remains the case that university students still tend to study away from their home town, though changes in government higher education funding policy are changing this state of affairs.) The characterisation of students as being 'away from home' facilitates their personification as elsewhere: as outsiders. Students as outsiders, facilitate the fragmentation of the unity and homogeneity that is the 'local' and assist in the characterisation of Lancaster as cosmopolitan.

Focus group discussions offer many insights into the social and cultural significance of students in Lancaster and provide examples of how students, as a sign of the cosmopolitan, impact upon the lives of lesbians and gay men in Lancaster. Dave, a gay man who grew up in Lancaster, described how he was outrageous when younger, wearing 'make-up and strange clothes' (L, gmfg, 5). He explained his ability to appear in this manner in such a small place because of Lancaster's cosmopolitanism. In response, Anthony specified that Lancaster's cosmopolitanism was due to the presence of the university.

Dave also offered his enthusiastic confirmation of this. Of importance here is the way students disrupt the imagined homogeneity and conformity that characterise Lancaster as the local. Students being outsiders, 'student' marked as difference, connotes Lancaster as a plurality, a certain freedom, a particular tolerance. This exchange offers an example of the way one difference (students) may impact upon another difference (sexuality).

Another example comes from Paula, a member of the lesbian group, who lived in a house which she described as being, 'on the edge of the Marsh', a poor working-class public housing estate. It was a location tinged with the threat of violence, 'quite a scary place to live really' (L, lfg, 1). Paula and her partner had experienced homophobia when they first moved into the house. Graffiti had been painted on the front door, the door was also smeared with dog shit, eggs had been thrown at the windows. Paula explained that her hairstyle had attracted particular threatening attention: 'I mean at one point I wouldn't cut my hair how I wanted it because I just felt very funny walking out of the estate. The neighbours in the wider area were a bit kind of "Ah ha! What's this?"' Paula went on to explain that this intense neighbourly interest, tinged with the possibility of violence, did not develop into interpersonal physical violence, suggesting the reason was because the neighbours believed she was a student. She concluded: 'It's alright if you're a student, you know.' She added another instance of her experience of misrecognition as a student in the following comment:

> I found it very hard to get a decent haircut in the area . . . There was one guy. I wanted it clipper cut basically, and he said, 'oh are you a student!' That was sort of a way of asking me, 'Am I gay?' I wasn't very impressed. I hadn't been a student for three years.
>
> (L, lfg, 1)

Paula's experiences offer further insights into the way student, as a sign of difference, works as a vehicle of cosmopolitan safety. It provides a respectable code of difference. By way of that code lesbian sexuality as difference is experienced as relatively invisible. This is also a significant dimension of the experience of Dave who wore make-up. Dave explained, '. . . students were a bit more outrageous at that time, say ten years, fifteen years ago . . . *you could stand out without standing out* in Lancaster' (L, gmfg, 5; emphasis added). While the use of make-up by men has long been read as a sign of sexual perversion/difference, when encoded by 'student' it can be read as a sign of a more respectable difference. The other dimension of Paula's experience of student, the way it produces misrecognition, ought not to be forgotten. The hairdresser's willingness to engage with the (student) other, to be an aficionado of that difference, produces a certain ignorance, a certain inability to read the signs of difference. It produces a (sexual) visibility that is simultaneously a (sexual) invisibility. For lesbians and gay men student might work to access identities, places and services that might otherwise be more difficult and dangerous. Students as the personification of cosmo-politan, by offering a variety of non-conventional appearances, stop the easy reading of appearance with sexuality, thus producing an experience of relative sexual safety and security.

However, student is far from being either a category of safety *per se*, or a category that all lesbians and gays can deploy to make themselves respect-able to heterosexuals. For example while students personify a certain respectability, they also personify difference. Some focus group participants commented that students are despised and hated in Lancaster and its environs, also subject to violence and threats of violence. This suggests that within Lancastrian cosmopolitanism an engagement with the student other has particular limits.

Another problem with students is that the category is not equally avail-able as a safety strategy to all. Many commented that student is a category that separates out lesbians and gay men as well as connects them to each other and to other groups. This is most apparent in discussions about the impact of the division between 'town and gown'. For various spatial, social and cultural reasons, lesbian and gay 'townies' (working-class) found it difficult to participate in student gay and lesbian groups, events, venues. Likewise, lesbian and gay students found it difficult to meet and mix with local lesbians and gay men.

Others emphasised the way students is a category limited by age. Student remains a category associated with youth thereby making it a problematic category of misrecognition for older lesbian and gay people. Thus as a sign of a cosmopolitan order of safety and security 'student' both facilitates a different safety from that of the local, being potentially more inclusive, but at the same time works to limit the operation of, and access to, that new order of security and safety.

We now want to turn to the uses of cosmopolitan to be found in the Manchester data. The context in which cosmopolitan emerges in this location is very different: in Manchester our focus is the gay Village, a dense concentration of sustainable, public, gay and to a lesser extent, lesbian, commercial and community businesses and organisations. It is located in the very heart not only of a large city but also a major urban conurbation that is racially and ethnically much more diverse than Lancaster. Manchester and the conurbation that surrounds it has a large student population. Earlier work on the gay Village (Whittle 1994) suggests that students play a different role in that location. Far from being a figure through which other sexualities might gain a certain visibility in the Village, students threaten to overwhelm the Village. Whittle suggests that they threaten the safety of lesbians, gays and transgender people in the Village. With these thoughts in mind we turn to the data on the uses of cosmopolitan in Manchester's Village.

We begin our examination with an extract from publicity produced by lesbian and gay campaigning group, Healthy Gay Manchester, a sexual health, HIV/AIDS organisation. In their *Lesbian and Gay Guide to Greater*

*Manchester* they give prominence to the cosmopolitan theme, declaring that the Village is a 'European gay Mecca'. Their guide to the Village explained that:

> Visitors flock from all over to sample its unique spirit. At the heart of this fast-growing, post-industrial city sits the eclectic café society of the Lesbian and Gay Village – *a cosmopolitan showcase* bursting with pride, and one of the queerest pieces of real estate Europe has to offer.
>
> (Healthy Gay Manchester 1998; emphasis added)

Similar sentiments are to be found in the focus group data. One of the participants in the straight women's group, Julie explained:

> I don't say, 'the gay Village'. I go, 'Oh it's really cosmopolitan!' Do you know what I mean? That is the word I would use to describe the Village . . . It is cosmo-village. That's what it seems like to me . . . there is this quite exciting buzz . . .
>
> (M, swfg (straight women focus group), 3)

Of particular interest is the association between the Village and the cosmopolitan. In the second extract they are reduced to one and the same in the new merged term: 'cosmo-village'. Cosmopolitan is also given a particular spatial inflection: European. Cath explains, 'You said it was more cosmopolitan . . . it is more like a European place in terms of nightlife, bars, and you know, places to hang out.' Jill, a member of the Manchester straight women's group, explained, 'You could be in Paris. You could be in Barcelona' (M, swfg, 1). Liz, in the same focus group, explained:

> It's an area of Manchester people go to. There's lots of nice bars, it's becoming like a European city with that sort of nightlife and so all these people are – all these other bars are springing up around it because they are catching on to a good thing.
>
> (M, swfg, 1)

Of interest here is the relation between the Village and the wider city. It is a metonymic relation of part to whole. The (continental) European[3] of the Village, which connotes the place as cosmopolitan, is the part that also signifies (is a metonym for) the cosmopolitanism of Manchester as a whole. These extracts suggest that the cosmopolitan imaginary is a feature not only of individual but also local government and voluntary organisational characterisations of the place.

Another aspect of these observations is the way they use aesthetic and spatial markers to describe their immediate location, the Village and Manchester more generally. What are the particular aesthetics through which the Village as 'elsewhere' is produced?

Various examples can be found in the data. Many of the bars in the Village, on the central drag Canal Street, have adopted a practice of using outside seating associated with the warmer climes of continental Europe, despite Manchester's often-inclement weather. Metz, situated on the canal side, is accessible via a bridge and keeps a boat on the Rochdale canal. This gives it a more exotic, almost Venetian, feel rather than being experienced as another bar in a rather dark basement in an ex-industrial building by the side of a dank, murky, disused canal in the North West of England. As another example of techniques of marking 'elsewhere' in this space the very name 'the Village' echoes with references to a pioneering and once vibrant gay culture in New York's Greenwich Village. The names chosen by voluntary organisations (Healthy Gay Manchester's use of Mecca to describe the Village) and by business initiatives reflect a conscious attempt to deploy exotic and glamorous associations connected to places and cities remote from Manchester (Tribeca, Metz, Prague and The Lexington) in the production and commodification of the location. This naming practice directly signals the attempt to brand difference.[4]

Through these various practices and techniques the local is reconfigured as the post-local and the trans-local: the cosmopolitan identified by Beck (2000). As Johnson (1998) notes, 'translocality is as much about fantasy and imagination, a traversing of conceptual spaces, as it is about the actual movement of goods and people. As cosmopolitan the Village is connoted as a located social order and security that is free from prejudice and a more tolerant place. At the same time it ought not to be forgotten that the dominant characterisation of the Village generates this image of safety and security in a specific context: consumption. This takes the form of a 24-hour economy, the entertainment industries and particular practices and institutions of civil society (cafés, bars, dance clubs). In this instance, that different order of safety and security that the Village stands for aligns safety and security with practices and institutions of excitement and pleasure. This is most vividly captured in the TV series set in the space of the gay Village broadcast on Channel Four, *Queer as Folk* (screened first in 1999, with a second series in 2000). The gay Village is represented as little more than a party space: a utopian hedonistic gay male space, a place of sexual diversity, of tolerance, with an absence of violence.

Business initiatives in Manchester have adopted and promoted policies of cosmopolitanism in various ways. Our first example is taken from the interview with John, the marketing manager for the gay-owned and operated business[5] that runs Metz, already mentioned in Chapter 5. Metz is a 'melting pot'. John explained:

> It's saying to gay men and women, you know, let's not live in an enclave which we've had to for political reasons for long enough. Let's integrate, we're realistic, with the wider community. It says to that wider community, 'You've got to integrate with gay men and women because

you're in their space.' That's what our business is about . . . There are three main groups that make up Metz. [We have the] gay community with all the diversity within that as a generic group. We've got the business community (we enjoy a lot of business lunching) and we have basically 25+'s. Our core customers are not kids, they are more mature people. People have described us as 'the 30-something venue'. That's fine . . . we actually target people who are more discerning, who are more mature . . .

(John, KII, Man., 1999)

The policy of 'integrate don't discriminate' incorporates an idea of the target market that is infused with qualities associated with cosmopolitanism. In general the customers in John's mind have a certain sophistication: 'Integrate don't discriminate' positions their customers, lesbians/gay men and straights, as having an orientation and a willingness to engage with the sexual other, an openness towards divergent cultural experiences. The term 'discerning' suggests that they already have a certain awareness of and desire for a bar that offers them a place of contrasts rather than a place of uniformity. As 'mature', '30-something' customers they are differentiated by reference to an established level of skill and competence that reflects their ability to respond to and manage the social and cultural dimensions of sexual difference. In this instance both lesbian/gay men and straights are represented as cosmopolitan.

This characterisation of the cosmopolitan nature of Metz's target customers is given prominence and has a wider significance in various strategies to market Manchester in general and the Village in particular. The marketing manager of Metz was chosen to be part of a team promoting Manchester as a destination for international tourism, for new businesses and for new capital investment. The tourist organisation, Marketing Manchester, has played an important role in this process. Joanna, a manager with Marketing Manchester, described the gay Village as 'a unique selling point' (Joanna, KII, Man., 1999). The Village, she explained, might be used to target both 'gay specific' audiences and wider audiences. She added that while she met some resistance to the use of the gay Village to market Manchester, she was working to ensure that marketing the gay Village to both gay and wider markets was incorporated into official policy. When asked why, she suggested that it is a sign of 'openness'. She illustrated this by reference to the choice of images used to represent the Village during the annual lesbian and gay Mardi Gras festival held in August. These, she explained, are images of 'the Village . . . with loads and loads of people', they signify 'the general feeling . . . of freedom of expression' and 'a very easy-going city on the whole', representing the city as a 'liberal' place. Mardi Gras is a symbol of the Village and thereby Manchester as a post-local, post-homogeneous, post-national place (Markwell 2002). This is a parochial politics of diversity, which, through marketing, has become a parochial politics of representation that has been given national and international significance.[6]

The Mardi Gras festival connects the policies of cosmopolitanism found in business and the tourist industry with local government policies and practices. Terry, the gay men's officer with the Manchester City Council, whom we met earlier in Chapters 5 and 6, explained that the City Council had taken a proactive role in promoting the annual lesbian and gay Mardi Gras festival. The Mardi Gras, he explained, had been a particular success attracting many heterosexuals as well as lesbians and gay men to the village and getting media coverage. He also provided several other examples of local government support of initiatives of cosmopolitanism. The council's regulatory functions, he suggested, provided a range of mechanisms to achieve this objective. One of these functions, which we considered in Chapter 6, was public hygiene initiatives. He suggested that they had an important role to play in promoting business in the Village. Other significant local government initiatives included financial support for the Healthy Gay Manchester's Village Guide referred to above. Policies and initiatives relating to urban regeneration were also important encouraging national and international visitors, jobs and money, to the area.

Before we leave the cosmopolitanism promoted by local government, businesses and tourism, we want to examine the way safety is imagined in this context. Joanna, a manager with Marketing Manchester, offers an illustration of the safety of this cosmopolitanism in the following example:

> I was walking down Oxford Street [a major thoroughfare near the Village in the city centre] into town . . . I was following a couple of guys that were holding hands. Now I didn't think anything of it . . . and I was watching the faces of the people coming towards them. Nobody batted an eyelid. Whether they didn't see, or whether they just weren't worried, they were just going about their own business . . . nobody bothered. Now it's that sort of example that would make the difference between going to one city or another, I think, as far as the gay tourist market is concerned. Some of the research that the BTA [British Tourist Authority] has done has shown that the gay and lesbian market aren't too worried about a city being gay friendly, it has to be gay neutral, or at least gay neutral. So long as nobody embarrasses them when they're checking into a hotel, or passes comment. It's the embarrassment factor I think rather than anything else.
>
> (Joanna, KII, Man., 1999)

Joanna offers an insight into the nature of this idea of the cosmopolitan city as a safer place for gay men (and one might add lesbians). In the context of this example of handholding, the safety produced by cosmopolitanism is characterised, in the first instance, as a gay visibility that is a relative invisibility to an imagined straight audience ('they didn't see'). In the second instance, it features as a particular indifference by the straight viewers ('they just weren't worried'). Another dimension of safety follows. The focus shifts to dwell on an experience of the lesbian and gay experience (as a tourist): the experience of checking into a hotel. Again gay, and in this instance, lesbian safety, is associated with practices of straight indifference ('nobody embarrasses them'). This indifference also informs the characterisation of a safer city for lesbians and gay men. It has to be, not so much gay friendly as 'at least gay neutral'.

We need to consider who is the cosmopolitan citizen being imagined here. The first is the speaker, Joanna. She indicates her sophistication, her cosmopolitanism, in the phrase, 'Now I didn't think anything of it . . .' Her own position, in the first instance in the shadow of the gay men who are the objects of her gaze, then shifts. She describes the practices and dispositions of a heterosexual cosmopolitan citizenry, 'nobody batted an eye lid'. The third cosmopolitan citizen is imagined not in terms of the wider city but in terms of the personnel involved in the tourist business. The sophistication that is cosmopolitanism is imagined through the manners of the hotel staff who perform 'gay neutral'. The knowledge, practices and skill necessary to perform the civility of straight indifference is at the heart of experience of cosmopolitan safety and security. Last, but not least, are the lesbian and gay tourists. As tourists they represent outsiders who come to consume 'other cultures', though in this instance that 'other culture' is also their 'own' culture made strange by way of geographical distance. The absence of embarrassment is the mark of an experience of belonging associated with the cosmopolitan.

So far we have focused largely upon the positive associations of cosmopolitanism. In doing so, following the insights provided by our exploration of 'home', there is a danger that such a partial representation of cosmopolitan may contribute to the myth of cosmopolitan safety. There is significant evidence in our data of negative associations. To ignore or avoid this dimension of our data would not only misrepresent the data but also erase the ambivalence of cosmopolitan. It is to these matters that we now turn.

## The trouble with cosmopolitanism: its limits and discontents

### (a) Cosmopolitanism and the (re)production of inequalities

The first issue we want to addresses is a problem raised by Brennan (1997) and Zizek (1997) earlier. Cosmopolitanism, they suggest, is a vehicle for the reproduction of inequalities rather than their erasure. We examine this problem through an analysis of data that focus on the gay Village in general and data about a specific event, the local lesbian and gay festival, the Manchester Mardi Gras. The Manchester event, like the Sydney Mardi Gras (Markwell 2002), from which it takes its name, has become a 'hallmark event' (Hall 1997). It is an event that has been used to symbolise Manchester more generally. The marketing and tourism organisation, Marketing Manchester, has used images of the Village during the Mardi Gras festival to promote the city both nationally and internationally. These are images of, 'the Village . . . with loads and loads of people'. They have been selected to connote Manchester as a place of difference; a place of 'freedom of expression' and a 'very easy-going city on the whole', a 'liberal' place. This annual event offers a pertinent example through which to explore the nature of cosmopolitanism.

We begin with some general reflections on the Village. The following comments were made during the course of a discussion about the results of the Manchester survey in the lesbian focus group. The survey found that most straight women interviewed in the gay Village were in the bars used by straight men. This was contrary to earlier suggestions made by both key informants and the focus groups. They had suggested that straight women came to the Village with their gay male friends, frequenting the gay bars with gay men in order to avoid straight men. Kath explained the different picture represented in the survey in the following terms:

> But that would make sense . . . There is no longer a need to be out [in the Village] with a gay man on your arm as your passport to get in somewhere because you can walk in.
>
> (M, lfg, 5)

Justine added, 'You can walk in with your boyfriend and they just won't say anything.' She went on to suggest that this represented a change. The sharp contrast between the past and the present was described in the following terms:

> I remember Cruise 101 [a gay club] that was very gay male, and women in there were 'fag hags' . . . There were no straight men at all and there were very few lesbians but that was many years ago . . . if we are looking at [the Village's] cosmopolitan air, then in some ways, it's legitimised heterosexual people going into the Village and going into gay bars. You know it's all about integration. I think it's quite interesting that lesbians are going to the two women-only spaces when they are available . . . but that the straight people and gay men can go to which ever venues they like . . .
>
> (M, lfg, 5)

Cosmopolitan is used here to name changes in access to and use of a particular place. It's a movement from a Village with 'no straight men at all and . . . very few lesbians' and limited access by straight women, who needed a 'passport' to facilitate entry, to a space that has a significantly enhanced and legitimised heterosexual presence. But, at the same time the enhanced mobility is partial. Straight men seem to be its primary beneficiaries. They have moved from a position of almost total exclusion to uninhibited access. Access by straight women is no longer subject to strict limits: they no longer need a passport. Gay men and lesbians seem to derive fewer benefits from this 'cosmopolitan air'. Gay men have unrestricted access, which we might presume is the freedom already associated with gay space or male space in general. The position of lesbians appears to remain as one of confinement and marginalisation in venues of questionable sustainability. There is perhaps a need for some caution here. The survey recorded a significant number of lesbians in the Village. Almost 20 per cent of those surveyed identified as lesbians in contrast to almost 36 per cent who were gay men. However, as Justine suggests, they were largely confined in two women-only spaces. Lesbians' confinement and containment in these bars suggests that while the Village may provide something of a haven for lesbians it is also organised by their relative exclusion.

Overall, this exchange draws attention to the potential for the cosmopolitan air to perpetuate inequalities and disadvantages. The beneficiaries of this cosmopolitan air are the already relatively powerful: straight people, especially straight men. As such this cosmopolitan instance stands as something rather less than an imagined plurality that is characterised as a universal equality, freedom, and a celebration of diversity.[7]

The annual Mardi Gras festival brings many of these matters into stark relief. Let's begin with a response that followed from a question posed by Karen acting as group facilitator of the third lesbian focus group in Manchester: 'How does Mardi Gras affect how you feel about the Village the rest of the year? If it does at all?' Zoe explained that originally the Mardi Gras:

> Was about celebrating your individuality and your sexuality . . . And now it's really about spending money, getting drunk and all those sorts of things.

Yoni added:

> The people who organise it create it into more of a festival and a carnival rather than a lesbian and gay event. Every year it gets more tourists and more straight people around. That seems to bring with it a feeling of less safety and less than an exclusive event.

Sarah commented:

> I think Mardi Gras has made the Village more like accessible to straight people. It has made straight people feel that it is OK to go to the Village. And I think that for me anyway that makes it feel not very safe. It doesn't feel safe particularly late at night.

Margo explained that the Village:

> was originally a gay space and it was small and it was nice and it felt safe and then suddenly somebody somewhere obviously cottoned on

that there was loads of money to be made and it became this huge thing that actually means nothing now.

(all extracts from M, lfg, 1)

These extracts draw attention to different features of cosmpolitanism. Far from being specific to these research participants, their comments echo sentiments expressed by the men in the gay focus group and many of the key informants. They all suggest that the experience of the Manchester Mardi Gras has promoted not so much a more sustainable celebration of lesbian and gay identity and community, but an experience of identity and community under threat and subject to transformation (Markwell 2002 on Sydney). As an experience of a loss of safety and security these extracts tell a story of a golden age of Mardi Gras in particular and of the Village more generally that is no more. The cosmopolitan is here a present and a future of danger and uncertainty in contrast to a recent past of safety and security.

The event of Mardi Gras as a medium of change has several dimensions. One is that it is an event that has promoted more easy access by straight people into the gay space of the Village. While in the first instance this is in the context of the event, it has a long-term effect, encouraging straight access at all times.

A second dimension is in the association between Mardi Gras, and consumption. While money-making was always an aspect of the Mardi Gras event (to raise money for HIV/AIDS charities) it is also associated with transformation. This is a shift from profit for the community to corporate profit, which we described in Chapter 5 as a shift from positive profit to negative profit. Margo, from the Manchester lesbian group, explained, 'I don't think the money goes to HIV at all' (M, lfg, 3). Others commented that the breweries are now the major beneficiaries of the event, making large profits from the consumption of beer. Frankie made a connection between the commercialisation of Mardi Gras and longer-term changes in the Village by way of a story about Manto's, one of the gay bars in the Village. She explained:

> I think that [the owners] would only let gays in and it was virtually empty. It was very quiet and really nice. People sat around chatting and drinking. But the next week they had no door policy because obviously they make their money off the straight young crowd. As a bar there is that dilemma between providing safe gay space and also making a profit. If the people you make your profit off are young, are straight, or they are young gay men, then that's who you are going to open your bar up to.

(M, lfg, 3)

In this instance the transformation of the bar from a gay and safer space to a mixed (and maybe more unsafe) space is connected to bar owner's search for ever-increasing profits. Profit is the impetus and rationale that promotes (market) diversification, bringing straights into lesbian and gay places and events. Here the diversity of cosmopolitan is aligned with local corporate greed. The pleasures of some within this plurality of consumers is experienced by others who are long-standing users of the place as a loss of pleasure and a loss of place, which is also a loss of safety and security, and the emergence of new dangers in that place.

There is much in the data pointing to the way the Mardi Gras event reproduced social marginality and exclusion by way of gender, class, race and ethnicity. We limit our examples here to instances focusing upon the reproduction of gender inequalities. The marginalisation of lesbians was evidenced in various ways. For example, it appears in the balance between gay men and lesbians in the planning meetings (60–80 men and five women). Such marginalisation has been a long-standing feature of the organisation of space at the event. Lesbian space, members of the lesbians focus group in Manchester explained, was always thought of by the organisers as 'added on', or 'extra'. The lesbian-women-only space at the 1998 Mardi Gras was described as an 'afterthought . . . a low priority'. It also had a symbolic spatial dimension: 'the women and the children were pushed to the outer boundaries of the space that was available . . .' (M, lfg, 1). In 1999 the women-only space was relocated to the centre of the event. In this location, we were informed, many lesbians were subject to verbal abuse and harassment by straight men visiting the Mardi Gras. In 2002 lesbians threatened to boycott the event when plans to organise a women's space were abandoned (*Pink Paper*, 16 August 2002). Zoe, one of the women in the focus group, concluded:

> I felt like it was just like, 'Well OK you lot can go and have that space over there and we're not going to make a great deal of effort and we're going to give you a marquee, but just do what you need to do over there and we'll do the proper stuff over here.' Because there isn't a lack of money or interest but it's always directed, almost always directed to male interests.
>
> (M, lfg, 1)

Here Zoe offers an example of the way in which existing hierarchies of gender are conjoined with the economics of cosmopolitanism (consumption and bigger profits) to reproduction of the social marginality and social exclusion of lesbians. Clarke (1991) suggests that lesbians are rarely addressed as consumers, rarely targeted as a specific group, and rarely identified as cosmopolitan (except with the short-lived 'lesbian chic'). This, she argues, is because they are not identifiable, accessible, measurable and profitable. The following comments by Justine develop the relationship between economics, power and lesbian marginality in the Village:

> I think it is because lesbians don't have money and power and I think it boils down to that in terms of who owns the village. There's very little

ownership in terms of lesbian-only space. If we sort of hark back all those many moons ago to Sappho's it obviously didn't make the money that people wanted it to make. They could fill it twice over with gay men and make lots and lots of money. I think that's got a lot to do with it. With money comes power. It's also in terms of supporters within the City Council, who are gay men. That's where the power is and that's why I feel there isn't a permanent home for lesbians within the Village. Also I don't think that lesbians in Manchester can speak to each other for long enough to establish a space [Lots of laughter].

(M, lfg, 5)

Justine's comments offer support for Clarke's arguments about the importance of economics and the limited significance of lesbians as a target market. At the same time her closing remarks suggest that there may be other social and cultural factors at work. Justine's comments also make a link between economic capital with social capital: gay men *both* have more money and are more likely to be in positions of power (gay men in local government) than lesbians. The slippage from economic to social capital is also reflected in the slippage from community by way of the commercial scene to community in and through the local state.[8]

Access to these resources Justine indicates, may facilitate or limit 'ownership' in the Village. Her use of 'ownership' in this context draws attention to the possibility of connections between the rhetoric and politics of property and cosmopolitan. In particular, it suggests that cosmopolitanism may be a context in which the rhetoric of property, as an intelligibility of belonging, changes its political significance, marking the limits of belonging (loss of ownership), and providing the means by which an experience of exclusion and marginalisation may be imagined. More specifically, our earlier analysis of the significance and use of the distinction between personal and fungible property has direct relevance (see Chapter 5). The shift from the personal to the fungible offers a way of making sense of the changes in perceptions of the relation between profit, identity and community described above. It also helps to explain changes in experiences of Manchester's 'hallmark event' and the gay Village more generally. Cosmopolitanism, rather than facilitating and nurturing those aspects of property and propriety that work to generate and sustain an experience of belonging, is shown, in the Mardi Gras event, to limit those uses of the rhetoric and politics of property, threatening to transform lesbian and gay experiences of property and propriety in that time and place.

Mardi Gras brings this into sharp relief. Frankie explained:

If they were honest then you could cope with that, but they pretend that it's a Mardi Gras for everybody, that everybody is welcome, that it is fantastic, but actually it's crap.

(M, lfg, 1)

In Mardi Gras, 'community' and 'charity' become a thin veil behind which a different political economy reproduces hierarchies of social distinctions. Gay men and straights, who are perceived to be already privileged, are the major beneficiaries. The search for profit and consumption practices generates partial 'access' to and power over the Mardi Gras event in particular and the place that is the Village in general. In turn it reproduces economic, social and cultural inequality, which for some makes 'community' and safety at best fragile and at worst impossible.

This offers a rather different experience of Mardi Gras from that promoted by the images of Mardi Gras used by Marketing Manchester. The representation of Mardi Gras as the quintessence of the cosmopolitan, as plurality, as freedom from prejudice, tolerance, equality, and a wholeness that incorporates all people, is something of a partial picture. Here Mardi Gras is made the image of the *myth of safe cosmopolitanism*.

There is another side to the cosmopolitan reported in our data. It is an experience of the privilege of some and the disadvantage of others. Cosmopolitan is a spatial experience of safety limited to those who already have the necessary economic, social and cultural abilities and resources to participate. The image of the Mardi Gras crowds needs to be treated with considerable caution. As an image of incorporation it is also an image of a moment in the operation of the hierarchies of inclusion and exclusion. This state of affairs echo's findings reported in Kevin Markwell's (2002) research on the impact of corporate consumerism and the international marketing of the Sydney Mardi Gras upon lesbian and gay perceptions of the event. As in the Manchester context, Markwell suggests that lesbian and gay criticism and disillusionment focuses on the lack of a sense of 'ownership' felt by many local lesbian and gay people.

### (b) Cosmopolitan dangers: 'dregs' and 'straights'

Our second reflection on the limits of cosmopolitan explores the distinction between good cosmopolitanism and bad cosmopolitanism as a distinction between safety and danger. An example of this distinction is taken from a conversation between participants in the straight women's focus group in Manchester. Having celebrated the plurality of the Village by use of the term 'cosmovillage', Julie went on to describe a rather different aspect of that cosmopolitan experience of place in the following way. During the course of a Saturday afternoon shopping trip with a gay friend, she visited Manto, a Village bar, to 'chill out'. She said, 'and we sat there and I can honestly say that it was all the dregs of society walking past me' (M, swfg, 2). This caused much laughter in the group. When calm returned she continued, 'I couldn't believe it'. Another member of the group responded, 'That is cosmopolitan though!' In this instance, rather than being a positive and safe multiplicity, 'cosmopolitan' is a multiplicity of people that is more threatening and more dangerous.

The specific context in which these remarks about the limits of cosmopolitan arose related to the presence of beggars and 'crack heads' in the Village. But we would suggest that it points to a more general dimension of the limits of cosmopolitanism. We want to explore the use of the distinction between the good/bad, safe/dangerous in the production of cosmopolitan in general and lesbians and gay man as a sign of the cosmopolitan.

As our opening snapshots suggested in some instances, gay men and lesbians have come to personify the good cosmopolitan. A good example of this is to be found in Richard Florida's (2002) work on urban regeneration. Florida suggests that gay men have come to signify diversity, tolerance and an openness to difference, all features of a community that are particularly attractive to others, in particular what he describes as the 'creative class'. At the same time we ought not to forget that gay men (and lesbians) have been (and in some contexts continue to be) a sign of difference that is threatening, dangerous and menacing.[9] The production of 'gay' as a sign of liberalism, tolerance and freedom from prejudice is a very recent invention. How has this been achieved and what is its significance?

John, the Metz Marketing Director whom we met earlier, explained: 'Obviously the Village has grown on the back of the fact that this is a lesbian and gay space. The reason that people come here is for the gayness of it, even if they are not gay' (John, KII, Man., 1999). Here he describes the way 'gay' has been used to market particular businesses and the Village more generally. This has been done not so much to attract gay men but also to draw people of other sexualities (heterosexuals) into the Village. In this context 'gayness' in general and gay men in particular are represented by very specific aspects of gay male culture: music styles, particular styles of dress, the aesthetics of particular bars and clubs. Annie, one of the women in the straight focus group in Manchester, explained, 'Gay people just have this liberated – you can do whatever you like' (M, swfg, 2) way of life. Gay as a sign of difference, diversity, liberation, liberal tolerance, freedom from prejudice is a very partial image of marginal sexualities. The gayness that is put to work in this cosmopolitanism is produced in and through a process of selection that limits the aspects of gay (and lesbian) life that can signify 'gay' (Litvak 1997). We should also notice the context in which the process of selection that produces these images is made. They are made in the service of marketing and promoting individual businesses and the entertainment and culture industries more generally. Often these marketing strategies are not directed exclusively, if at all, to gay or lesbian audiences. Richard Florida's work provides an example of their use in the context of a straight audience. In his work gay appears as one of a series of social and cultural indicators associated with successful urban regeneration. These indicators are used to develop strategies to attract capital and new information and cultural businesses to an area. The social mobility of the 'creative classes' that provide the capital and labour force in these industries, Florida suggests, is influenced by a variety of cultural factors. The 'gay index' Florida identifies generates a correlation between high profile gay male communities and the successful attraction of creative industries. Thus initiatives such as the establishment and promotion of a gay Village may work to attract capital to a city or a region. This gay index is not so much an index of all dimensions of gay life but the 'myth of the safe gay'. At the same time, we would add, it must also be the production of the dangerous gay.

This use of 'gay' in the first instance foregrounds pleasure rather than safety. More specifically in targeting other sexualities the pleasure that is being singled out, marketed and commodified by way of this 'gay' is a pleasure for heterosexual consumption. More specifically, Rushbrook suggests that:

> The perception that homosexuality is closely associated with sex may encourage straight-acting couples, unaware of their performance of heterosexuality in 'normal' everyday public space, to perform their hetero-sexuality to 'excess' in queer space.
>
> (2002: 196)

One example that stands out from our research data is the use of the Village by straight women as the location for hen parties. Thus, the reduction of gay men to a sign of 'freedom' and 'liberation' enables straights to practice their own desires in those terms. At the same time this particular gay has to be produced and contained as a pleasure and a difference that is safe for heterosexuals. Julie's comment about the problem of 'dregs' (albeit in a different context) offers an instance of the operation of the limits of this safety. Young explains:

> But we also take pleasure in being open to and interested in people we experience as different. We spend a Sunday afternoon walking through Chinatown, or checking out this week's eccentric players in the park. We look for restaurants, stores, and clubs with something new for us, a new ethnic food, a different atmosphere, a different crowd of people. We walk through sections of the city that we experience as having unique characters which are not ours, where people from diverse places mingle and then go home.
>
> (1990: 239)

This is heterosexual pleasure that is aligned with respectability. Pratt and Hanson (1994) suggest that Young's reflections on urban difference are somewhat idealistic, maintaining, 'She is using a moment in the city to attempt to speak, to represent, a type of association between individuals that does not require identification and a type of identification that does not rest on exclusion' (p. 7). We would add that she is also using the same moment to forget both the nascent and the actual violence of heterosexual cosmopolitan respectability upon lesbians and gay men. In the example which opens this section, the phrase, 'dregs of society' offers an instance in which cosmopolitanism as respectability shifts into something that is much less sanitised, more troubling and more problematic for straight consumers.

The power and seduction of these images of pleasure marketed to and for a heterosexual audience (as well as a gay audience) should not be underestimated. After the broadcast of the UK's *Queer as Folk* TV series, which occurred during the course of the data-gathering stage of the research, dramatic increases in the levels of tourism, particularly straight tourists, in the Village were reported to us.

Nor is the power and seduction of these images limited to straights. It ought not to be forgotten that the Village may also offer a resource of pleasures, safety and respectability for gay men and lesbians who visit the Village. It offers a respite from the everyday vilification and hostility that imprisons them within the category of 'dregs of society' in other locations, both near and far. This was vividly illustrated during the early stages of the research. Police arrested and prosecuted several gay men for consensual sex in private in Bolton, less than 10 miles north of the gay Village. Bolton falls under the same police service as the Village (see Moran 2002). Likewise, this cosmopolitan safety appears to have little significance in other spatial contexts in which violence and the threat of violence may occur such as the home, the neighbourhood, the workplace, the school or college.

The data generated by the survey of the gay Village indicate that we need to exercise some caution here. In the survey the gay men who lived in areas away from the centre of Manchester and visited the Village less frequently reported higher experiences of safety in the Village than the gay men who lived locally and visited the Village more frequently. This suggests that the pleasures, safety and dangers of the gay Village are relational.

The fact that, in part, the pleasures and safety being imagined are not limited to those of the gay and lesbians who use the space is particularly significant. The pleasures of some, especially those of the dominant group in a society, may be the dangers of others, especially those that are and remain marginal and socially excluded in and through those pleasures. These are matters we will return to in the following chapter.

## *(c) The location of cosmopolitanism*

This brings us to our third study of the limits of cosmopolitanism. While Lancaster is also imagined as a place by investments in ideas of the cosmopolitan, the use of gayness as its personification is very different. For example, the refusal of gay business owners to nominate their businesses to the wider public as 'gay' offers a sharp contrast to the Manchester experience. As we noted in our exploration of the rhetoric and politics of property in Chapter 5, in Lancaster economics plays an important factor in the refusal of 'gay' to name or brand a business. Gayness in this context has little or no marketability.[10] The gay and lesbian market is perceived by gay business owners to be too small. Nor is gayness a viable brand to be marketed to other sexualities (heterosexuals) in this context. Our key informants suggested that using gayness to brand a business would result, at worst, in homophobic violence, at best in heterosexual flight from the business leading to its likely collapse. At the same time gay key informants running bars and cafés used by lesbians and gay men branded their businesses as 'mixed', which brought lesbians, gay men and heterosexuals together with considerable success.

It is useful to reflect at this point on the differences between 'mixed' and 'integrate don't discriminate' as brands. In the latter 'gayness' is always already a thing that is marketable. In good part 'integrate don't discriminate' is about extending the market for 'gayness' to include straights. In sharp contrast to this, in the context of 'mixed', 'gayness' is not merely an impossible brand but a name associated with various dangers: of heterosexuals and to the business.

How does cosmopolitanism map on to this branding? 'Mixed' is more likely to be a coded way of communicating to lesbian and gay consumers in a hostile heterosexual context. Certainly, in the context of Lancaster, 'mixed' appears only in listings in gay and lesbian magazines, indicating the possible gay and/or lesbian presence in a place. Its formal use in marketing a place to straights would potentially expose the business to the dangers outlined above.

In analysing the data on the use and experience of the brand 'mixed' we want to ask two questions. What is the relationship between 'mixed' and cosmopolitanism? Second, who is able to take up the position of the cosmopolitan in this context?

If cosmopolitanism is a part of this experience it might, in the first instance, be a position taken up by the straight. Richard and Freddie, owners of No. 6 Café in Lancaster, described the mixed experience as a straight experience in the following terms. Freddie began:

> We've got some straight men friends who are really comfortable with it as well. Yeah, they're extremely comfortable with it all. They come in to the opening previews to the art exhibitions [in the Café] and all that and they're really nice. They're quite professional folk.

Richard continued:

> Yeah! We get quite a lot of office people, solicitors and all that, people from around; there's lots of solicitors' offices around. They all know that there's a good number of gay people in here and none of them could care less.
>
> (Freddie and Richard, KII, Lan., 1998)

The knowing heterosexual who connects with the 'exotic' world of lesbians and gay men who visit the café are here described in terms we have already identified as associated with the cosmopolitan. In particular, Richard and Freddie describe the straight men in terms of showing a willingness to engage with the sexual other, an openness toward their culture, being competent at recognising and managing interaction with difference. The manners of indifference ('they couldn't care less') seems to be a key dimension of the straight relation to the sexual other in this place

It is perhaps a little more difficult to characterise the lesbian and gay experience of mixing with heterosexuals in the same space in the same terms. The lesbian and gay focus group members described their experiences of the No. 6 Café in various ways. The following illustrate the most common of these. Gill described the café as 'my place', and continued, 'where I can go to hold Paula's [her girlfriend's] hand and feed her bits of cheesecake . . . in the ideal world, that's what I want.' Paula described No. 6 as 'gay owned' with a 'straight atmosphere'. She added that the atmosphere varied to a degree from time to time depending upon the clientele: 'very straight' on Saturday afternoon when lots of 'straight people wandered in there by accident' and 'more or less obviously gay' at the café's World Aids Day event. One of the gay men offered the following example of an experience in the café:

> I was there I think about a month or two ago with a friend. I'm afraid I have one of these catalogues from an organisation called Regulation which sell all sorts of weird and wonderful things [SM and fetish goods]. Jeff wanted to lend it to Freddie, who is the chef there. When Jeff was handing it over to Freddie it had a rather lurid picture on the back. I saw somebody in the café looking at this lurid picture. I thought, 'I wish Jeff had been more discreet handing it over'. Not everybody wants to see lurid pictures. I think this person took it, you know, in the 'best possible taste!' I just thought he should have been a bit more discreet in handing it over.

Various dimensions of these practices and characteristics previously identified as cosmopolitanism are lacking here. For example, there is little evidence of lesbians and gay men visiting the café to engage with the heterosexual as sexual other. Heterosexual remains the 'I' over against which the lesbian and gay experience remains that of the 'other'. While there may be a certain lesbian and gay openness toward straight culture this arises and remains in a context in which they are sexual outsiders. In this context it is an 'openness' of necessity rather than one of choice. Likewise, lesbian and gay competence in recognising and managing interaction with the heterosexual world is a necessary part of managing survival and safety in an often hostile world (Corteen 2002). The sophistication and manners at work here, referenced by way of the failure to be 'discreet', is very different. While it is clearly concerned with recognising and respecting straight culture, this respect is born more out of fear of the violence and hostility commonly associated with that culture rather than out of a more positive curiosity in, celebration of, or appropriation of, that other sexual culture. Lesbians and gay men have a great knowledge of the heterosexual as 'other' and all the necessary skills to engage with that sexual other. However, in Lancaster this intelligence and these skills are not about being in the dominant position of the cosmopolitan subject or an equal citizen, or of pursuing and practising the consumption of the safe pleasures of sexual otherness. Nor is it about the process of reconstituting themselves in the dominant or even equal position, or producing one's place within it. This 'cosmopolitanism' is a survival strategy born out of being and remaining marginal.

No. 6 Café provides a temporary respite from an otherwise hostile environment. At best it is a place where identity affirmation is contingent and quixotic (Bell and Binnie 2000). This is not about identification, as Pratt and Hanson (1994) argue, but it is about safety from heterosexism and the heterosexual dispositions that are carried on the body. It is not Beck's (2002) desire to recognise the similarity of others as a universalism, but a recognition produced through danger and difference.

## Understanding cosmopolitanism

Our data and analysis offer various contributions to the way we understand cosmopolitanism. The first contribution arises in the context of Zizek's suggestion that there are only two contemporary alternatives for belonging. He describes these as either a cosmopolitan global capitalism or totalitarianism, nationalism and fascism. Our analysis suggests that these two positions are not so much alternatives (in a relationship of either/or), but intimately connected (cosmopolitan capital *and* totalitarian, global *and* local, etc.), one and the same. Let us return to one of the key features of that opening definition of cosmopolitanism, produced by a binary opposition of cosmopolitan and local. These two terms connote a range of respectively positive and negative meanings: the global, universal, the whole, the heterogeneous (plural), freedom from prejudice, equality over against, the parochial, the particular, the limited, the homogeneous (the singular), the restricted, the prejudiced, the totalitarian. The list could go on. It is of particular interest that Zizek's two alternatives reflect these two poles of the binary. He presents them as being in an either/or relationship. Our analysis suggests that their connection needs to be understood instead by the conjunction 'and', as they are two sides of the same coin. What Zizek offers is two different but intimately connected images of the cosmopolitan subject. In contrast, our data and analysis offer an insight into the way both cosmopolitan *and* local are put to work to fabricate the experience of the subject. Furthermore, our analysis demonstrates the need to focus on the specific and parochial use of the various attributes of the cosmopolitan, local relation.

A second contribution relates to the argument that cosmopolitans are at the privileged, empowered end of what Doreen Massey (1993) has famously termed the power-geometry of time-space compression. Cosmopolitans, she argues, are most frequently characterised as being social elites (professionals in high-status occupations), members of what Leslie Sklair (2001) defines as the transnational capitalist class, or what Robbins (2001) calls 'the liberal managerial class'. While our analysis offers some evidence in support of this, it also challenges this picture. Like Pnina Werbner (1999) who maintains that working-class labour migrants, as a category of social marginality, in certain contexts might be cosmopolitan, our data offer some support for sexual minorities as cosmopolitans. We argue that sexual minorities in a context of social exclusion, Lancaster, may use cosmopolitanism as a survival strategy to facilitate access to places and services that might otherwise be denied. But we also suggest that there is a need for caution. The Lancaster and Manchester experiences demonstrate that there is a need to expand the ways of thinking about the strategic and tactical use of cosmopolitan and its limits. There is also an urgent need to explore this in more detail, as it provides a way of challenging the reduction of gay cosmopolitanism to the more derogatory category of global gay. The latter threatens to reproduce many of the negative associations associated with gay male mobility as danger, by connecting those negative connotations with the dangers of global capitalism (Altman 1996, 1997, 2001; Evans 1993).

The Manchester data relating to the use of the Village by white working-class heterosexual women offers another contribution to our understanding of cosmopolitanism, which may work to empower these otherwise excluded women in various ways (see Skeggs 2003). These women use the Village to assert their claim on public space not of their own making. Finally, the Village provides a place for the voyeuristic pleasure of looking. It is in this context that their presence is also revealed as more problematic, particularly for lesbians (see Skeggs 1998). Writing about the structuring of difference within the city, Pratt and Hanson argue:

> In real cities, different groups and inequalities are structured relation-ally; a celebration of alterity (especially one premised on the denial that different groups can or even should understand each other) would seem to draw attention away from the relations of power and domination that structure difference and the very real *connections* that exist between groups.
>
> (1994: 7)

Our data and analysis offer many instances of this relationality. Differences *and* connections are drawn in the gay space but these have very particular effects.

## Conclusion

We began this chapter with a series of questions. Who can take up the position of the cosmopolitan? What factors facilitate the adoption of a cosmopolitan position? What factors limit its use? What are the effects of cosmopolitan-ism? More specifically, what are the everyday practices of cosmopolitanism? What practices might be rendered more difficult or impossible? So, what answers do we provide?

In different ways the data from the two research locations points to the importance of knowledge and cultural competence in being cosmopolitan. In Lancaster this takes the form of an ability to perform and to be read as a student. In Manchester, for lesbians and gay men it takes the form being a 'good commodifiable gay' in contrast to a 'bad user-unfriendly gay'. As we have shown in this and other chapters of this book, this distinction is fabricated by a range of economic, social, cultural and spatial distinctions: class, age, race, ability, ethnicity, location. In this chapter we explored the ways in which all these features inform a distinction between the cosmopolitan and the local, between the 'good cosmopolitan' and the 'bad cosmopolitan'. Again, knowledge and performance are central to these distinctions. As one of the straight women in the Manchester group explained: 'But it is all to do with education you know. We all mix with all sorts of people, those types of people just don't because they are uneducated and they are a bit more careful.' As another women from the same group illustrates, this is produced through a distinction between 'little towns' (the local), in this instance Knutsford, a small respectable middle-class town south of Manchester and the city (the cosmopolitan). The 'little town' is where she 'wouldn't have met a gay man' in contrast to the city which symbolises diversity. Here, the participants define themselves against those who clearly don't know any better. Connected to this is the problem of how to behave. The 'good cosmos' are those who celebrate knowing the other by a performance of manners, of respect for the other. The practices of 'sophistication' are of particular importance here. Cosmopolitanism is an attitude and a practice based on education, knowledge and appropriate behaviour.

Key to this is intellectual and capital appropriation that distinguishes which forms of gay and lesbian cosmopolitanism are worth knowing about, worth exploiting, worth excluding. These questions underline the recent debates about cultural omnivores (Erickson 1991, 1996; Peterson 1993; Peterson and Kern 1996; Warde 1994). Some of these scholars suggest that social class is being broken down because people are consuming lots of different types of culture rather than conforming to the established distinc-tions between high and popular, whilst others show that the range of culture consumed only adds to the ability of the middle class to expand its distinc-tions and power. Our data suggests that only some groups have access to all the varieties of culture available, making it much more difficult for those who do not embody or personify high economic, social and cultural capital to be able to access and exploit other cultures.

A central point here is not just about access to the different cultures, but also about what is seen as worth appropriating into the omnivore subjectivity. Our analysis suggests that we are at the stage of late capitalism identified by Zizek, in which multi-cultures can be commodified through their reduction to an 'essential' difference, used to generate profit, enabling social divisions to be (re)drawn by the distinction between the profitable and the non-profitable. This suggests that it may be marketability rather than sexuality that is the issue for marginalised sexual groups. Are our differences worth knowing, having, experiencing? Are they marketable and consumable?

However, incorporation into an imagined wholeness by commodification, as our analysis suggests, is not entirely straightforward. There are cosmopolitan winners and cosmopolitan losers. Sexuality, gender and class have intervened in the commodification of gay space. Moreover, whether the use of this space by lesbians and gays makes them complicit with hetero-capitalism is still open to debate (who isn't?). It certainly does not guarantee that they take an uncritical stand towards the territorialisation of gay space. In fact, our research suggests that because they struggled most and have the greatest investment in the space, they are its most critical users. Yet we can still see how gay men and lesbians (not to mention transvestites and transgendered people) do become objects for the straight fetishisation of difference.

The attempts to generate a cosmopolitan character who is socially mobile and can cross the boundaries of social class in a particular location are dependent upon fixing others in place (making them local over against our cosmopolitanism). Cosmopolitanism is the means by which the new cultural omnivores can assert themselves in a particular place through their accumulated knowledge of cultures that signify 'else-where' to which previously they would have been denied access. It is about re-figuring and re-imagining the dominant, however defined, through the appropriation of others; but only those others who have already been turned into a sign of, and commodified with, (sub-cultural) value.

What this does suggest? Following Gramsci (1971) and Williams (1973), it is that partial, not full, gay male incorporation has occurred. The commodifiable bits have been hived off (Manchester's Mardi Gras is a good example of this), and the gay struggle for space has been turned into the search for economic rent. From our research it seems that what has been left out is subject to change but it is usually the less commodifiable. It is nearly always those who do not do respectability in order to make consumption by others safe, the 'dregs of society'. As terms like cosmopolitanism come to replace those of inequality, distinction and difference, we should remember the political and economic impetus behind them, which is to divide social groups by class, gender, sexuality, location in order to make them amenable to commodification.[11]

As an alternative image and practice of safety and security cosmopolitanism has some positive but also many negative features. Our data suggests that there is a need to pay careful attention to the contradictory effects and the ambivalence of cosmopolitanism. It may be aligned with both safety and danger. Many aspects of cosmopolitanism in Lancaster produce safety only by misrecognition, which perpetuates absence. In this context it is an invisibility that may in turn perpetuate a failure and a refusal by those with official responsibility for safety and security services to take lesbian and gay needs more seriously.

In Manchester, both local state and business policies and practices have produced and promoted a new visibility, a new presence, although these changes have been geographically limited in their impact. At the same time it would be wrong to conclude that this does not generate a potential for wider changes both within the areas that are geographically connected to the Village and those that are more remote. In addition our research suggests that these changes have both amplified the dangers of homophobic violence and at least, in a limited way, generated in that location a demand for new strategies and responses to danger and insecurity. We now want to examine one of the lesbian and gay strategies which emerged in response to these cosmopolitan dangers and insecurities: the politics of estrangement.

# 8   Stranger danger

## The uses of estrangement and the politics of fear

There are friends and enemies. And there are *strangers*.

(Bauman 1991: 53; emphasis in original)

Understanding strangeness requires an examination of the regime that creates it.

(Phelan 2001: 37)

These opening quotations eloquently pinpoint the two key concerns of this final chapter: strangers and the politics and practices of making strange (what we call estrangement). The quotation from Zygmunt Bauman's *Modernity and Ambivalence* (1991) highlights the peculiar position of the stranger. The stranger is presented as a third figure. In the first instance, Bauman suggests, there is the relation of friend to enemy, which he explains, is a 'master opposition': between inside and outside, which:

> sets apart truth from falsity, good from evil, beauty from ugliness. It also differentiates between proper and improper, right and wrong, tasteful and unbecoming. It makes the world readable and thereby instructive. It dispels doubt . . . It assures that one goes where one should.

(1991: 54)

The relation of friend to enemy described here is a violent hierarchy with a very specific quality: an effect of certainty and stability. Bauman describes the relation as a 'cosy antagonism' and a 'collusion' (p. 55), where the 'enemy' is always represented as distinct, separate and distant from the friend; geographically, socially and culturally. The third term, 'stranger' is a figure that disrupts this stable and comfortable state of affairs.

The stranger, Bauman tells us, is '. . . neither friend nor enemy; because he may be both' (p. 55). The stranger conflates opposites. Thus the stranger is truth and falsity; good and evil; propriety and impropriety. The figure of the stranger also has a spatial dimension: the stranger is distant and proximate. This characterisation of the stranger is in sharp contrast to the friend/enemy dichotomy in which opposites are managed by way of a clear and relatively stable distribution of the positive (friend) and the negative (enemy). The figure of the stranger embodies and personifies a troubling and persistent ambivalence, representing the world as an unreadable place, a place of doubt and uncertainty. It is a figure that gives form to an experience of loss, of orientation, of direction and place. As a relation of 'both', 'and', the stranger personifies a special threat and an exceptional danger 'more horrifying than that which one can fear from the enemy' (p. 55).

What is the relationship between lesbians, gay men and this idea of the stranger? Shane Phelan's (2001) study of contemporary dilemmas of sexual citizenship suggests that lesbians and gays occupy the position of strangers in the heterosexual body politic: both within the body politic, but not of it. Likewise, for Arlene Stein (2001), lesbians and gay men are the quintessential 'strangers' in American society at the beginning of the new millennium. Her study of lesbians and gay men as strangers focuses upon struggles for lesbian and gay civil rights within a small-town in the US Pacific Northwest. She explores the way lesbians and gay men are simultaneously in that small town community, but for some, not of that community: made distant and alien from it. Both Phelan and Stein suggest that the concept of the stranger outlined may have particular significance for the study of sexual politics in general.

The preliminary exposition of the concept of the stranger draws attention to its connection to other themes explored in this book. Of particular significance is the spatial dimension of the concept of stranger: of inside and outside. We noted in Chapter 5 the importance of the distinction outside/ inside in the formation of boundaries. The stranger, as the embodiment of spatial ambivalence (being both inside and outside), is a key figure through which boundary formation, boundary violation and boundary (re)inscription is imagined, embodied and enforced. Likewise, Bauman's suggestion that the stranger is both 'proper and improper' also has a familiar ring to it. Both connect the stranger to the theme of property as a rhetoric and politics of belonging.

The stranger is also a figure that haunts debates about cosmopolitanism, as a return to one of the snapshots that opened the chapter on cosmopolitan safety illustrates. Steve explained:

> I've never been so petrified in my life. It was the Red Cross [a pub] in Skirton just by the bridge. I walked in and the whole place went completely quiet. Everyone was staring at the door. I had my brolly with me, and my record bag. I had a cap on. I'd been strutting around [with friends] and I strutted right in there. It went quiet. I just stood there. I was looking at the floor all the time we were in there. I just wanted to get out as fast as I could. I looked round and there were like slash marks in the chairs.
>
> (L, gmfg, 2)

Here Steve rehearses an experience of being out of place in a particular location: a pub in a central neighbourhood of Lancaster, but in the context of a particular community, the local. What role does the stranger play in the constitution of the experience of the individual and community here? This close encounter in the confined space of a pub is produced as an experience of social and cultural proximity and remoteness, qualities that are a key dimension of the practice and politics of estrangement. As we noted in the last chapter, to be in this relation is to be in a position of exposure, vulnerability and danger in relation to those who embody the dominant order.

If the stranger plays an important role in the constitution of the community as local what role does this figure play in the production of the community as cosmopolitan? Within a cosmopolitan setting the encounter with strangers and strangeness would appear to be the basis of a different community in which strangeness is not antithetical to safety, but instead part of its reason. It is the role of the stranger and the uses of estrangement in the context of the cosmopolitan that provides our point of departure in this chapter.

In the last chapter we noted that Manchester's gay Village has been characterised and promoted as a 'cosmopolitan showcase' (Healthy Gay Manchester 1998). In part, the phrase 'cosmopolitan showcase' is a reference to the high spatial concentration and resulting visibility of gay-identified businesses, organisations and people, at the 'heart' of the city, which is presumed to be overwhelmingly heterosexual. Also the 'cosmopolitan' nature of that 'showcase' is a reference to heterosexual access to, and presence, in the gay Village. While the phrase 'cosmopolitan showcase' makes no explicit reference to safety, as Castells and Murphy (1982) and Castells (1983) have demonstrated in their work on the Castro district in San Francisco, the spatial concentration of gay men is associated with social justice. Safety from homophobic violence and harassment is an important dimension of that social justice. In the guide to the Village, while there is no formal reference to the Village as a space of safety for gay men and lesbians, certain information suggests that this is a significant dimension. In general the safety of the gay space is connoted by spatial concentration, visibility, vibrancy, strength and pride. More specifically references to the Lesbian and Gay Policing Initiative and details of a help-line dedicated to 'Action on Hate Crime' offer some indication of dimensions of the Village that have an overt safety and security focus. But this paints a somewhat partial picture. The research data offer some alternative and unexpected challenges to these connotations of safety and security.

What are the experiences of safety and danger in this 'cosmopolitan showcase'? Our survey, the UK's largest survey of lesbian and gay experiences of safety and danger to date, generated some startling data. The first surprise is that gay men in the Village sample (37 per cent – the largest group of survey respondents in the Village) were the group most likely to find Manchester's gay Village unsafe.[1] Another unexpected result is the stark difference between gay and lesbian respondents using the space. Gay men are twice as likely to perceive the Village as unsafe than lesbians. When we examine the gay men's responses in more detail, we find that those who have closest contact with the Village, living in, or near the City centre, and/or making regular visits to the Village, report the lowest safety ratings. In sharp contrast, gay men from out of town report the highest safety ratings.[2]

These findings are perhaps even more surprising when we compare the Manchester 'cosmopolitan showcase' data with the survey data from 'small town' Lancaster, which has none of the resources and characteristics associated with visible and vibrant concentrations of lesbians and gay men. In Lancaster lesbians and gay men are more likely to find Lancaster safer than straight women. There is also little reported difference between the 84.1 per cent of gay men and the 85.9 per cent of lesbians who reported Lancaster to be safe.[3] In the first instance these findings appear to offer a challenge to a baseline hypothesis of the research: that the Village, 'one of the most vibrant Lesbian and Gay communities in the country', offers and is experienced as safer space.

But the challenges didn't stop there. When we asked our Manchester survey participants to tell us their reasons for avoiding parts of the Village (its streets or bars), we were surprised by the responses. Manchester's gay men and lesbians rarely mentioned experience of violence. In fact, they reported the lowest levels of experience of violence. The most important reason given for avoiding bars and areas is 'perceptions of danger'.[4] Lancaster differed in this respect. Experiences of violence played a much more prominent role in the rationalisation of avoidance behaviour by both gay men and lesbians. Gay men reported the highest level of experiences of violence as the basis for avoidance (41.7 per cent). In Manchester gay men reported the lowest level of experiences of violence (9.8 per cent) of any sexual category. Violence also played a more important role for Lancaster lesbians (30.6 per cent) in stark contrast to low reports of violence by lesbians in Manchester (8.9 per cent). Another difference between the two locations is to be found in the categories of danger offered by the survey respondents. In Manchester 'straights' appear as a distinctive category of danger, a category that has little significance for the Lancaster respondents.

How are we to make sense of these findings? We begin by returning to the scholarship on strangers in order to develop a more detailed understanding of the category of the stranger. We then explore the connection between the stranger and fear, in particular fear of crime. In their conjunction we offer a new approach to understanding the phrase 'stranger danger'. We then return to explore the empirical data, undertaking an analysis of research which suggests that lesbians and gay men are made strange in the constitution of the hetrosexual community. We then explore data which suggest that the politics of making-strange is not a politics peculiar to the constitution of the hetero-community. There is much to suggest that making-strange is a practice and politics also in use in the constitution of the homo-community.

## The stranger

We begin our exploration of scholarly work on the stranger with Georg Simmel (1964) whose reflections produce the 'stranger' as an ideal type: a conceptual tool that can help to isolate, analyse and offer an explanation of social relations.

For Simmel, the 'stranger' is a figure that embodies particular positive relations and a specific form of interaction, a set of relations through which the dynamics of both the individual and the collective, the group, come into being. As Simmel notes, the stranger connects the two, being, 'an element of the group itself': both a fully fledged member *and* one who is perceived to be, 'outside it and confronting it' (1964: 402). This is echoed in the work of Bauman (1991) on strangers. As we noted above, for Bauman the stranger is a particular characterisation of relations of inclusion and exclusion, a social dynamic that creates the possibility of a particular form of incorporation into the group, assimilation. At the same time, the stranger produces the limits of incorporation, in the reproduction of a social order based upon particular exclusions. The stranger, Simmel suggests, is constituted by way of an interaction between the abstract (as the general), which generates an experience of remoteness, and the specific, which produces a particular intimacy. The stranger is also a very distinct spatial relation: a 'unity of nearness and remoteness'. In the figure of the stranger the 'distant is actually near'. The stranger also personifies a particular temporality, the one who comes today and stays, a durable presence (Simmel 1964). The combination of these themes in the stranger makes it a figure that is particularly troubling.

Bhabha (1996) notes that it is the proximity that forces, figures and enables the production of difference. It is not always the dangerous other that threatens (Bauman's enemy), but the proximate stranger who is not as easily identifiable. The stranger personifies anxieties to do with reading, interpretation and judgement. Ahmed (2000) develops Bhabha's work, by drawing attention to a pervasive concern with strangers (which she describes as stranger fetishism) by exploring the ways in which the stranger figures difference in contemporary societies. She argues that stranger fetishism is in part a displacement of social relations on to an object (in the traditional Marxist take on fetishism). But it is more than this: it transforms objects into figures: 'stranger fetishism is a fetishism of figures; it invests the figure of the stranger with a life of its own insofar as it cuts "the stranger" off from histories of its own determination' (2000: 5). Narratives that construct 'the strange culture' as their object (distance) are also contaminated by that very object (by proximity). They involve, simultaneously, social and spatial relations of proximity and distance. 'Others' become strangers (the ones who are distant), and 'other cultures' become 'strange cultures' (the cultures that are distant), only through coming too close to home, that is, through the proximity of the encounter or 'facing itself' (2000: 12). It is in the moment and location of that close encounter that they have to be located out of place primarily because they inhabit the same space (Sennet 1992).

## A figure of fear: stranger danger

The stranger, Bauman notes, is also a figure of fear: 'more horrifying than that which one can fear from the enemy' (1991: 55). Much recent scholarship has suggested that fear is a dimension of contemporary society that has grown in significance (Davies 1998; Ellin 1997; Furedi 2002; Glassner 1999). Scholarship on fear of crime is a particular growth area: crime surveys, which were invented in the USA in 1960s, record and document the fear of crime becoming a everyday part of the law and order landscape (Stanko 2000). Their popularity has given fear of crime a particular prominence in contemporary politics. In turn, fear of crime has been a key theme in criminological and criminal justice work, not only within the academy but also within the context of practical interventions and policy (Hale 1996). Ditton and Farrell (2000) reported an explosion of interest in this area: in a four-year period, conference papers, monographs and books on the subject increased from just over 200 too more than 800.

It is now a commonplace in criminology literature that fear of crime is much more important than experience of crime in the generation of experiences of, and reactions to, crime (Hale 1996). However, reviews of the fear of crime literature draw attention to the highly problematic and contested nature of the domain. Most recently, Bannister and Fyfe (2001) have proposed that the recent explosion in the literature indicates that interest has outstripped conceptual development. We want to offer a contribution to the conceptual development of fear of crime scholarship by exploring the connection between the stranger as a figure of fear, and fear of crime.

The figure of the stranger associates and locates fear in a character with particular social, cultural, spatial and temporal dimensions. In the context of our study of violence and safety, the relation between the stranger and fear is a concern with fear of crime in general, and fear of violence in particular. We therefore focus, in particular, on three aspects of the fear of crime literature: fear and the problem of defining 'crime'; the nature of fear; the geography of fear.

What, if any, is the connection between the fear associated with the stranger and 'fear of crime'? In order to answer this question we need to examine the meaning of the phrase 'fear of crime'. Some scholars have suggested that 'fear of crime' is a phrase that should only be used in the context of a fear of a particular range of legally proscribed acts, usually limited to serious physical violence and property crime (serious crime) (Hale 1996). Others have challenged resort to this narrow, pedantic definition of crime. Some scholarship on fear of crime has also made links between fear of crime and fears associated with well-being, quality of life, lifestyle (Hindelong *et al.* 1978). This is a formulation of fear of crime more closely associated with the fear connected to strangeness, but this has been challenged on the basis that it is too general. While the fear associated with the stranger is not reducible to a narrow definition of crime, we would question the validity of the resort to such a narrow definition of crime in any attempt to make sense of fear of crime.

For us 'crime' (and our interest here is focused on violence as crime) must be widely construed. In part, this takes account of feminist (Kelly 1987, 1988) and lesbian and gay scholarship (Onken 1998) which draws attention to the urgent need to recognise the multiple forms of violence and its different effects. There is also support for this position within fear of crime literature. Sally Merry's (1981) work has particular significance, challenging resort to narrow definitions of crime, arguing that broad definitions are necessary: a whole range of experiences generates fear of crime (fear of violence), from physical injury to experiences of minor improprieties and incivilities that threaten ontological security and belonging. The adoption of broad definitions enables a full account of the 'multi-dimensional nature of fear of crime' to be generated (Hale 1996). As we demonstrated, for example, in Chapter 6 on comfort, there is much evidence to connect fear of violence (widely defined) to ontological security (Giddens 1991; Beck 1992), the sense of being safe, of having some control over one's life, of being able to make sense of being. It is in the link between ontology, fear and crime widely defined, so as to include the minor incivilities (Kelling and Coles 1996), that connects the stranger and fear of crime.[5]

Within the stranger literature the fear associated with the stranger has a particular intensity; it is represented as 'more horrifying' than 'ordinary' fear (associated with the enemy). The ambivalence of the stranger seems to be at the heart of this fear, which is associated with experiences of irresolvable doubt, uncertainty and confusion. Fear of crime literature is dominated by a similar characterisations of 'fear': threat and danger is produced by a set of associations – with the unknowable, the unruly, and that which is beyond control (Bannister and Fyfe 2001; Wurff *et al.* 1988). The literature on the stranger foregrounds the body as an object of fear, just as the fear of crime literature foregrounds the body in the context of the production of the subject of fear. Here, fear is emotion, pain, uneasiness, anxiety, caused by the sense of impending danger and doom (Bannister and Fyfe 2001). These two 'bodies of fear' have different histories and political effects. The fear of crime appears in a context in which fear has been personalised, individualised and dismissed. Until recently fear of crime was degraded and dismissed as irrational and unreasonable (Hale 1996; Sparks 1992).

Engagement with the fear of crime literature does pose some other problems. The language of 'fear' may on occasion be substituted by other terms such as terror, anxiety, worry, anger and loss of trust (Jefferson and Hollway 2000; Stanko 2000; Walklate 2000). These distinctions, their individual significance, their inter-relation and their connection to fear, have been used to challenge quantitative research on fear of crime (Hale 1996). Also calls have been made for new approaches (a new language) to describe fear of crime research (Ditton *et al.* 1999). Whilst we agree that we should take these different terms and the discourses to which they connect seriously, we do not agree that the plurality of terms is a problem. Different terms point to the role and importance of many and various disciplinary engagements with the affects associated with danger and insecurity both social and individual. It is in their plurality (their different ontological, political contexts and histories) that the very idea of 'fear of crime' is being produced in many different contexts within contemporary society.

The third and final connection we want to explore between the stranger and fear of crime focuses upon spatial themes found in the two related literatures. Both connect danger and fear to the spatial order, with an increasing amount of work highlighting the spatial dimension of fear (Gold and Revill 2000; Tuan 1979). In general, this literature is concerned with how people experience and interpret (urban) space. Fear of crime is assigned an important role in the production of social division and social exclusion by its psychological, physical and economic impact on individuals. Fear of crime (victimisation), Bennett (1990) and Hale (1996) suggest, is closely associated with a breakdown in social order and control, closely associated with the urban environment. Likewise, the stranger literature focuses upon the spatial disruptions arising out of proximity, where, in spatial terms, fear is associated with danger in the public realm, resulting in withdrawal into the private realm. In turn, this withdrawal accelerates the decline and deterioration of the community and the public realm and gives rise to more crime in public places (Hale 1996). Further withdrawal takes the form of displacement leading to the abandonment of places.

As we have already noted, the stranger is an important figure through which the physical and social characteristics of place and the familiarity of that space are produced, a trope through which people effectively read the environment as a barometer of risk and protective factors. In order to make these readings they draw on the discourses of the stranger to make sense of their own and others' occupation of space. This always involves visual evaluation of the built environment as well as visual evaluation of others. Space is always discursive space; for the individual it cannot be known beyond the information that is used to make sense of it, or even feel it. This information is not equally available and is dependent upon the prior social positioning of the reader (Skeggs 2000b).

Before we leave the relation between the fear associated with the stranger and the debates on fear of crime, we need to add another piece to the puzzle. So far, the relation between the stranger and fear has been framed by danger. Our opening comments suggested that this relation might be specific to the role of the formation of particular types of community, which we called the local. In turning to communities, which might be characterised as cosmopolitan, we suggested that the fear associated with the stranger might play a different function. As we read figures and spaces for fear, in order to know what to avoid, we may also, as Walter Benjamin suggests, seek out figures and places of fear (see Gilloch 1996). William Neill (2001) proposes that we need to understand how urban fear can attract as well as repel. He suggests, following from Benjamin, that fear can be a better release from boredom and consumerism, which now threatens to totalise. Fear, Neill maintains, has a close relationship to desire, which may be institutionalised (made safe?) through commodification. It holds out the illusory possibility of an experience of escape from anxiety and the heroic conquest of fear.

Finally, we want to draw some of these strands together to offer a challenge to the traditional understanding of 'stranger danger'. As much current work on violence demonstrates, most instances of violence take place in the context of situations in which the perpetrator and victim have a prior relationship. In part, this work seeks to challenge the preoccupation with and the priority given to, stranger danger. 'Stranger danger' in this context is a phrase that appears to refer to random violence by persons who are unknown to the victim. The analysis of the stranger above draws attention to a rather different meaning of the phrase 'stranger danger'.

We would suggest that the phrase 'stranger danger' is also a phrase that emphasises the importance of the proximity of the perpetrator. The stranger that personifies danger in the phrase 'stranger danger' is a figure that embodies social, cultural and spatial proximity, as well as remoteness (distance). In turn the fear (of crime) referenced through stranger danger is not a fear limited to spatially and temporally remote acts and persons. Stranger danger is a phrase that also explains a key feature of the fear associated with perpetrators, violence and the threat of violence proximate to us. Paraphrasing Bhabha (1996), it is the close relation of proximity and distance that forces, figures and enables the production of fear and the figure of fear as a stranger. It is not the remote dangerous other (Bauman's enemy) that the phrase 'stranger danger', necessarily refers to, but also the one who is intimate (known). 'Stranger danger' we want to suggest, is a useful term that can offer insights into the nature of the most common everyday experiences of violence, and the threat of violence which is the violence of those already known to the victim.

We now want to turn to our empirical data to explore these themes in the context of our two locations.

## Making-strange 1: lesbians and gay men as figures of fear

Lesbians and gay men have long been produced and examined as objects of fear (Duggan 2000; Hart 1994; Moran 1996). We ask what regime of strangeness (Phelan 2001) is at work in this production? And what is the lesbian and gay experience of this regime of strangeness, which positions lesbians and gay men as 'outside' and 'alien' to the hetero? As outsiders, lesbians and gay men are portrayed as 'the unknown' to the known of heterosexuality (McGhee 2001). It is as the 'unknown' that a will to know subjects lesbian, gay, homosexual, to endless documentation, analysis and categorisation (Moran 1996). They are both unknown yet already known, always absent but present. Being both known (inside) and unknowable (outside), they are made objects of knowledge (and ignorance) that embody ambivalence. So positioned these figures have a spectral quality (Castle 1993). They personify a horror, paraphrasing Bauman, more terrifying than the fear of the enemy. Through this regime of strangeness lesbians and gay men are produced as 'stranger danger'.

The spatial dimension of the estrangement of the lesbian, gay, homosexual (nearness and distance) is generated across a wide range of social relationships and places: we are predominantly the children of heterosexual families, spouses and ex-spouses, parents and grandparents, in those families. We are neighbours, friends, school and work colleagues in a heterosexual world. These different social settings offer contexts, forms of intimacy and proximity that the figure of lesbian, gay, homosexual, as stranger, radically disrupts. In such settings these figures are rendered remote by projections and perceptions about the different nature and practices of desire.

A second aspect of the stranger (the one who comes today and stays) suggests a prior absence of lesbian and gay people followed by a persistent presence, connoting a journey and a movement, away from a prior location of belonging, a home(land), to a place where belonging is frequently challenged and sometimes denied. In some respects this is a more problematic dimension of the stranger in the lesbian and gay context. Many have noted the exodus of lesbians and gay men away from the home(land), be it the family home, or the hometown, to the relative anonymity of cities (Weston 1995). However, following on from our analysis of home in Chapter 6, it would be wrong to conclude that the estrangement and subsequent abandonment of home is necessarily a geographical displacement. It may, in the alternative, be a movement that works at the level of metaphor: while remaining in the same place it is also experienced as a social and a cultural displacement, exodus, and re-placement produced in and as an experience of identity. Thus while a physical dimension to that journey may be sufficient it is not a necessary requirement. On the other hand, at the level of metaphor, the spatial dislocation (Smith and Katz 1993) appears to be a necessary requirement of estrangement and one that resonates with the lesbian and gay experience of estrangement, be it in the family, the neighbourhood, the home town or the nation.

### Locating estrangement

Let's consider two instances of a regime of strangeness as a heteronormative practice. Both are drawn from lesbian experiences. One is taken from Lancaster, the other from Manchester. The Lancaster example relates an experience of a lesbian couple living on what many considered to be a very rough, poor working-class council housing estate, close to the centre of the city. Gill explains:

> When we moved onto the Marsh [a council estate] it actually was quite in your face homophobia . . . We did get graffiti on the door and dog

shit on the door [and eggs at the windows] . . . which was extremely unpleasant . . . [It] caused us an enormous amount of problems and took a long time to get over . . . [B]ecause of the particular financial situation we were in, we couldn't move for a long time . . .

She adds:

> I've worked for Social Services in Lancaster for some time, which is a bit of an eye-opener to say the least . . . I still can't find anybody who is prepared to refer to Paula other than 'my friend' or 'your friend'. 'Does your friend do this? Does your friend do that?'

(L, lfg, 1)

Gill's observations offer two contexts of estrangement: the neighbourhood and the workplace. She reports a range of techniques of estrangement. Let us begin with the spatial contexts. Both the council estate and the workplace provide locations (respectively poor working-class and respectable, professional middle class) of geographical and social proximity, being the neighbours next door and a colleague. Gill also reports a series of practices through which intimacy is both recognised and brought to an end. The estrangement documented here involves the physical marking of a particular location as alien, by symbols of excess: graffiti, food (as waste rather than life-giving nutrition) and dog shit. Through these markings the 'neighbour', reflected in the aesthetics of mass state housing, is fractured and the home is desecrated, turned from a sanctuary into a place of insecurity. The second practice of estrangement reported is the use of language to break the bond of intimacy. In this instance the context of belonging is the workplace and a group of work colleagues. Proximity is fractured by the use of the term 'friend', rather than the use of 'partner', 'lover', 'wife', 'husband' and so on. In different ways these techniques generate experiences of the presence of the lesbian as stranger: both near and far.

The invisibility of lesbians and gays is a prerequisite of a sexual politics of estrangement. It is also an important strategic lesbian and gay safety response, used to preclude the physical and symbolic violence of the practices of estrangement. A small provincial city, such as Lancaster, offers a particularly dense landscape of places and institutions of proximity, and multiple opportunities for repeated interpersonal interaction. As one of the key informants explained, Lancaster is a place where 'everybody knows everything'. The community in this context, as we noted in Chapter 7, is experienced in many instances as 'local' in contrast to cosmopolitan. Together, these factors make anonymity both highly desired and highly problematic. Invisibility and privacy take priority over visibility and publicity.

The many contexts and formations of invisibility that take shape in the context of Lancaster have a familiar ring to them. For example, in that place lesbians and gay men were and continue to be largely absent from the local institutions of governance. There is a lack of local policies, little awareness of issues and an absence of 'out' gay and lesbian representatives and officials. Within the wider community, voluntary and community groups, when present (for example in the form of the lesbian and gay youth group, the gay walking group, *The Gutter Girls* – a lesbian magazine, events organisation) are politically, socially, culturally and economically marginal, largely invisible. As we noted in the Chapter 7 they may also be subject to systematic misrecognition and misreading, being imaged through the relatively safe category of student.

Many of the various gay and lesbian events and venues that have arisen from time to time in Lancaster share the common characteristic of being entirely inconspicuous (Brown 2000): the entrance is 'discretely positioned', 'hard enough to find', 'down a flight of stairs', 'difficult to get in'. Many are here today gone tomorrow. Our informants offered an instance of this enduring public invisibility in the following example. Some years before the research, the main gay venue in the town was a pub, The Ring O' Bells, well known to local gay men. Thursday night was 'gay night' and everyone used to meet there. Nor was this information limited to the locality, the pub had a listing as a gay venue in a national gay monthly magazine. However, the landlady and landlord, who were described to us as 'an odd old couple' either didn't realise they had a strong gay presence on that night or were unwilling to publicly acknowledge the fact. This remained the status quo despite (so the story goes) various incidents such as their invitation to a 'leather party'. The 'open secret' (Sedgwick 1990) of the gay presence in the pub continued until a gay political campaign against Clause 28, the notoriously successful attempt by the Thatcher government to ban 'the promotion of homosexuality' in local government and education (Smith 1994). Requests to the landlord to allow the circulation of campaign leaflets and a plea to use the bar for a campaign meeting were refused. The landlord responded that he didn't have and didn't want to encourage, 'that sort of clientele'. The formal denial of a gay presence precipitated a boycott of the pub by many of the regulars. The tradition of Thursday gay nights in The Ring O'Bells, we were told, never recovered from the blow.

At the time of the research the main lesbian and gay venue, The Navigation (described by the gay owner as 'mixed') was a bar based in a small, previously derelict, canal-side, industrial building. The location of the bar is significant. On the edge of the city centre and close to the main police station, it was barely visible from the main road, its presence marked by one sign situated some distance from the bar. The building itself had no signs and it was only accessible across a temporary car park, the result of a subsequently abandoned road scheme. It was remote from and largely invisible to passers by. We were also told that the inside of the bar was policed to ensure that it was sexually inconspicuous. As one key informant explained: 'he has been known to sort of tell people to leave if they're sort of . . . getting a bit loud or anything, he'll tell them to leave because he's got straight people in the bar' (Richard, KII, Lan., 1998). Another explained, '[the owner] once banned a friend of mine because he was a bit camp.' (Freddie, KII, Lan., 1998). When asked why the bar was not marked or advertised as a 'gay bar' the owner explained, 'you would get your windows broken'. In addition, he explained, 'you wouldn't get any customers' (Dennis, KII, Lan., 1998). While the former suggests that invisibility is a response to the threat of heteronormative violence, the latter suggests something more, explained by the owner in terms of the needs of gay men who were not out of the closet and in terms of his own economic needs. He also ran a business that provided tourist canal trips from the location.

The latter draws attention to the economic rationality connected to the production of invisibility in certain locations (Brown 2000). In a small provincial city like Lancaster, economic factors inform invisibility (as we noted in Chapter 7). Commercial gay and lesbian space is difficult to sustain. As Freddie, one of the gay owners of the No. 6 Café, explained,

> Lancaster is not the sort of place you can do anything that's gay . . . I think it's too fickle. It's too close to Manchester and Blackpool. You couldn't be totally gay as a café in Lancaster because there's not enough trade.
>
> (Freddie, KII, Lan., 1998)

The combination of proximity to established concentrations of gay and lesbian venues and the relatively small size of the lesbian and gay presence in the locality make it difficult to establish sustainable gay and lesbian focused businesses and thereby a visible presence. Most venues and events are mixed. However, it ought not to be forgotten that the economics of invisibility may work as a mechanism that enables particular sexualities to foster capital accumulation. This may take the form of economic wealth of the particular venue owner or it may take the form of social and cultural capital. Over time the many inconspicuous venues have provided an important local resource for lesbians and gay men. An example that relates to the café comes from the lesbian couple whose home was smeared with dog shit and eggs. They explained, 'the only place that I feel completely safe and completely out, is The No. 6 Café . . .' (L, lfg, 1).

Before leaving Lancaster we want to briefly examine another aspect of this regime of strangeness, that which demands a reading of the environment as a barometer of risk and protective factors. How does this work for those who are made strange in Lancaster? An example is found in response to Paul's question to the gay men's focus group: 'What about the *safe* thing though? How do you tell? What are the ingredients of a safe place?' In response, Phil explained:

> Your brain [is] working overtime [it] picks up on all different subconscious things . . . Like the body language and whether they stare at you for

more than a fraction of a second . . . .your subconscious is working a million miles per hour just calculating, 'Is this a nice safe place to go or is it dodgy? Should I go out again before I get my head panned in?' I think it's just one scan along the room and you can see whether all these people are sort of like staring at you with venomous eyes and things saying, 'You're not welcome here. Go away!'

(L, gmfg, 2)

The experience described here is one of an intense moment of surveillance and reading. While some in the group connected this moment of surveillance to a search for signs of physical violence, 'slashed seats' and 'blood on the floor', in general, as illustrated above, the search for signs of safety is wider than this. It involves a reading of the place and more specifically, a reading of those found in that place. Many of the focus group participants draw particular attention to the way perceptions of safety are produced reading the types of people in the place. One participant described this in terms of reading signs of 'lifestyle'. He explained, the presence of 'people with dyed hair' is a 'good sign', being read as an indicator of an individual's alignment with the politics of the 'left' rather than the 'right', and a sign of non-conformity rather than conformity. As such, for this participant 'dyed hair' was a metonym of safer persons and thereby of safer space.

Discourses of the stranger are drawn upon in this process of reading in order to make sense of their own and others' occupation of space. In these examples the regime of strangeness works not only to produce the signs of danger but also signs of safety. In the former context, strangeness produces a distinction that is experienced as being out of place; in the latter it is read as a sign of belonging. As we suggested earlier both may not be equally available.

Let us turn now to the second example, which comes from the Manchester Lesbian focus group. Leslie recounts an incident with a neighbour whom she describes as an elderly chap, 'always chatty and always really nice'. Leslie lives in a north Manchester suburb with her partner. In some respects it appears to be very different from the Lancaster setting, being described by Leslie as 'a nice, very Jewish leafy area and very private'. In other respects it is perhaps not so different from the Lancaster neighbourhood described above. Leslie explained:

It was never mentioned that there were just the two women who bought this house. We'd been there for about three years and the old guy next door said to me, 'Oh I'm really pleased, I've just found out that my niece is expecting her first baby.' I said 'Oh that's great when is she due?' She was due on the 1st April, so I said, 'Well I'm due on the 1st March' and he blanked it, you know, totally blanked it. It was like I never said it.

She then went on to describe a second related incident with the same neighbour:

About a month later we were chatting. We had very high trees in the garden that was blocking the sunlight. He said, 'Well I'll hold the ladder and you go up' I said 'You wouldn't send a pregnant woman up there?' He said 'Who are you trying to kid?' I said, 'Nobody! I definitely am pregnant.' But it was like he could acknowledge I lived with my girlfriend but it was like, 'How could she get pregnant living with her girlfriend? She must be mad! This woman's telling everyone she's pregnant.'

(M, lfg, 2)

It was, she concluded, 'very strange'. What is the context of estrangement reported here and what are the practices of estrangement?

One context of estrangement is the neighbourhood. In this instance practices of neighbourliness take the form of a conversation over a garden fence. In contrast to the Lancaster example, in the first instance, the conversation is a practice of intimate familiarity (Stein 2001). There is also a second setting of intimate familiarity, to be found in the reference to the idea of motherhood. Intimate familiarity is produced about a particular idea of motherhood that is subject to disruption. Lesbian motherhood disrupts the social and cultural proximity informed by the heterosexual assumptions that shape and focus motherhood as a sign within an economy of everyday intimacy. In Leslie's example, estrangement is marked by various practices: a silence, a formal denial, and an accusation. Through these practices motherhood is fractured and lesbian motherhood is (re)made proximate and distant. In turn the nearness, associated with neighbourliness, is made remote.

Thus far, the two examples from Lancaster and Manchester draw attention to a range of places and institutions, the neighbourhood, the workplace and motherhood, which are contexts in which lesbian estrangement is both produced and experienced by way of a range of techniques. As such they have a certain familiarity and appear to have much in common.

However, it should not be forgotten that the second example occurs in a northern suburb of Manchester, no more than a couple of miles from the 'cosmopolitan showcase' of the gay Village. In many respects the wider sexual political landscape of Manchester differs significantly from that found in Lancaster. In Manchester lesbians and gay men are represented in the local institutions of governance, local government has established policies on homosexuality. Considerable efforts have been made over a period of time to develop awareness of issues, and 'out' gay and lesbian representatives and officials, both formally and informally, facilitate awareness. Beyond the institutions of the local state, there is also a sustainable world of lesbian and gay commerce (bars and businesses), and voluntary and community organisations, that produce a degree of presence and visibility absent from Lancaster. At the same time many of these manifestations of the strong and vibrant communities are highly concentrated and have limited effects. In addition, while the political profile of some community and voluntary organisations is high, most remain economically, if not socially and culturally, marginal and relatively invisible.

The estrangement documented in our second example offers an illustration of the close proximity of the continuing estrangement of lesbians (and one could add gay men) that takes place in the shadow of the 'European gay Mecca'. Lesbians and gay men are in various combinations spatially, socially, culturally and economically remote and proximate (Bell and Binnie 2000). The example draws attention to the importance of taking seriously *the limits* of the impact of the Village as a resource.

At the same time there is much that separates these two examples. Perhaps the most obvious difference is the respective absence and presence of a gay Village. While there is a need to take the spatial limits of its economic, social and cultural impact seriously, at the same time there is also a need to take account of its wider impact. As others have noted, gay spaces are always 'host spaces' (Berlant and Warner 1998), providing a resource for those who do not and could not (for social and economic reasons) live there or use the space more regularly. We have already noted evidence which indicates that the Village may be a variable safety resource for some. The survey data suggest that those gay men in the Village who were from out of town reported the highest levels of safety in the Village. In sharp contrast the gay men who lived closest to the Village and used it most regularly reported the lowest levels of safety. So Manchester's Village may be a resource not only for the lesbians and gay men in the suburbs and towns, but also for lesbians and gay men in Lancaster, in particular those who have the economic resources to facilitate the necessary mobility. It may function as a respite from, and a counterpoint to, a pervasive regime of strangeness.

## Making-strange 2: lesbians and gay men as subjects of fear

So far we have focused on one regime of strangeness in which lesbians (and gay men) are made strange in the production of straight communities. In that context lesbians and gay men are made objects of fear. We now want to examine another regime of strangeness, in which straights are made strange (objects of fear), in the production of a homo community. This provides an opportunity to examine gay men and lesbians as subjects of fear. Manchester's gay Village, we suggest, is one location of such a regime of strangeness. In the 'cosmopolitan showcase . . . where the pleasure never stops', gay men were the group most likely to describe the place as unsafe. Those gay men who had the closest contact with the Village reported the lowest perceptions of safety but this perceived absence of safety and experience of insecurity was *not* connected to experiences of violence. Manchester's gay men and lesbians reported the lowest levels of experiences of violence amongst the groups questioned. The most important reason given for avoiding bars and areas is 'perceptions of danger'. How are we to make sense of this state of affairs?

The picture painted in the survey suggests that fear is a key factor in the production of the space that has been described as the 'strongest and most vibrant lesbian and gay communities in the country'. The literature on fear of crime suggests that this is far from an exceptional state of affairs. It is now perhaps a trite point, but one worth repeating within the frame of a lesbian and gay politics of violence, that fear of crime is for many more important than direct experience of criminal acts in the generation of experiences of danger and safety. In the remainder of this chapter we want to offer an analysis of this fear. More specifically we offer an exploration of a regime of strangeness through which this politics and geography of fear is produced.

First, we contextualise the picture that emerges from the survey data. During the period we were gathering our data, it was apparent that, at least for gay men, talk of danger and safety had a high profile in the 'gay Mecca', central to campaigns about hate crime, local crime reporting initiatives, particular events (the annual lesbian and gay Mardi Gras) and policing and security issues more generally. Within a longer time frame and a wider political agenda, incorporating HIV/AIDS, danger and safety has regularly had a high profile in the Village. In crude terms the priority of safety and danger articulated by gay men in our survey data, and particularly by those gay men who use the Village most frequently, might be a manifestation of a wider culture that promotes, produces and gives priority to issues of danger and insecurity (Stanko 1997, 1998).

Another piece of the puzzle comes from information generated through structured interviews with key informants in Manchester. These informants included gay and lesbian bar and business owners in the Village, people in lesbian and gay related voluntary organisations, local government, the police and private security services. A dominant theme of many of these interviews was the problem of straights in the Village, which was most commonly characterised as straight 'invasion'. Straights were said to pose a threat in many different ways. New straight venues threatened to dilute the concentration of gay and lesbian bars and clubs; straights on the streets and in the gay and lesbian venues put in jeopardy the high visibility of lesbians and gay men. Straights were associated with abuse, threats, harassment and occasional violence against lesbians and gay men in the Village. The invasion also had a temporal dimension, being mainly concentrated at the weekends. In response gay men and lesbians, we were told, had to leave the Village for safer spaces.

Partly in response to these stories of 'heterosexual invasion', we undertook our survey at a time, Friday, particularly associated with the invasion of straights and with the flight of lesbians and gay men from the Village. It is obvious that a Village survey would not get to the lesbians and gay men who had fled the Village so we were not recording their perceptions. Our survey offers an insight into the nature and effect of the 'heterosexual invasion' upon perceptions of danger and safety and upon the management of safety of those who remained in the Village.

We did not have the resources to survey all gay and lesbian venues in the Village and so made an informed selection to ensure a cross section of venues. Of the 733 respondents, 34 per cent were straight (19.5 per cent women, 13.6 per cent men). Our reading of the heterosexual invasion story from key informants had created an expectation that the straights would be in gay and lesbian venues. We found a slightly different state of affairs. Straights were largely concentrated in a small number of bars that were described as 'mixed'. The lesbian and gay respondents were largely concentrated in the lesbian and gay venues in the Village. We certainly found that lesbian and gay men respondents associated straights with danger in the Village. However, despite this anxiety and concern about the danger of 'straights', those expressing anxiety, including the gay men who reported the greatest anxiety about safety, persistently remained in the Village.

Also, our data offered a more nuanced representation of the nature and effect of the straight invasion story, demonstrating the spatial dimension of categories of danger. 'Straights' is a category of danger associated with particular locations, perhaps unsurprisingly, 'straight bars and areas' and 'central drags', being the main thoroughfares around and through the Village. The data also indicated gender differences in the spatialisation of fear and danger.

Before continuing further let's put this in the context of the Lancaster data which painted a picture of higher levels of safety reported by both lesbians and gay men *and* at the same time higher reports of incidents of violence. The Lancaster survey questions necessarily had to reflect the specifics of the location; as Lancaster does not have a lesbian and gay Village we asked about bars and clubs. Likewise, when enquiring about avoidance of 'streets and bars' our question related to Lancaster in general, rather than a more specific central area like Manchester's Village. While this draws attention to the need to be cautious in undertaking comparisons it fails to account in full for the differences in lesbian and gay experiences between our two locations.

In an attempt to explore the meaning of our Lancaster data further we asked our local lesbian focus group for their thoughts on the Lancaster findings (Corteen 2002). One response is of particular interest: the safety reported, they suggested, may record effects that flow from the daily challenges and threats of an ever-present and overwhelming hostile straight environment. In a more hostile environment, such as Lancaster, the experiences of safety, they argued, are a reflection of the fact that *lesbians and gay men excel in safety management*, more specifically the safety afforded by diverse practices that make lesbians and gay men invisible in a straight world; the logic being that as long as that invisibility is maintained experiences of safety follow.

Together our initial reflections on the data produced what, in the first instance, might appear to be a rather counter-intuitive picture of safety. A politics and a space of visibility, pride and strength, that offers a challenge and limit to an otherwise pervasive, oppressive straight culture, may lead to lower perceptions of safety. Whereas in a location that has few if any of these resources, where the impact of hetero-society is more pervasive and unrelenting, lesbians and gay men report higher levels of safety.

In part perhaps these preliminary conclusions are neither so unexpected nor surprising. Myslik's (1996) study of the gay area of Washington DC documents how, while a spatial concentration of gays may provide a degree of safety for those using the space, the opposite may also be the case. More specifically, the concentration and visibility of gay men in that space may also facilitate access to gay men (and lesbians) by those who seek to perpetrate harm against them. Others have made wider connections between a politics of visibility and violence in reflections on the rise of hostility, towards gay men in particular, in the wake of the HIV/AIDS pandemic (Gross 1993; Herek and Berrill 1992; Johansson and Perry 1994). But there is a need for some caution here. The Manchester data does not record high levels of violence as a major factor informing experiences of danger and safety. Experiences of violence seem to play a more prominent role in the lives of the lesbians and gay men we surveyed in Lancaster. In short, experiences of violence seem to be a more important element in a location of lesbian and gay invisibility, and not in the context of an out and proud lesbian and gay population. In the 'gay Mecca' our data record the importance not of violence but of fear of violence, in the form of anxiety about straights and in the more diffuse category of 'perceptions of danger'.

In the remainder of this chapter we want to focus upon the regime of strangeness that informs the generation of this fear in the 'gay Mecca'.

### New strangers, new dangers in the gay 'cosmopolitan showcase'

> . . . who commits the violence . . . it's definitely heterosexual people.
>
> (M, gmfg, 5)

Here, Peter, one of the participants in the Manchester gay men's focus group, pinpoints the problem: heterosexuals personify danger in the Village. Others in the focus groups suggested the problem was more specific: the problem is straight men. Many different forms of danger are associated with 'straights', from physical attacks to verbal abuse and more abstract characterisations of danger such as 'hostility'. Peter offers another manifestation of danger in the following comments;

> A small but very obnoxious group of straight people, unreasonably pissed [were] affecting the whole character of the bar . . . they were dancing, there's a dance floor downstairs, but you don't do it in the middle of a busy bar . . . and it was done in a particular way [with their elbows out] that I don't expect in a gay bar . . . they seem to be more controlled in gay bars . . . but the aggression that goes with heterosexual people . . . was self-evident to the extent that they literally fell over.
>
> (M, gmfg, 5)

Here heterosexual danger takes the form of unruly behaviour. Its unruliness is signified by reference to location (being out of place), and more specifically by contravening the conventions of that place, in the mode of dancing. These unruly acts take the form of minor incivilities. Frankie, a member of the Manchester lesbian focus group, characterised the problem as 'sheer lack of respect' (M, lfg, 1). One of the incivilities most commonly referred to in the focus group data is 'looking'. As Gail, another member of the group explained:

> There has been a lot of straight people in there and I've been in there with my partner and we don't even hold hands . . . because we feel as though we are being looked at and stared at . . . we were surrounded by heterosexual people who were snogging.
>
> (M, lfg, 1)

Here the danger associated with the incivilities of heterosexual looking (and 'snogging') is marked in the change ('policing') of behaviour. The threat is experienced as a restraint upon lesbian behaviour, arising out of a located experience of challenged legitimacy. We have already explored in some detail, in Chapters 5 and 6, the ontological significance of such encounters and explored how these lesbian and gay experiences are respectively informed by a rhetoric and politics of property and comfort.

Another feature of the ontological dimension of straight danger is to be found in a comment by Gary, who characterised safety in a particular gay club in the following terms:

> 0.2 per cent straight people are there. You know it is just fully gay . . . you just go there to lose your inhibitions . . . to be who you want to be.
>
> (M, gmfg, 5)

Safety, in this instance, is an experience of ontological belonging and security which takes the form of ontological purity: the virtual absence of 'straights'.

This talk of danger, safety and ontology also has another dimension. It is, as Girling *et al.* (2000) note, talk about place. Place-talk takes various forms. As we have already noted the Manchester survey data suggests that experiences of danger, and their composition, are place-specific. For example, straights as danger was particularly associated with straight bars:

> When I go into a straight bar then my direct experience is there [i]s an expectation of violence . . . [gay men] have a sensitivity that they will pick up more quickly that there is something going on . . . In the straight scene [violence] seems to be the first option.
>
> (Peter, M, gmfg, 5)

The experience of 'straight bars' as places of violence brings together direct experience of straight violence in straight bars and expectations of danger. The bus station is another location of danger highlighted in our survey data:

The bus stop is a bit of a black spot . . . if you start going in that direction basically then there's a lot more drunkenness, but straight drunkenness or people pissing in corners and that kind of romantic behaviour, then you start feeling a bit more kind of self-conscious basically as opposed to just letting your mind drift or be happy or whatever.

(Adam, M, gmfg, 4)

The danger/safety of the place is explained not in terms of direct violence, but by reference to a reading of the urban landscape and particular practices as signs of an incivility and thereby signs of danger.

Reading bars and clubs by the relation between straight and danger produces those places not only as 'straight bars' or, 'gay places', but also maps those places respectively as dangerous and safe. There is an 'expectation of violence' associated with straight bars, whilst 'gay bars' are associated with an expectation of safety. In turn, there is an expectation of safety associated with the Village, which places the expectation of danger (be it straights or straight space) as elsewhere. This makes the Village as a place of safety over against danger, which is always already elsewhere. Paraphrasing Bauman, this produces safety and danger as a cosy spatial antagonism, where spatial distribution takes on the form of a comfortable 'collusion'.

On the theme of straight invasion, straight 'colonisation' and straight 'takeover', Bricknell (2000) suggests that the 'straight' is not only a figure of the enemy/danger over against the gay as friend/safe, but also a figure that disrupts this 'cosy antagonism'. The invasion narrative is a pervasive story of straights in the Village. Ben, the manager of one of the most long-standing and popular gay bars in the Village, explained:

Most gay people feel [the Village is] their space. . . . It's their only place and it's being invaded. Invade sounds a bit dramatic but it is being invaded somewhat by straight people. So there is a bit of animosity.

(Ben, KII, Man., 1998)

Sue, who was sometime organiser of a lesbian group in South Manchester, offered the following invasion story:

You see, it doesn't bother me, the fact that there's a lot of straight people in at the weekend, because I'm not there. But for the [gay] men who traditionally go out, it obviously seems to affect them because their own private space is being invaded in their eyes.

(Sue, KII, Man., 1998)

The invasion is usually temporally more specific: 'Friday and Saturday it can be straights-ville'. Others pinpoint particular times of the day:

Come twelve o'clock all the gay people piss off to Cruz and Paradise and Poptastic and then all the straight people who don't want to come into any clubs or anything know these places are still open till two.

(Carl, M, gmfg, 5)

The regime of strangeness in these invasion stories has a temporal and a spatial dynamic. The temporal dimensions generate a certain nostalgia, whereby the gay Village is constituted as having a past of spatial purity (a time of a more perfect safety) in contrast to the present, which is a time of spatial confusion and uncertainty as a result of the 'new' straight presence. Straights no longer figure distance in relation to gay space, they now figure proximity; they not only pass by the gay bars and clubs, but they have come to stay. The invasion story tells of a change in the status quo. Straight is now a figure that disrupts that cosy antagonism that once made the experience of the Village as safe; that which was understood as distant is now experienced as proximate. This produces various effects: that which is outside is also inside; evil now also occupies the place of good; the improper is close to the proper; the tasteful is no longer remote from the unbecoming. From the Village as a world that is readily readable and free from doubt, straights in the Village disrupt; the Village is now a world made unreadable and thereby dangerous. As Carla, one of the Village bar owners, explained, the threat is being in a gay bar and 'being in a situation where it could be a gay man or straight man you are talking to and you're not sure. It's dangerous so people then go on to the street' (Carla, KII, Man., 1998). However, this is experienced as another location of danger. Straights are also on the streets of the gay Village. In this regime of strangeness, straights as strange disrupt the comfortable collusion of opposites that informs the production of gay space as safe: gay/straight. The figure of the stranger gives prominence to boundaries (through their violation), a matter we explored in some detail in Chapter 5.

It is in the context of this stranger that attention focuses on the failure of Village gate-keepers to patrol and maintain boundaries, which are experienced as too porous. For example, Gail from the Manchester lesbian focus group explained, 'a billboard outside said 'Integration not Segregation' which I think is a fantastic idea but unfortunately . . . it has become too top heavy the other way' (M, lfg, 2). Boundaries are not taken seriously: 'a lot of bars are gay but in a very trivial sense', they are 'token', and a 'camouflage' for 'straight businesses'. The stranger is one context in which the limits of the rhetoric and politics of property is thrown into stark relief. In turn, this regime of strangeness threatens to bring the possibility of comfort to an end and to elevate its political importance. We now want to turn our attention to the politics of this regime of strangeness.

## The politics of estrangement: power and ontology

But you are in the majority and for the very first time in your life you are in the majority and it's a fantastic feeling to know that you are with other people who are exactly like you and all the others fade into insignificance.

(M, lfg, 1)

This observation by Gail, a member of the Manchester lesbian focus group, draws attention to a key feature of the lesbian and gay experience of the Village, an experience of being in the majority, for a change, putting you into the position of, 'the one in power'. The estrangement of straights in and through the gay and lesbian space of the Village is about power over against the power of straights. Barry, from the gay men's focus group, notes:

> I feel like when a couple of straight people are in a gay place I am the majority, I'm the one in power here, I can do what I want in front of them and they've got to like it or they've got to get out the door.
>
> (M, gmfg, 4)

Being dominant in a particular place is explained here in terms of a capacity to dictate and enforce the forms and boundaries of civility within that place: to name the stranger. This politics of power has ontological significance, informing lesbian and gay 'confidence' and 'self-assurance'. Another onto-logical dimension mentioned in the gay focus group discussions is the place of danger in gay identity. Peter proposes:

> We are less tolerant of violence as gay men than heterosexuals are . . . they go out for a good night out on a Saturday night and . . . they're expecting [violence] so our tolerance of violence is lower than that . . . in the heterosexual environment.

He added:

> We will pick up more quickly that there is something going on and our expectations of a civilised response to a challenge is higher . . . that we don't immediately go to fisticuffs if there was a problem.
>
> (M, gmfg, 5)

These extracts suggest that the gay regime of strangeness appears to produce a particular relation between violence and the ontology of the gay subject: gay as a particular sensitivity to violence, a greater awareness of the possibility of violence and a greater intolerance of violence. The differences may be given form in, and be institutionalised by, demands for a different civility by straights in gay space; they may also inform new sensitivities and different expectations of safety and security. Gary, a member of the gay men's focus group, suggests it may make lesbians and gay men 'more conscious of straight people being on the scene' (M, gmfg, 5), resulting in the number of straights being 'overestimated', and producing particular amplification effects, for example within the context of the 'invasion' story. 'Playing devil's advocate' Gary also comments:

We don't necessarily like straight people accessing the scene quite as much and in order to justify that to ourselves we say it compromises our safety whereas it might not necessarily. But it makes us feel better. It sits better on our shoulders if we believe that that's the reason we do not like it.

(M, gmfg, 5)

Gary points to the comforts generated by the cosy antagonisms and comfortable collusion associated with a 'simpler' world of friends and enemies.

But, we would suggest, there is a need for caution; this cosiness has an air of nostalgia about it, being nothing more than a 'myth of the safe Village'. As we noted in Chapter 7, the past of the Village is associated with more limited and more difficult access by straights.

While this regime of strangeness appears to produce a gay and lesbian identity formation as an experience of being in power, it is also a regime that makes this an experience of fragility. Allegories of invasion are one context in which the fragility of gay power over straights is spoken. In the following extract this is articulated in a contrast between the straight invasion of gay bars and the gay invasion of straight bars. Adam contends, 'there aren't many bars . . . that have been straight but invaded by gay people . . . it doesn't happen . . .' (M, gmfg, 2). This allegory of power imbalance between gay and straight is told by resources, of unequal capacities to achieve a successful invasion. Invasion also provides a vehicle for other metaphors of inequality that focus on the fragile temporality and the instability of relations of gay to straight. Another instance of the fragility of gay power is explored in the following exchange in the gay men's focus group. Gary proposed that 'a couple of straights . . . slightly enriches [a gay club] a bit', and while Adam agreed, he also added a note of caution, 'it's when it starts going over the line . . . when it starts to shift that percentage too much' (M, gmfg, 4). Here, the fragility of power takes the form of the difficulty of deciding the undecidable; how many straights does it take to move from an experience of safety to one of danger? This exchange also draws our attention to another dimension, implicated in the generation of the pleasures of the place, which problematises the reduction of straights to danger in the gay regime of strangeness.

While 'straight' might stand as a totalising category of sexualised danger over against lesbian and gay, we also need to take account of more nuanced and particular formations of straight danger which appear, for example in the relation between straight and lesbian and straight and gay:

There are different issues for men and different issues for women. Straight women can't stand lesbians. Although they like to be around gay men they are really threatened being around lesbians . . . people have had arguments with straight women in gay bars.

(Frankie, M, lfg, 1)

In contrast, Simon notes:

> It's a power thing, isn't it? It's about fear, its about being frightened . . . I certainly don't feel frightened by straight women, but I do feel frightened, threatened by straight men.
>
> (M, gmfg, 4)

When read together these two extracts draw attention to a more complex gay and lesbian regime of strangeness. While 'straight', as stranger danger, may be sex/gender neutral strangeness, is also a category informed by gender differences. In particular contexts straight danger may be 'straight men', in others it may be 'straight women' (see Skeggs 1998, 2002). Furthermore, as Simon's observation illustrates, 'straight', or more specifically 'straight women', may also connote safety. Combinations of sex, gender and sexuality work to manage the ambivalence of the category 'straight' (as both safe and dangerous) by way of fragmentation of that category. As Gary notes, there is a tendency to assume that, 'all heterosexual people are gay-men haters or that there is some element of homophobia going on with straight people' (M, gmfg, 5). But he quickly followed this up with the conclusion that this is problematic: 'Some heterosexual people are being really violent to some gay men – you know its not generic.' Resort to categories that connote singularity, such as 'straight' are perhaps particularly seductive because of the way they seek to erase ambivalence.

Nor is this regime of strangeness only subject to qualification by reference to gender. Our data also suggests that class is significant in the management of ambivalence, although rarely directly spoken, most frequently referenced through geography (housing estates or named areas), or appearance (hair=big, clothing=sports wear, opal fruit, i.e. checked shirts, mini-skirts, fluffy bras, platform shoes), or the terms 'lad' and 'scally'. For example, Norman, whom we met in Chapter 5, a gay man with several businesses in the Village, narrates:

> You only need a couple of straight lads to come down here and have a good time and they start fetching their friends. It's when you get gangs of 12 or 15 leaving pubs in Salford and it's like 'Let's go down the Gay Village and kick a fucking queer's head in.' It happens, believe me.
>
> (Norman, KII, Man., 1998)

The use of terms such as 'lads' (and in other examples, 'yobs') and the reference to 'Salford' (a city that adjoins the northern borders of Manchester and is always historically represented as working-class), are terms that give the gendered danger of 'straight' a strong working-class inflection (Moran 2000). Our exploration of how class informs the reading of feminine-appearing women (as straight), making the femme invisible[6] (Skeggs 2000, 2001) is also significant here. Fear is figured through class-defined respectability. It is those who threaten respectability that produce a disruption of the space; their difference is institutionalised in bar policies.

Another dimension appears in the following exchange. Evelyn comments:

> I stopped going to that lesbian mothers' group, there were women who had their children by insemination and they were all fantastic pure lesbian mothers and there was I, this sullied woman who had my children through a heterosexual relationship. So the flip side of it is that there is a hierarchy . . .

Leslie asks:

> Is that the way it is or is that your perception of it though? I certainly don't consider myself to be any better because I had my children by . . .

Evelyn continues:

> I'm not saying that. I'm not saying you. I'm saying, maybe it's the people I have been around. It's taken a long time to stop feeling inferior as a lesbian mother because my children weren't donor babies . . . that's why I stopped going. I felt inferior to that group of women.

The transcript continues:

> Leslie: [shocked] Really?
> Evelyn: I don't know if they did it consciously or subconsciously. That's how I felt. Also, I was the only Black woman there. I always ended up making the tea and washing up. Something very strange going on there. I just thought I can't be bothered and just left . . .
>
> (M, lfg, 2)

Evelyn draws attention to a politics of estrangement within lesbian space that has reproductive and racial distinctions.

A gay regime of strangeness not only (re)produces totalising identity categories of danger (straights) and safety (gays), but it also gives them a problematic characteristic: ambivalence. The examples above point to the uses of gender and class to manage that ambivalence, erasing it by way of distinctions that seek to isolate the 'true' danger and at the same time reinstalling it in the figuration of danger by a logic of estrangement. This is also a process that produces a possibility of assimilation, but it is a process of incorporation based upon (more refined) categories of exclusion: a narcissism of minor differences (Stein 2001).

The fragmentation of the straight/danger correlation by gender and class also draws attention to the differences within the totalising categories of lesbian and gay. Conceptualisations of danger in lesbian and gay space that fail to move beyond the dynamic of straight/gay straight/lesbian will produce very partial accounts of the experiences of lesbian and gay conceptualisations of risk, danger and safety. While there is some work on violence in same-sex domestic relations which challenges the totalising categories of lesbian and gay, there is little work focusing on these problems in other lesbian and gay contexts. And although there is much in the data that reinforces the idea and experience that lesbian space and lesbian community is 'where its safe to be lesbian', there is also data which suggests a different experience of same-sex space.

## Conclusion

In this chapter our analysis has focused on the ways in which a regime of strangeness works to produce experiences of danger and safety, of insecurity and security. Danger and safety, insecurity and security, are figured through the stranger. The stranger personifies exceptional danger to the social order, calling for vigilance and action to (re)secure good order. Lesbians and gay men have long been produced as strangers for a heterosexual politics of social order. Through this deployment of a regime of strangeness lesbians and gay men have been produced as objects of fear. In general, the safety and security of heterosexual order has demanded their exclusion and invisibility. We offer examples which suggest that this state of affairs still persists. Yet at the same time, as we noted above, this same regime of strangeness produces lesbian and gay as figures and places of fear that can attract.

The gay Village in Manchester is a place that is at least, in part, informed by a heterosexual politics that produces gay men and lesbians as objects of fear that both repel and attract. It is a place that has been promoted locally, nationally and internationally to lesbians and gay men as a safe haven from the hetero world. While safety has not been the only criteria informing its development (Quilley 1997), it has been an important concern, central to inner city regeneration and redevelopment, promoted to heterosexuals as a 'cosmopolitan showcase'. In this context lesbians and more specifically gay men as the exotic 'dangerous other' are subject to commodification and made safe for a straight audience.

It is in the context of the commodification of the Village that a lesbian and gay regime of strangeness has emerged producing a 'new' stranger (straights), which gives form to new perceptions and experiences of insecurity and danger. The straight as stranger produces danger and safety, insecurity and security for a different sexual spatial politics, of lesbian and gay safer space, using fear, not against a lesbian and gay politics of recognition, but for it. The way violence and safety are imagined is linked to the generation of experiences of sexualised belonging, which in turn are experiences of the sexualised self. The power to exclude and to estrange is part of building identity; articulating threat and fear is part of community formation

(Sennet 1992). The regime of strangeness binds together as it separates. The reported anxieties and fears of crime in the Village work to promote resistance to hetero-violence that masquerades as (cosmopolitan) universalism. One of our objectives in this chapter has been to understand how a regime of strangeness works to transform lesbians and gay men who have for so long been subjected to exclusion as objects of fear into subjects of inclusion, as subjects of fear.

There is little evidence to support a conclusion that the politics of estrangement works to produce the dominant gay or lesbian subject as the cosmopolitan subject in and through that place. For example there is little evidence that the straight as other is produced as an exotic sexual object of lesbian or gay consumption or pleasure. If straight is aligned with safety, then it is primarily by way of a heightened awareness of straight as a category of danger: that they become known. The survey of the Village produced a picture of sexual segregation rather than one of close proximity. Lesbians and gays avoid straight bars for fear of violence. The high reports of safety in the Village, recorded by straights in the survey, can be contrasted with reports of the gay men who recorded the lowest levels of safety in that place, but who were subject to the straight cosmopolitan pleasures of looking, characterised as 'being gawked at' and experienced as 'feeling like being in a zoo'. In good part the lesbian and gay regime of strangeness is a response to the violence and threats of violence that are associated with a politics of heterosexual cosmopolitan consumption.

A second objective of this chapter has been to avoid the either/or that these two manifestations of a politics of estrangement threatens to generate; of visibility, pride and strength (subjects of fear), against invisibility, shame and weakness (objects of fear). Both provide mechanisms for the management of safety and more needs to be done to examine the interconnection between the two modes of estrangement that produce these different lesbian and gay experiences of the self.

It is premature to draw grand conclusions from our data about the complex relationship between fear and sexuality, and its impact upon individuals and communities in different locations. But we do want to draw attention to some of the contexts in which the geographies and politics of estrangement and fear discussed above have emerged and need to be understood (Walklate 2001).

The first context is the fear of crime debates. To date, within studies on fear of crime, little attention has been paid to the impact of sexuality. Likewise, the significance of fear in lesbian and gay experiences of danger and safety associated with violence remains largely unexamined (although see Myslick 1996; Valentine 1989, 1990, 1992). In many respects our data offers many surprises and poses many challenges. Stanko (2000) suggests fear of crime is 'a proxy term for social disadvantage' (p. 23) and that higher levels of anxiety evidence social discrimination. While we would in general agree with Stanko, our research points to the urgency to take account of the multiple, not singular categories of stratification in the generation of fear. In turn, our preliminary thoughts on the use of these various categories to manage the ambivalence of strangers points to the need to examine the strategic and tactical significance of their co-existence (de Certeau 1988).

Second, our data on the politics of estrangement in the Village come in the main from those who use the Village. Those who contributed to the Manchester survey were in the Village on a Friday lunch time and evening which, key informants suggested, was the time associated with high levels of 'straight invasion'. Those who expressed the highest concerns about danger were the people who had the highest frequency of use. This is significant within the context of fear of crime debates, which associates fear with with-drawal. In our sample those who expressed most concern about fear of crime had not withdrawn from the public sphere even though their mode of occupation may have been affected by fear. Nor does it suggest that fear of crime does not have dramatic damaging consequences for lesbian and gay individuals and communities.

Third, in most references to straights as danger, violence and the threat of violence are not so much reasons for invasion as its effects. Straight use of the space is explained in terms of access to late-night drinking and access to straight women who use the space. Other explanations, given by lesbians and gay men include, straight desire to access the sub-cultural capital associated with gay male culture – it is sometimes 'trendy', 'fashionable', 'cool'.[7]

Finally, Manchester's gay Village is predominantly a commercial space, which may manifest safety and danger in very particular forms. While these spaces of entertainment were initially generated from political campaigning, they are now resolutely commercial. The demand for profit generates its own instability. The form and impact of fear on these particular spaces may differ from its impact upon 'neighbourhoods' characterised predominantly as locations of privacy and domesticity (Valentine and Johnston 1995). However, at the same time, for lesbians and gay men, commercial and entertainment spaces may have a different significance than that associated with the hetero-sexual. As we noted in Chapter 6, these 'public' spaces are an important location for experiences of privacy, intimacy comfort, domesticity and home.

The data collected in our research suggest that a politics of identity that challenges myths of the lesbian and gay as dangerous other, of a politics of estrangement, may actually re-invent myths of the stranger for a different politics. Rather we don't use the term 'myth', in this context, but this is not in order to connote the need to move from the falsehood of myth to the truth of post-myth condition (Gilloch 1996). We use 'myth' to point to the very limited repertoire of ways of making sense of being, belonging and social order. There is a long history, from the Greeks and the Romans onwards, of imaginary geographies, in which the members of certain social groups locate themselves at the centre of the universe. It is a world made through the location of threatening monsters and grotesques at the spatial periphery (Hubbard 2000; Morley 2000; Sibley 1998). The powerful project these images to both centre themselves and exclude others. The example of the 'cosmopolitan showcase' of the gay Village suggests that the concentration of difference in the same space does not bring this way of imagining the world to an end. In a space where many different groups come together, Bourdieu (1986) and Bhabha (1996) would argue that the ability to identify differences in proximity requires an ability to read and identify the potential threat in order to produce 'the self' as safe. This chapter therefore has offered an example of a logic of exclusion deployed for an identity politics of recognition. In the context of the rest of the book, our analysis in this chapter illuminates the specific historical and, we would add, the spatial particularities of this logic.

# 9 Conclusion
## The challenges of safety and security

Violence, property, comfort, cosmopolitanism and estrangement are different (and connected) rhetorics and political strategies through which lesbians and gay men produce themselves as objects and subjects of violence and safety. While our analysis separates them out, in practice their operation is often simultaneous. The boundary is a pervasive spatial trope in our study of safety and security. The recurrence of the theme of the boundary is implicated in the production of these regimes as distinctive and separate. At the same time it works to connect them all, enabling the easy substitution of one for another. In turn, by way of metaphor and metonym their inter-relation also becomes the possibility of the simultaneous operation as both different and the same registers and practices of safety and security. Boundary as metaphor produces their mobility. In many respects it is key to understanding the institutional and conceptual framework of the sexual politics of violence and safety.

Boundaries both divide and join, they are never foolproof. Boundary-drawing is always associated with the possibility of boundary-crossing. Boundaries generate clear meaning and pose problems of meaning (Bauman 1991). Boundaries locate ambivalence. What are the perils to be found here?

### Naming the perils of emancipatory politics

Being deployed in order to promote safety and security from heterosexist violence, these various regimes of safety and security appear to promote an emancipatory political project: freedom from heterosexist violence. At the same time, in different ways, they seem to fall foul of such an objective in various ways. Demands for violence (even when tempered by the gloss of reason) seem to be somewhat out of place in the context of a politics that seeks to bring violence to an end. The resort to what might be described as neo-liberal ideas of property and propriety are usually more closely associated with the political thinking of the conservative right, a political economy of possessive individualism. Likewise, resort to home and comfort, as we indicated in Chapter 5 can be a politics of nostalgia more closely aligned with a conservative and, some would argue, a reactionary politics. Home and comfort are the cornerstone of a myth of safety. The promotion of home as a location of safety may expose the already vulnerable to further danger. In turn, our analysis of cosmopolitanism suggests that its promotion as a new model and reason of safety and security by both individuals and policy-makers falls short. Last but not least, the demands for and techniques of social justice, arising in a location that has been described as one of the 'strongest and most vibrant lesbian and gay communities in the world' (Healthy Gay Manchester 1998), are equally problematic. In that place we found evidence of a politics of estrangement, a politics long used to produce hierarchical regimes predominantly associated with modalities of subordination and exclusion. One of our most disturbing conclusions is that the emancipatory sexual politics against heterosexist violence is all too closely associated with social and cultural trappings of our unfreedom.

## The challenge of ambivalence

This brings us to another conclusion. Ambivalence is a feature of each of the different rhetorical and political regimes of safety and security analysed in this study. Law's violence is both good and bad, it creates and destroys. For lesbians and gay men, in the past and for many in the present, the violence of law is bad violence. At the same time lesbians and gay men are engaging in a law and order politics that seeks to transform that bad violence into the good violence of law. Property talk is talk of order, of belonging and of security. Particularly in its relation to boundaries, it gives form to fears, anxieties and insecurities. Comfort, and its location, home, is not only a haven associated with strength and support, sanctuary, retreat, refuge, privacy, but also experienced as oppression, surveillance, scrutiny, judgement, exposure, weakness and vulnerability. Likewise, cosmopolitanism is celebrated and promoted as a new order of equality, liberty and freedom associated with plurality; but our analysis suggests, simultaneously, it reproduces dominant orders, generates inequalities, and imposes familiar limits on freedom and liberty. The figure of the stranger offers to bring these different registers of ambivalence together. The stranger embodies the ambivalence of boundaries, being separate from and connected to: the stranger is both proximate and distant. Ambivalence, Bauman (1991) suggests, is experienced as uncertainty, confusion and discomfort. It 'carries a sense of danger' (p. 56). The stranger gives these affects physical and human form.

   The ambivalence of the various political strategies draws us to a perhaps unexpected conclusion. The rhetorics and strategies we have explored in terms of a response to danger, and in the name of order and safety, appear to promote the opposite: a sense of disorder and danger.

   Functional, spatial and temporal distinctions play a central role offering to distinguish and distribute that which is indistinguishable and proximate: to divide danger from safety, to separate disorder from order, to disconnect insecurity from security. In Chapters 2 and 3 we noted the particular significance of the functional distinction between, a violence associated with law's rule and reason (good violence), and an unruly violence associated with disorder (bad violence). In the lesbian and gay demand for access to state violence the good violence of the criminal justice system is separated out from and set against bad (heterosexist) violence. The temporal divide between the past and the present also helps to distinguish good (nostalgic, safe) from bad (present, dangerous). An example of this is to be found in Rosga's (2001) characterisation of the challenge facing lesbians and gay men who seek to gain access to state violence by turning the state against itself. To do this bad state violence has to be distinguished from good state violence by a temporal distinction: a division between a past of heterosexist (bad) state violence and a present/future of good state violence, which is put to use to bring that bad violence to an end. In our exploration of comfort, in Chapter 5, spatial distinctions play a key role. The spatial distinction between the parental home and the home of choice is a distribution of disorder and danger in contrast to order and safety.

Likewise, in the first instance cosmopolitanism offers to challenge the ongoing political significance of these divisions. Cosmopolitanism is a term that suggests a proximity of those who have previously been separate and apart, a bringing together rather than a making of distinctions. Cosmopolitan suggests the inclusion of those previously excluded, connoting multiplicity. In a lesbian and gay context this multiplicity offers the possibility of inclusion of (sexual) differences and a visibility without violence, a new universality that is associated with equality, liberty and freedom rather than social hierarchy and exclusion. However, our analysis offers many illustrations of the ways in which cosmopolitanism is another context in which functional, spatial and temporal distinctions are put to work to limit access to these goals.

The safety and security of cosmopolitanism is made by a spatial division that produces danger and insecurity as a location that is always elsewhere, which in our data is characterised as the local. In turn, cosmopolitan safety is also a periodisation of safety and danger: of a danger and insecurity that is past, and a present/future that is safe and secure. The functional dimensions that inform the politics of cosmopolitanism are most evident in the context of the processes of selection that make the cosmopolitan encounter into an encounter with a carefully crafted exotic other: the good gay and the good heterosexual. The safety supposedly offered by the cosmopolitan is not open to all; rather it is constituted by exclusion. Respectability informed, at least, by distinctions of gender, class, race and age, is central to the dispositions and discourses of cosmopolitanism.

When refracted through the lens of a political project of safety and security the problem of ambiguity and the urgency of the need to resolve ambiguity is perhaps at its most extreme. At the heart of the distinctions between the unsafe and the safe, insecurity and security is the distinction between disorder and order. A politics of safety and security is an obsession with order. Ambivalence is a threat to order and a call for order. Functional, spatial and temporal distinctions play a central role in the (re)production of order. Violence, property, comfort, cosmopolitanism and estrangement are different regimes and practices through which ambivalence and order are imagined and practised.

In this book, the challenge of Brown (2001), warning of the possibility that the emancipatory objectives of progressive politics may have counter-intuitive effects, points to the perils and problems of ambivalence; this also points to the importance of taking ambivalence seriously.

Our reflections emphasise the need to avoid an either/or response to ambivalence. It is by the logic of either/or that the false opposition of emancipation against oppression is produced and sustained. A focus on ambivalence and the management of ambivalence enables us to examine their proximity and their inter-relationship. Far from being a disturbing and threatening sign of chaos and disorder, taking ambivalence seriously facilitates an examination of the generation of order. The challenge is to understand the political effects and affects produced by the functional, spatial and temporal distinctions that play such an important role in the management of ambivalence and thereby the production, management and maintenance of order. For example, while lesbian and gay resort to the politics of estrangement, to make straights strange, echoes a reactionary politics of lesbian and gay exclusion, it may have strategic political significance for a more progressive politics. Bauman (1991) suggests that the, 'burden to resolve ambivalence falls, ultimately, on the person cast in the ambivalent condition' (p. 75). Through the experience of estrangement, straights (at the level of both individuals and institutions) may be forced to be reflexive about their particular practices of straight (in)civility and straight order (Phelan 2001). However, we would add a word of caution: the prospects of social transformation in such situations should only be imagined as a possibility rather than a probability. There is a contingent rather than a necessary relation between reflection and transformation. Likewise, reflection creates the possibility rather than the probability of justice.

For us the logic of either/or brings reflection and understanding to an end. In drawing attention to the importance of ambivalence we seek to open up debate and to foster understanding. The challenge raised by this book to present and future scholars, policy-makers, practitioners and activists is to take ambiguity seriously. Violence offers some of the most troubling instances of ambivalence. For example, women's experience of domestic violence has long drawn attention to the fact that those whom you know the best, those who are most intimate, those you trust, are also those who are most likely to be the most dangerous and the most violent. It is not a situation specific to violence against women but one that is still difficult to secure in the political and public imagination. To deny ambivalence is extremely dangerous and damaging. The urgency of the need to take the violence of those most intimate to us seriously is also a call to take ambivalence seriously. This is a project that will require much vigilance if we are to avoid the unthinking and unreflexive slippage into a cosy and comfortable logic of either/or.

Our challenge generates a major task for those in institutions, such as the police but also in the proliferating number of participants in the safety and security networks that make up the contemporary landscape of crime control. These institutions have a major investment in order, their practices are dedicated to the eradication of ambiguity. The urgent need is to make sense of ambivalence and its resolution: to engage in a project of critical reflection in order to develop policies and practices which take ambivalence seriously. Our hope is that this book will be used to facilitate that project.

# Notes

## 1 Violence, sexuality and cultures and spaces of safety

1 McVeigh *et al.* (2001) argue that law can neither be simply violent nor simply just. 'Law's violence is different from brute force precisely because force and justice are together the impossible conditions of law's possibility' (p. 12).

2 'Governance' is distinguished from 'government' in that the former is not restricted to the practices of a formal public authority, but emphasises 'private' modes of regulating social and economic life.

3 See, for instance, Hennessy (1995) for a critique of how consumption has had paradoxical effects, both generating visibility but confining those made visible to class-divided aesthetic forms of recognition.

4 This is a different definition of misrecognition from that of Bourdieu (1992) who argues that misrecognition operates in the interests of the powerful to disguise their power. Here it is used as a way of making value that is attributed to different groups (see Skeggs (2003) for an extended discussion of this process).

5 Lisa Bower (1997) shows how in the US claims for recognition have taken a legal form, what she names as 'official recognition'.

6 With a cumulative conception of nationality, Hage (1998) shows how we can capture how governmental belonging gives one not only the position of cultural dominance within the nation, but also the power to position others within it.

7 See Callinicos (1999) for an exposition of the neo-liberal politics of Giddens and Beck.

8 As Perry (2001) points out, turning the state against itself is not a challenge unique to exclusions that work through the context of sexual identity; it is to be found in all contexts of social exclusion.

9 The project on 'Violence, Sexuality and Space' was funded by the ESRC (grant no. L133251031) from May 1998 to May 2001. The research data was produced by Bev Skeggs, Les Moran, Paul Tyrer, Karen Corteen and Lewis Turner. See http://www.les1.man.ac.uk/sociology/vssrp for an outline overview of the project and list of publications.

## 2 Violence for safety

1 The heteronormative is also incorporated in the institutional structure that brings state violence into operation. Work on the experiences of gay and lesbian police

officers and officials in the wider criminal justice institution offers some evidence of this (see Burke 1993; Doan 1997).

2 It is wrong to assume that all interpersonal homophobic violence is understood as bad violence over against the good violence of the state. In some jurisdictions such interpersonal violence is also defined as good violence. One context in which this takes place is the defence of 'homosexual panic'. Here the one accused of murder gives a defence that he used reasonable force in response to a homosexual advance or proposition. For example in the context of Australia see Howe (2002) and Meure (2001).

3 In *Bowers* v. *Hardwick* this strategy failed. Keen and Goldberg (2000) suggest that, subsequent to the Supreme Court decision *Romer* v. *Evans*, which dealt with an attempt to restrict lesbian and gay access to anti-discrimination laws, the 'legacy of *Bowers* v. *Hardwick* might soon draw to a close" (p. 236). In June 2003 the US Supreme Court overruled *Bowers* v. *Hardwick*.

4 Scholars have also noted that in some jurisdictions one of the effects of decriminalisation of same-sex genital relations has been an increase in police activity and criminalisation of those engaging in such activity outside of the narrow context of decriminalisation. For example, in the context of England see Walmsley (1978) and, more recently, in the wake of reforms in Tasmania initiated after criminalisation was successfully challenged using the UN Charter of Civil and Political Rights, see Baird (1997).

# 3 Attachment to hate: the emotional dimensions of lesbian and gay crime control

1 Stolcke (1995) insists that the conceptual move from racism to cultural essentialism should not be seen as a new form of racism, but rather is a qualitatively different comparative discourse (see also Cronin 2000a).

2 Jacobs and Potter (1998) offer the most sustained, albeit problematic, critique of this orthodoxy. They question the veracity, not of the claims of harm *per se*, but of the claims of exceptional harm. Associated with this is the challenge to suggestions that violence motivated by hate or bias is an exceptional problem: an epidemic of violence. They suggest that the enactment of legislation against special hate crimes will itself promote harm, arguing that rather than offering a solution that prevents community fragmentation, the very category of hate crime further institutionalises the distinctions that promote fragmentation and institutionalise conflict.

3 In the UK, while the phrase 'hate crime' is a part of the common currency of the contemporary landscape of political activism around violence, it remains a political and bureaucratic category, rather than as it is found in the USA and Canada, a legislative term. While recent reforms under the Crime and Disorder Act 1998 have introduced the idea of sentence enhancement as well as the creation of a new offence in the context of racially aggravated violence, the government refused (and continues to refuse) to extend what might be called 'hate crimes' to other identity categories. Despite the absence of 'hate crime' as a legislative category, in the UK there is evidence that 'hate crime' is in practice already a significant organising category for policing, with many local initiatives in place.

4 And as such it is the feminine antithesis of law's masculine form: the Law of the Father.

5 The phrase is attributed to H. L. A. Hart who was responding to Lord Devlin's suggestion that law should reflect popular sentiments.

## 4 The limits of law and order: individual responsibility

1 It was prepared by an organisation made up of the senior police officers in the UK, the Association of Chief Police Officers (ACPO).

2 In our research on Manchester's gay Village, policing in the main was carried out by private security firms with minimal formal state policing.

3 See Valentine (1998) on lesbians subject to violence from the known as much as the unknown: known danger rather than stranger danger.

4 GALOP is the London gay and lesbian anti-violence and police monitoring organisation.

5 There is an extensive literature that explores a similar problem with safety literature that addresses women's needs. See, for example, Stanko and Curry (1997).

6 A lesbian and gay reading of the idea of ontological insecurity, embedded in and through safety literature, offers a different political and temporal dynamic to that offered by either Giddens or Garland. To reduce insecurity to a loss of trust, as a feature of modernity, is problematic. Lesbian and gay personal safety expertise is associated with different and longer histories of practices of social exclusion based upon same-sex genital relations. Nor can the experience of ontological insecurity be reduced to a relation to professionals.

7 Other research suggests that even when police recording mechanisms isolate incidents of homophobic violence there is little evidence of police use of that data to combat violence and little evidence of successful prosecutions. See Stanko (2002).

## 5 The rhetoric and politics of property

1 Danielle was interviewed in her capacity as a worker with the Manchester City Council. She advised us that she made the observation about the Village in her private not professional capacity.

2 Formally, the legal and the political are taken to be separate from each other. The relationship between political and legal claims is traditionally a hierarchical relationship of the legal over the political. In this scheme of things property as a legal relation is always more than property that is merely a political relation. As a legal relation property is enforceable by way of highly honoured processes, the courts, and ultimately esteemed officials associated with the state, the judiciary. In turn these officials may resort to specific sanctions imposed by way of particular institutions of legitimacy which gives rise to an enforceable claim: the good violence of the state. At the same time it is important to recognise that this hierarchy is unstable: it may be inverted. Property as a phenomenon of law may be highly problematic. It may be a social practice and strategy that is more limited as a legal than a political strategy. For example it may be of more limited availability, presupposing official recognition of the political claims of property. It may be confined to recognition by way of particular institutions. A political

relation may have wider and more effective significance. An objective here is to examine the interface between political and the legal aspects of everyday property talk.

3  The names of key informants, with the exception of elected representatives, have been changed. The names of certain locations have also been changed for reasons of security.

4  This is far from an accurate picture of Norman's property interests in the bar. His use of the bar in particular is subject to many limits, for example those which are related to the regulation of the consumption of alcohol.

5  The interview was conducted with an Assistant Planning Officer for the Manchester City Council who suggested that the personal dimension of property was treated rather ambiguously. The city's Unitary Development Plan makes reference to the city's willingness to support and foster development within the gay Village. In response to a question, 'Is there anything that your department can do to support [the gay Village]?', we were told: 'Not as such, because we . . . are not allowed even to look at the clientele of a bar. What is a gay bar one week could become an Irish pub the next . . .' Here the bar is characterised as fungible property, having no special relation to a particular clientele in this instance. However, shortly after we were informed that when an application is made for planning permission, there is a general understanding of the need for 'an element of honesty' about the particular use to which the premises are to be put. One reason given for this focus on the fungible is that it 'is designed to protect minorities' from the planning process and from planners who might use their powers to prevent facilities opening (Mark, KII, Man., 1998).

6  The Manchester focus group participants drew attention to the dangers of marking the boundary in this way. Wearing the band was experienced by some as a form of 'outing' that made them feel exposed and vulnerable. Many also complained that the band was not an effective gate-keeping mechanism as it gave access to all who could afford to buy one, gay or straight. Thereby it functioned to make the boundary more permeable to the danger of 'straights'.

7  This provides an interesting example of profit that is indifferent to the sexuality of the bar's customers being aligned with community needs.

8  The relationship between the aesthetics of the place and safety from drunken violence is also a feature of boundary-making and marking in Lancaster. Dennis, the gay owner of a bar in Lancaster which was described by him as a 'mixed' bar, offers an example of this. He explained that while his bar was remotely situated across a car park it was close to several other pubs and bars where violence was common. He did not employ door staff. One of the techniques he used to regulate access was described in the following terms. He explained that if male 'lager louts' came to the bar, 'they just stand out and they just feel uncomfortable and that in itself makes them leave . . . it's a bit too pretty for them.' He described the aesthetics of the bar as 'relaxed', which he explained in the following terms: 'no juke box, no loud music, no pool table, no darts, no big screen, just a bar, a meeting place, with this big conservatory and a macaw [named Oscar]' (Dennis, KII, Lan., 1998).

9  Much work has been done on the 'problem' of young people in public places. In the UK reform initiatives have focused on the need to remove young people from public spaces. See the Crime and Disorder Act 1998 relating to anti-social behaviour orders (s. 1) and 'Youth crime and disorder' (ss. 8–16)

10  The relation between gender and property is more complex than this would suggest. For example, Naffine (1998) has explored the juxtaposition of masculinity and secure and impenetrable boundaries in contrast to femininity as porous and penetrable boundaries. The latter has significance in the context of femininity as that which can be possessed/penetrated in contrast to masculinity as that which can penetrate and is impenetrable.

11  The relation between 'women's space' and 'lesbian space' is explored in the research data, especially in discussions about the Pankhurst Centre in Manchester. Women's space has particular significance, as it is space that is 'the most comfortable [where as a lesbian I could] . . . do anything I want to . . . in other places I am slightly more on my guard so to speak' (L, lfg, 2) This seems to develop, particularly in the Manchester focus groups, into a division between those straight women who 'fear' lesbians and who want to spend time with gay men, for safety's sake: 'straight women . . . hiding in gay men in some places just to have a dance . . .' (L, lfg, 2), and straight women who are not threatened by lesbian desire. See also Skeggs (2001).

12  During the course of the interview 'Rose' commented: 'I used to do a transvestite night on Wednesday, on the first of the month on a Wednesday, and then they stopped coming, they said they didn't feel safe coming down into the village . . . But they used to come down to our place but they said they felt intimidated walking about.' This draws attention to a relation between marginality and safety. There is a need for caution in reducing the marginality/safety relation in this instance to economic marginality. Transvestites are not necessarily economically marginal. Research on the economic impact of gender performance on transgender people suggests that change of gender has a potentially dramatic impact on economic status (see Perkins 1994; Hooley 1996).

## 6  Comfort and the location of safety – home

1  'Scally' is Liverpool slang for violent and unruly working-class men. Other terms include 'yob' and 'yobbo'.

2  The Editor notes that 'uncanny' is the English term for the German '*unheimlich*', unhomely (Freud 1985: 339ff.).

## 7  Cosmopolitan safety

1  Zizek could be criticised on the basis that he focuses his attention on corporate multi-culturalism, rather than that which has not yet been in/corporated.

2  Higher education institutions in the city house and contribute much larger numbers to the racial and ethnic mix of the city. A more recent addition to the ethnic mix of Lancaster has been the establishment of a private Islamic school for girls.

3  Also of interest here is the way this use of European presupposes that the UK is not in the first instance European.

4  Not all attempts to brand the area as European have succeeded however– witness the closure in 2000 of a Belgian-themed bar and brasserie in a prime location on Canal Street.

5 The company also operates Metz bars in other UK cities, Liverpool, Leeds and most recently Glasgow.

6 The use of these specific connotations of the Village is not only to be found in tourist and business promotion literature, but also in local and national listing magazines, in TV lifestyle programmes on Manchester (on loft-living) and in the publicity produced to promote the sale of homes in the city.

7 We should also note the speakers' qualification of 'cosmopolitan'. The reference to the village as a place with a 'cosmopolitan air' is a qualification of the term. This might suggest that for this participant cosmopolitanism, while not fully realised, is preserved as an objective as a utopian model of social order as diversity.

8 Her closing comment ties this back into the problematic nature of community.

9 There is an extensive body of literature that documents and analyses this relationship (see Moran 1996 and Edelman 1994).

10 Subsequent to the completion of the project a gay bar opened in Lancaster. It has high visibility, located on one of the major arteries through the city centre and flies the rainbow flag in its windows and over the door.

11 Here we want to bring together the insights gained from feminist theories on sexuality with more recent developments in class analysis from Bourdieu (1979, 1985); Butler (1997, 1999); Lovell (2000); McCall (1992); McNay (1999, 2000); Moi (1991); Skeggs (1997). However, this is not to ignore the important historical work on class, gender and sexuality such as Davis and Kennedy (1986); Nestlé (1987, 1997). Peter Cohen's (1997) study of AIDS activism in New York shows that for many middle-class gay men in the US, AIDS represented a 'class dislocation'.

## 8 Stranger danger: the uses of estrangement and the politics of fear

1 Our statistical analysis (using logistic regression) confirms that being a gay man is significant.

2 Our Manchester survey data suggests use of the Village was important; the more you use the gay Village the less safe you perceive that space to be. Gay men were the group that used the Village the most: 86.5 per cent of the gay men surveyed visited the Village once a week or more. The analysis also suggested that address was significant. Individuals living outside Manchester perceived the Village to be safer than individuals from Manchester. Those who were most remote from the Village (i.e. from outside Manchester) scored the highest rating for perceptions of the Village as 'safe' (80 per cent) in contrast to those living in the city centre who had the lowest rating for perceptions of 'safety' (48.6 per cent).

3 In Lancaster straight men were the group with the lowest perceptions of safety. Straight men were almost twice as likely to find Lancaster unsafe than our lesbian and gay respondents. There is a need for some caution here as the sample of straight men surveyed is small.

4 This was the most popular reason given by all groups.

5 Stanko (2000), who provides a critique of the resort to narrow definitions of 'crime' in the context of fear, is also of importance here. She suggests that it has had both particular and more general effects. It has been an important factor in

reducing fear of crime to a debate about victims, more specifically a debate about good victims and bad victims and the needs of the former and the culpability of the latter, highlighting the connection between fear of crime and social hierarchies and inequalities that are at work in the production of the stranger.

6  There is a long and detailed historical debate within lesbian literatures on how femme is taken as straight: see Martin (1996); Butler (1998).

7  In contrast, the straight women's group had stopped using the space because it was no longer seen to be cool.

# References

ACPO (Association of Chief Police Officers) (2000). *Guide to Identifying and Combating Hate Crime: Breaking the Power of Fear and Hate*. London, ACPO.

Adkins, L. (2002). 'Sexuality and Economy: Historicisation vs Deconstruction', *Australian Feminist Studies* **17**(37): 31–41.

Adler, S. and J. Brenner (1992). 'Gender and Space: Lesbians and Gay Men in the City', *International Journal of Urban and Regional Research* **16**(1): 24–34.

Ahmed, S. (1998). 'Tanning the Body: Skin, Colour and Gender', *New Formations* **34**: 27–43.

Ahmed, S. (2000). *Strange Encounters: Embodied Others in PostColoniality*. London, Routledge.

Ahmed, S. and J. Stacey (eds) (2002). *Skin*. London, Routledge.

Altman, D. (1996). 'Rupture or Continuity? The Internationalisation of Gay Identities', *Social Text* **48**: 77–94.

Altman, D. (1997). 'Global Gaze/Global Gays', *GLQ: A Journal of Lesbian and Gay Studies* **3**: 417–36.

Altman, D. (2001). *Global Sex*. Chicago, Chicago University Press.

Aries, P. *et al.* (eds) (1989). *A History of Private Life*. London, Harvard University Press.

Bachelard, G. (1963). *The Poetics of Space*. Boston, Beacon Press.

Baird, B. (1997). 'Putting Police on Notice: A South African Case Study', in *Homophobic Violence*. G. Mason and S. Tomsen (eds). Sydney, Hawkins Press.

Balibar, E. (1999). 'Class Racism', in *Race, Identity and Citizenship: A Reader*. J. X. Inda (ed.). Oxford, Blackwell: 322–35.

Bammer, Z. (1992). 'Editorial "The Question of Home"', *New Formations*: vii–xi.

Bannister, J. and N. Fyfe (2001). 'Fear of Crime', *Urban Studies* **38**(5–6): 807–13.

Bar On, B.-A. (1993) 'Marginality and Epistemic Privilege', in *Feminist Epistemologies*. London, Routledge.

Bauman, Z. (1991). *Modernity and Ambivalence*. Cambridge, Polity Press.

Bauman, Z. (1997). *Postmodernity and its Discontents*. Cambridge, Polity Press.

Bauman, Z. (2000). 'Time and Space Reunited', *Time and Society* **9**(2/3): 171–85.

Bauman, Z. (2002). 'Violence in the age of uncertainty', in *Crime and Insecurity: The Governance of Safety in Europe*. A Crawford (ed.). Cullompton, Willan Publishing: 52–74.

Beck, U. (1992). *Risk Society: Towards a New Modernity*. London, Sage.

Beck, U. (2000). 'The Cosmopolitan Perspective: Sociology of the Second Age of Modernity', *British Journal of Sociology* **51**: 79–105.

Beck, U. (2002). 'The Cosmopolitan Society and its Enemies', *Theory, Culture and Society* **19**(1): 17–44.

Bell, D. (1995). 'Pleasure and Danger: The Paradoxical Spaces of Sexual Citizenship', *Political Geography* **14**: 139–53.

Bell, D. and J. Binnie (2000). *The Sexual Citizen: Queer Politics and Beyond*. Cambridge, Polity Press.

Bell, D. and G. Valentine (eds) (1995). *Mapping Desire*. London, Routledge.

Bell, J. (2002) *Policing Hatred: Law Enforcement, Civil Rights, and Hate Crime*. New York, New York University Press.

Bennett, T. (1990). *Tackling Fear of Crime*. London, Home Office.

Berlant, L. (1997). *The Queen of America Goes to Washington City: Essays on Sex and Citizenship*. Durham, NC and London, Duke University Press.

Berlant, L. (2000). 'The Subject of True Feeling: Pain, Privacy, Politics', in *Transformations: Thinking Through Feminism*. S. Ahmed, J. Kilby, C. Lury, M. McNeil and B. Skeggs (eds). London, Routledge: 33–48.

Berlant, L. (2001a). 'Trauma and Ineloquence', *Cultural Values* **5**(1): 41–58.

Berlant, L. (2001b). 'Remembering Love, Forgetting Everything: Now Voyager', paper presented at University of Manchester.

Berlant, L. and M. Warner (1998). 'Sex in Public', *Critical Inquiry* **24**(Winter): 547–66.

Betsky, A. (1997). *Queer Space; Architecture and Same Sex Desire*. New York, William Morrow.

Bhabha, H. (1996). 'Rethinking Authority: Interview with Homi Bhabha', *Angelaki* **2**(2): 59–65.

Blackstone, W. (1979). *Commentaries on the Laws of England*. Chicago, University of Chicago Press.

Blomley, N. (1994). *Law, Space, and the Geographies of Power*. London, Guilford Press.

Blomley, N. (1997). 'The Properties of Space: History, Geography and Gentrification', *Urban Geographer* **18**(4): 286–94.

Blumenfeld, W. J. (1992). *Homophobia: How We All Pay the Price*. Boston, Beacon Press.

Bourdieu, P. (1979). 'Symbolic Power', *Critique of Anthropology* **4**: 77–85.

Bourdieu, P. (1985). 'The Social Space and the Genesis of Groups', *Theory and Society* **14**: 723–44.

Bourdieu, P. (1986). *Distinction: A Social Critique of the Judgement of Taste*. London, Routledge.

Bourdieu, P. (1987). 'What Makes a Social Class? On the Theoretical and Practical Existence of Groups', *Berkeley Journal of Sociology*: 1–17.

Bourdieu, P. (1992). *Language and Symbolic Power*. Cambridge, Polity Press.

Bouthillette, A. M. (1997). 'Queer and Gendered Housing: A Tale of Two Neighbourhoods in Vancouver', in *Queers in Space*. G. B. Ingram *et al.* (eds). Seattle, Bay Press.

Bower, L. (1994). 'Queer Acts and the Politics of "Direct Address": Rethinking Law, Culture and Community', *Law and Society Review* **28**(5): 1009–33.

Bower, L. (1997). 'Queer Problems/Straight Solutions: The Limit of the Politics of "Official Recognition"', in *Playing with Fire: Queer Politics, Queer Theories*. S. Phelan (ed.). New York, Routledge: 267–91.

Bowley, M. (2000). 'A Cancer at the Heart of Society', *New Law Journal* 4 August 2000: 1203–4.

Boyd, E. A., R. A. Berk and K. M. Hamner (1996). '"Motivated by Hatred": Categoriz-ation of Hate-motivated Crimes in Two Police Divisions', *Law and Society Review* **30**(4): 819–50.

Brennan, T. (1997). *At Home in the World: Cosmopolitanism Now*. Cambridge, MA, Harvard University Press.

Bricknell, C. (2000). 'Heros and Invaders: Gay and Lesbian Pride Parades and the Public/Private Distinction in New Zealand Media Accounts', *Gender Place and Culture* **7**(2): 163–78.

Brown, M. P. (2000). *Closet Space: Geographies of Metaphor from the Body to the Globe*. London, Routledge.

Brown, W. (1995a). *States of Injury*. Princeton, Princeton University Press.

Brown, W. (1995b). Rights and Identity in Late Modernity: Revisiting the "Jewish" Question', in *Identities, Politics and Rights*. T. Kearns (ed.). Michigan, University of Michigan Press: 85–130.

Brown, W. (1995c). 'Wounded Attachments: Late Modern Oppositional Political Formations', in *The Identity in Question*. J. Rajchman (ed.). New York and London, Routledge.

Brown, W. (2001). *Politics out of History*. Princeton, NJ, Princeton University Press.

Bumiller, K. (1987). 'Victims in the Shadow of the Law: A Critique of the Model of Legal Protection', *Signs: Journal of Women in Culture and Society* **12**(3): 421–39.

Burke, M. (1993). *Coming out of the Blue*. London, Cassell.

Butler, J. (1997a). *Excitable Speech: The Politics of the Performative*. New York and London, Routledge.

Butler, J. (1997b). 'Merely Cultural', *Social Text 52/53* **15**(3 & 4): 264–77.

Butler, J. (1998). 'Afterword', in *Butch/Femme: Inside Lesbian Gender*. S. Munt (ed.). London, Cassell: 225–31.

Butler, J. (1999). 'Performativity's Social Magic', in *Bourdieu: A Critical Reader*. R. Shusterman (ed.). Oxford, Blackwell: 113–29.

Butler, T. and M. Savage (eds) (1995). *Social Change and the Middle Classes*. London, University College London Press.

Callinicos, A. (1999). 'Social Theory Put to the Test, or Politics: Pierre Bourdieu and Anthony Giddens', *New Left Review* **236**: 77–102.

Cant, B. (1993). *Footsteps and Witnesses: Lesbian and Gay Lifestories from Scotland*. Edinburgh, Polygon.

Carrington, C. (1999). *No Place Like Home: Relationships and Family Life among Lesbians and Gay Men*. Chicago, University of Chicago Press.

Castells, M. (1983). 'Cultural Identity, Sexual Liberation and Urban Structure: The Gay Community in San Fransisco', in *The City and the Grassroots: A Cross-Cultural Theory of Urban Social Movements*. M. Castells (ed.). Berkeley, University of California Press.

Castells, M. and K. Murphy (1982). 'Cultural Identity and Urban structure: The Spatial Organisation of San Fransisco's Gay Community', in *Urban Policy under Capitalism*. F. Fainstein and S. Fainstein (eds). Beverly Hills, Sage.

Castle, T. (1993). *The Apparitional Lesbian*. New York, Columbia University Press.

Cheah, P. (1998). 'Introduction Part II: The Cosmopolitical – Today', in *Cosmo-politics: Thinking and Feeling Beyond the Nation*. P. Cheah. Minneapolis, Uni-versity of Minnesota Press: 20–41.

Clarke, D. (1991). 'Commodity Lesbianism', *Camera Obscura* **25–6**: 181–201.

Cohen, P. (1997). ' "All they needed": AIDS, Consumption, and the Politics of Class', *Journal of the History of Sexuality* **8**: 86–115.

Comstock, G. (1992). *Violence Against Lesbians and Gay Men*. New York, Columbia University Press.

Cooper, C. (1994). 'The House as Symbol of the Self', in *Designing for Human Behaviour*. J. B. Lang, C. Burette, W. Maleski and D. Vaslon (eds). Philadelphia, Dowden, Hutchinson and Ross: 130–46.

Cooper, D. (1998). *Governing Out of Order: Space, Law and the Politics of Belonging*. London, Rivers Oram Press.

Corteen, K. (2002). 'Lesbian Safety Talk: Problematizing Definitions and Experiences of Violence, Sexuality and Space', *Sexualities* **5**(3): 259–80.

Corteen, K. M., L. Moran, B. Skeggs and P. Tyler (2000). Citizens' Inquiry Reports: Lancaster and Manchester 2000, Violence, Sexuality and Space Research Project. Manchester, University of Manchester (http://www.les1.man.ac.uk/sociology/vssrp).

Cover, R. (1986). 'Violence and the Word', *Yale Law Journal* **95**: 1601–29.

Crawford, A. (1997). *The Local Governance of Crime: Appeals to Community and Partnerships*. Oxford, Oxford University Press.

Cronin, A. (2000a). *Advertising and Consumer Citizenship: Gender, Images and Rights*. London, Routledge.

Cronin, A. (2000b). 'Consumerism and "Compulsory Individuality": Women, Will and Potential', in *Transformations: Thinking Through Feminism*. S. Ahmed, J. Kilby, C. Lury, M. McNeil and B. Skeggs (eds). London, Routledge: 273–88.

Davies, M. (1994). 'Feminist Appropriations: Law, Property and Personality', *Social and Legal Studies* **3**: 365–91.

Davies, M. (1998). 'The Proper: Discourses of Purity', *Law and Critique* **IX**: 147–73.

Davies, M. (1999). 'Queer Property, Queer Persons: Self-Ownership and Beyond', *Social and Legal Studies* **8**(3): 327–52.

Davies, M. and N. Naffine (2001). *Are Persons Property? Legal Debates about Property and Personality*. Aldershot, Ashgate.

Davis, M. and E. Lapovsky Kennedy (1986). 'Oral History and the Study of Sexuality in the Lesbian Community: Buffalo, New York 1940–1960', *Feminist Studies* **12**(1): 7–25.

de Certeau, M. (1984/1988). *The Practice of Everyday Life*. Berkeley, University of California Press.

de Lauretis, T. (1990). 'Eccentric Subjects: Feminist Theory: Historical Consciousness', *Feminist Studies* **16**(1).

Derrida, J. (1992). 'Force of Law: The Mystical Foundation of Authority', in *Deconstruction and the Possibility of Justice*. D. Cornell, M. Rosenfeld and D. G. Carlson (eds). London, Routledge: 3–67.

Dikec, M. (2002). 'Pera Peras Poros; Longing for spaces of Hospitality', *Theory Culture Society* **19**(1–2): 227–47.

Ditton, J. and S. Farrell (2000). *The Fear of Crime*. Aldershot, Ashgate.

Ditton, J. *et al.* (1999). 'Afraid or Angry? Recalibrating the 'Fear' of Crime', *International Review of Victimology* **6**: 83–99.

Doan, L. (1997). 'Gross Indecency Between Women: Policing Lesbians or Policing Lesbian Police', *Social and Legal Studies* **6**(4): 533.

Donzelot, J. (1979). *The Policing of Families: Welfare versus the State*. London, Hutchinson.

Douglas, M. (1966). *Purity and Danger: An Analysis of Concepts of Pollution and Taboo*. London, Ark.

Douglas, M. (1991). 'The Idea of a Home; A Kind of Space', *Social Research* **58**(1): 287–307.

Douzinas, C. (2000). *The End of Human Rights*. Oxford, Hart Publishing.

Duggan, L. (2000). *Sapphic Slashers: Sex Violence and American Modernity*. Durham, NC, Duke University Press.

Duncan, N. (1996). *Body Space: Geographies of Gender and Sexuality*. London, Routledge.

Dunne, G. (1997). *Lesbian Lifestyles: Women's Work and the Politics of Sexuality*. Basingstoke, Macmillan.

Edelman, L. (1994). 'Tearooms and Sympathy, or the Epistemology of the Water-closet', in *Homographesis: Essays in Gay Literary and Cultural Theory*. L. Edelman (ed.). New York, Routledge.

Ellin, N. (ed.) (1997). *Architecture of Fear*. Princeton, Princeton Architectural Press.

Erickson, B. (1991). 'What is Good Taste for?' *Canadian Review of Sociology and Anthropology* **28**: 255–78.

Erickson, B. (1996). 'Culture, Class and Connections', *American Journal of Sociology* **102**: 217–51.

Evans, D. (1993). *Sexual Citizenship: The Material Construction of Sexualities*. London, Routledge.

Florida, R. (2002). *The Rise of the Creative Class: And How It's Transforming Work, Leisure, Community and Everyday Life*. New York, Basic Books.

Forest, B. (1995). 'West Hollywood as Symbol: The Significance of Place in the Con-struction of Gay Identity', *Environment and Planning D: Society and Space* **13**: 133–57.

Forty, A. (1986). *Objects of Desire: Design and Society 1750–1980*. London, Thames and Hudson.

Fraser, M. (1999). 'Classing Queer: Politics in Competition', *Theory, Culture and Society* **16**(2): 107–31.

Fraser, N. (1995). 'From Redistribution to Recognition? Dilemmas of Justice in "Post-Socialist" Age', *New Left Review* **212**: 68–94.

Fraser, N. (1997). 'Heterosexism, Misrecognition and Capitalism: A Response to Judith Butler', *Social Text 52/53* **15**(3 & 4): 279–89.

Freud, S. (1985). 'The Uncanny', in *The Pelican Freud Library*. 14 'Art and Literature'. A. Dickson (ed.). London, Penguin Books: 335–76.

Furedi, F. (2002). *Culture of Fear*. London, Continuum.

GALOP (2001). *The Low Down: Black Lesbians, Gay Men and Bisexual People Talk about their Experiences and Needs*. London, GALOP.

Garland, D. (1996). 'The Limits of the Sovereign State: Strategies of Crime Control in Contemporary Society', *British Journal of Criminology* **36**(4): 445–71.

Garland, D. (2001). *The Culture of Control: Crime and Social Order in Contemporary Society*. Oxford, Oxford University Press.

George, R. M. (1999). *The Politics of Home: Postcolonial Relocations and Twentieth Century Fiction*. Cambridge, Cambridge University Press.

Giddens, A. (1990). *The Consequences of Modernity*. Cambridge, Polity Press.

Giddens, A. (1991). *Modernity and Self-Identity: Self and Society in the Late Modern Age*. Cambridge, Polity Press.

Gilloch, G. (1996). *Myth and Metropolis: Walter Benjamin and the City*. Cambridge, Polity Press.

Girard, R. (1989). *Violence and the Sacred*. Baltimore, Johns Hopkins University Press.

Girling, E., I. Loader and B. Reed (2000). *Crime and Social Change in Middle England: Questions of Order in an English Town*. London, Routledge.

Glassner, B. (1999). *The Culture of Fear: Why Americans are Afraid of the Wrong Things*. New York, Basic Books.

Gluckman, A. and B. Reed (1997). *Homo Economics: Capitalism, Community and Lesbian and Gay Life*. London, Routledge.

GML & GPI (1999). *Lesbian's Experiences of Violence and Harassment*. Manchester, Greater Manchester Lesbian and Gay Policing Initiative.

Gold, J. R. and G. Revill (2000). *Landscapes of Defence*. Harlow, Prentice Hall.

Goldberg, D. T. (ed.) (1994). *Multiculturalism: A Critical Reader*. Oxford, Blackwell.

Goldberg Hiller, J. (2002). *The Limits of Union, Same Sex Marriage and the Politics of Civil Rights*. Ann Arbor, University of Michigan Press.

Goodrich, P. (1990). *Languages of Law*. London, Weidenfeld.

Goodrich, P. (1992). 'Poor Illiterate Reason: History, Nationalism and Common Law', *Social and Legal Studies* 1: 7–20.

Gould, C. (1988). *Re-Thinking Democracy*. Cambridge, Cambridge University Press.

Govier, T. (2002). *Forgiveness and Revenge*. London, Routledge.

Gramsci, A. (1971). *Selections from Prison Notebooks of Antonio Gramsci*. London, Lawrence and Wishart.

Green, J. N. (1999). *Beyond Carnival: Male Homosexuality in Twentieth Century Brazil*. Chicago, University of Chicago Press.

Grewel, I. and C. Kaplan (2001). 'Global Identities: Theorising Transnational Studies of Sexuality', *GLQ* 7(4): 663–79.

Gross, L. (1993). *Contested Closets: The Politics and Ethics of Outing*. Minneapolis, University of Minnesota Press.

Grosz, E. (1995). *Space, Time and Perversion*. London, Routledge.

Hage, G. (1998). *White Nation*. Melbourne and London, Pluto Press.

Halberstam, J. (1998). *Female Masculinity*. Durham, NC and London, Duke University Press.

Hale, C. (1996). 'Fear of Crime: A Review of the Literature', *International Review of Victimology* 4: 79–150.

Hall, S. (1997). *Representation: Cultural Representations and Signifying Practices*. London, Sage.

Hannerz, U. (1996). *Transnational Connections: Culture, People, Places*. London, Routledge.

Hart, L. (1994). *Fatal Women: Lesbian Sexuality and the Mark of Aggression*. London, Routledge.

Healthy Gay Manchester (1998). *Healthy Gay Manchester's Lesbian and Gay Guide to Greater Manchester*.

Heaphy, B. (1999). 'Sex, Money and the Kitchen Sink: Power in Same Sex Relationships', in *Relating Intimacies: Power and Resistance*. J. Seymour and P. Bagguley (ed.). Basingstoke, Macmillan: 222–45.

Heidegger, M. (1997). 'Building Dwelling Thinking', in *Basic Writings*. D. F. Krell (ed.). New York, Harper Collins: 319–41.

Hennessy, R. (1995). 'Queer Visibility in Commodity Culture', in *Social Post-modernism: Beyond Identity Politics.* L. Nicholson and S. Seidman (eds). Cambridge, Cambridge University Press.

Herek, G. M. and K. T. Berrill (eds) (1992). *Hate Crimes.* London, Sage.

Herman, D. (1994). *Rights of Passage: Struggles for Lesbian and Gay Legal Equality.* Toronto, University of Toronto Press.

Herman, D. (1997). *The Anti-Gay Agenda: Orthodox Vision and the Christian Right.* Chicago, Chicago University Press.

Hindelong, M., M. Gottfredson and J. Garofalo (1978). *Victims of Personal Crime.* Boston, Bollinger.

Hobsbawm, E. (1991). 'Introduction', *Social Research* **58**(1 Spring): 65–68.

Holliday, R. (1999). 'The Comfort of Identity', *Sexualities* **2**(4): 475–91.

Honneth, A. (1995). *The Struggle for Recognition: The Moral Grammar of Social Struggles.* Cambridge, Polity.

Honnig, B. (1994). 'Difference, Dilemmas and the Politics of Home', *Social Research* **61**(3): 563–97.

hooks, b. (1990). 'Marginalising a Site of Resistance', in *Out There: Marginalisation and Contemporary Culture.* C. West, R. Ferguson and M. Gevee (eds). New York and Cambridge, New Museum of Contemporary Art and MIT Press.

Hooley, J. (1996). *The Transgender Project.* Sydney, Central Sydney Health Authority.

Howe, A. (2002). 'Provoking polemic: provoked killings and ethical paradoxes of the postmodern feminist condition', *Feminist Legal Studies* **10**(1): 39–64.

Hubbard, P. (2000). 'Desire/Disgust: Mapping the Moral Contours of hetero-sexuality', *Progress in Human Geography* **24**(2): 191–217.

Iganski, P. (1999). 'Why Make Hate a Crime?' *Critical Social Policy* **19**(3): 385–94.

Ingram, G. B., A. Bouthillette and Y. Retter (1997). *Queers in Space.* Seattle, Bay Press.

Irigaray, l. (1985). 'Commodities among themselves', in *This Sex which is not one* (trans). C. Porter. Ithaca, Cornell University Press: 192–7.

Irigaray, L. (ed.) (1993). *An Ethics of Sexual Difference.* Ithaca, Cornell University Press.

Jacobs, J. B. and K. Potter (1998). *Hate Crimes: Criminal Law and Identity Politics.* New York, Oxford University Press.

Jacobs, J. M. (1998). 'Staging Difference: Aestheticization and the Politics of Difference in Contemporary Cities', in *Cities of Difference.* R. Fincher and J. M. Jacobs (eds). London and New York, Guilford: 252–78.

Jagose, A. (1994). *Lesbian Utopics.* London, Routledge.

Jefferson, T. and W. Hollway (2000). 'The Role of Anxiety in Fear of Crime', in *Crime, Risk and Insecurity.* T. Hope and R. Sparks (eds). London, Routledge: 13–30.

Jenness, V. and K. Broad (1997). *Hate Crimes: New Social Movements and the Politics of Violence.* Hawthorn, Aldine De Gruyter.

Jenness, V. and R. Grattet (2001). *Making Hate a Crime: From Social Movement to Law Enforcement.* New York, Russell Sage Foundation.

Johansson, W. and W. A. Percy (1994). *Outing: Shattering the Conspiracy of Silence.* Binghampton, Harrington Park Press.

Johnson, M. (1998). 'Global Desirings and Translocal Loves: Transgendering and Same-sex Sexualities in the Southern Philippines', *American Ethnologist* **25**: 695–711.

Johnston, N. (1990). 'The Territoriality of Law: An Exploration', *Urban Geography,* **11**(6): 548–65.

Johnston, L. and G. Valentine (1995). 'Wherever I Lay My Girlfriend, That's My Home: The Performance and Surveillance of Lesbian Identites in Domestic Environments', in *Mapping Desire: Geographies of Sexualities*. D. Bell and G. Valentine (eds). London, Routledge.

Kantorowicz, E. H. (1957). *The King's Two Bodies. A Study in Mediaeval Political Theology*. Princeton, Princeton University Press.

Keen, L. and S. Goldberg (2000). *Strangers to Law*. Ann Arbor, University of Michigan Press.

Keith, M. (1993). 'Ethnic Entrepreneurs and Street Rebels: Looking Inside the Inner City', in *Mapping the Subject: geographies of cultural transformation*. S. Pile and N. Thrift (eds). London, Routledge.

Kelling, G. L. and C. M. Coles (1996). *Fixing Broken Windows: Restoring Order and Reducing Crime in our Communities*. New York, The Free Press.

Kelly, L. (1987). 'The Continuum of Sexual Violence', in *Women, Violence and Social Control*. J. Hamner and M. Maynard (eds). Basingstoke, Macmillan.

Kelly, L. (1988). 'How Women Define Their Experiences of Violence', in *Feminist Perspectives on Wife Abuse*. K. Yllo and M. Bograd (eds). London, Sage: 114–32.

Kinsman, G. (1987). *The Regulation of Desire*. Montreal, Black Rose Books.

Knopp, L. (1994). 'Social Justice, Sexuality and the City', *Urban Geography* 15: 644–60.

Kuehnle, K., and A. Sullivan (2001). 'Patterns of Anti-Gay Violence: An Analysis of Incident Characteristics and Victim Reporting', *Journal of Interpersonal Violence* 16(9): 928.

Laplanche, J. and J. B. Pontalis (1988). *The Language of Psychoanalysis*. The Institute of Psychoanalysis, Karnac Books.

Lauristen, J. and D. Thorstad (1974). *The Early Homosexual Rights Movement (1864–1935)*. New York, Times Change Press.

Lawrence, F. M. (1999). *Punishing Hate: Bias Crimes under American Law*. Cambridge, Harvard University Press.

Lefebvre, H. (1991). *The Production of Space*. Oxford, Blackwell.

Leventhal, B. and S. Lundy (1999). *Same Sex Domestic Violence: Strategies for Change*. Thousand Oaks, Sage.

Levin, B. (1999). 'Hate Crimes. Worse by Definition', *Journal of Contemporary Criminal Justice* 20(1): 6–21.

Litvak, J. (1997). *Strange Gourmets: Sophistication, Theory and the Novel*. Durham, NC and London, Duke University Press.

Lobel, K. (ed). (1986). *Naming the Violence: Speaking out about Lesbian Battering*. Boston, Seal Press.

Loffreda, B. (2000). *Losing Matt Shepard: Life and Politics in the Aftermath of Anti-gay Murder*. New York, Columbia University Press.

Lovell, T. (2000). 'Thinking Feminism with and against Bourdieu', *Feminist Theory* 1(1): 11–32.

McCall, L. (1992). 'Does Gender Fit? Bourdieu, Feminism and Concepts of Social Order', *Theory and Society* 21: 837–67.

McGhee, D. (2001). *Homosexuality, Law and Resistance*. London, Routledge.

MacKenzie, C. (2000). *A Guide to Personal Security*. Manchester, Greater Manchester Police.

McNay, L. (1999). 'Gender, Habitus and the Field: Pierre Bourdieu and the Limits of Reflexivity', *Theory, Culture and Society* 16(1): 95–119.

McNay, L. (2000). *Gender and Agency: Reconfiguring the Subject in Feminist and Social Theory*. Cambridge, Polity.

McVeigh, S., P. Rush *et al.* (2001). 'A Judgement Dwelling in Law: Violence and the Relations of Legal Thought', in *Law, Violence, and the Possibility of Justice*. A. Sarat (ed.). Princeton, Princeton University Press: 101–42.

Madriz, E. I. (1997). 'Images of Criminals and Victims: A Study of Women's Fear and Social Control', *Gender and Society* **11**(3): 342–56.

Majury, D. (1994). 'Refashioning the Unfashionable: Claiming Lesbian Identities in the Legal Context', *Canadian Journal of Woman and the Law* **7**(2): 286–306.

Markwell, K. (2002). 'Mardi Gras Tourism and the Contruction of Sydney as an International Gay and Lesbian City', *GLQ* **8**(1–2): 81–99.

Martin, B. (1996). *Femininity Played Straight: The Significance of Being Lesbian*. New York, Routledge.

Martin, B. and C. T. Mohanty (1986). 'Feminist Politics: What's Home Got to do with it?', in *Feminist Studies/Critical Studies*. T. De Laurentis (ed.). Bloomington, Indiana University Press: 191–211.

Mason, A., and A. Palmer (1996). *Queer Bashing: A National Survey of Hate Crimes against Lesbians and Gay Men*. London, Stonewall.

Mason, G. (1995). '(Out)Laws: Acts of Proscription in the Sexual Order', in *Public and Private: Feminist Legal Debates*. M. Thornton (ed.). Melbourne, Oxford University Press: 66–88.

Mason, G. (1997a). 'Sexuality and Violence: Questions of Difference', in *Faces of Hate: Hate Crime in Australia*. C. Cunneen, D. Fraser and S. Tomsen (eds). New South Wales, Hawkins Federation Press.

Mason, G. (1997b). 'Boundaries of Sexuality: Lesbian Experience and Feminist Discourse on Violence against Women', *Australasian Gay and Lesbian Law Journal* **7**: 40–56.

Mason, G. (2001). 'Body maps: Envisaging Homophobia, Violence and Safety', *Social and Legal Studies* **10**(1): 23–44.

Mason, G. (2002). *The Spectacle of Violence: Homophobia Gender and Knowledge*. London, Routledge.

Mason, G. and S. Tomsen (1997). *Homophobic Violence*. Sydney, Hawkins Press.

Massey, D. (1993). 'Power-geometry and a Progressive Sense of Place', in *Mapping the Futures: Local Cultures, Global Change*. J. Bird, B. Curtis, T. Putman, G. Robertson and L. Tickner (eds). London, Routledge: 56–69.

Merry, S. (1981). *Urban Danger: Life in a Neighbourhood of Strangers*. Philadelphia, Temple University Press.

Merry, S. (1995). 'Resistance and the Cultural Power of Law', *Law and Society Review* **29**(1): 11–26.

Metropolitan Police. (2002). *Understanding and Responding To Hate Crime*. London, Metropolitan Police.

Meure, D. (2001). 'Homo panic in the High Court: The High Court in *Green* v. *R.*, *Griffith Law Review* **10**(2): 240–58.

Mohanty, C. T. (1992). 'Feminist Encounters: Locating the Politics of Experience', in *Destabilising Theory: Contemporary Feminist Debates*. M. Barrett and A. Phillips (eds). Cambridge, Polity Press: 74–92.

Mohr, R. D. (1992). *Gay Ideas: Outing and Other Controversies*. Boston, Beacon Press.

Moi, T. (1991). 'Appropriating Bourdieu: Feminist Thought and Pierre Bourdieu's Sociology of Culture', *New Literary History* **22**: 1017–49.

Moran, L. J. (1996). *The Homosexual(ity) of Law*. London, Routledge.

Moran, L. J. (2000a). 'Homophobic Violence: The Hidden Injuries of Class', in *Cultural Studies and the Working Class: Subject to Change*. S. Munt (ed.). London, Cassell: 206–19.

Moran, L. J. (2000b). 'Victim Surveys and Beyond', *Scolag, Legal Journal* **275**: 10–13.

Moran, L. J. (2001) 'Affairs of the Heart: Hate Crime and the Politics of Crime Control'. *Law and Critique* **12**(3): 331–44.

Moran, L. J. (2002). 'The Poetics of Safety:  Lesbians, Gay Men and Home', in *Crime and Insecurity: The Governance of Safety in Europe*. A. Crawford (ed.). Cullompton, Willan Publishing: 274–99.

Moran, L. J. and D. McGhee (1998). 'Perverting London: Cartographic Practices of Policing', *Law and Critique* **ix**(2): 207–24.

Moran, L. J. and B. Skeggs (2001). 'Property and Propriety: Fear and Safety in Gay Space', *Social and Cultural Geography* **2**(4): 407–20.

Morley, D. (2000). *Home Territories: Media, Mobility and Identity*. London, Routledge.

Morrison, C. and A. Mackay (2000). *The Experience of Violence and Harassment of Gay Men in the City of Edinburgh*. Edinburgh, Scottish Executive Central Research Unit.

Mouzos, J. and S. Thompson (2000). *Gay-Hate Related Homicides: An Overview of Major Findings in New South Wales*. Canberra, Australian Institute of Criminology.

Murphy, J. G. and J. Hampton (1988). *Mercy and Forgiveness*. Cambridge, Cambridge University Press.

Myslick, W. D. (1996). 'Renegotiating the Social/Sexual Identities of Place: Gay Communities as Safe Havens or Sites of Resistance', in *BodySpace: Destabilising Geographies of Gender and Sexuality*. N. Duncan (ed.). London, Routledge: 156–69.

Naffine, N. (1998). 'The Legal Structure of Self Ownership: Or the Self Possessed Man and the Woman Possessed", *Journal of Law and Society* **25**(2): 193–212.

National Advisory Group (1999). 'Breaking the chain of hate: A national survey examining the level of homophobic crime and community confidence towards the police service'. London, National Advisory Group.

Nava, M. (2002). 'Cosmopolitan Modernity: Everyday Imaginaries and the Register of Difference', *Theory, Culture and Society* **19**(1): 81–99.

NCAVP (1999). *Anti-Lesbian, Gay, Bisexual and Transgender Violence in 1998: A Report of the National Coalition of Anti-Violence Programs*. New York, National Coalition of Anti-Violence Programmes.

Nedelsky, J. (1991). 'Law, Boundaries and the Bounded Self', in *Law and the Order of Culture*. R. Post (ed.). Berkeley, University of California Press: 162–90.

Neill, W. J. V. (2001). 'Marketing the Urban Experience: Reflections on the Place of Fear in the Promotional Strategies of Belfast, Detroit and Berlin', *Urban Studies* **38**(5–6): 815–28.

Neocleous, M. (2000). *The Fabrication of Social Order: A Critical Theory of Police Power*. London, Pluto Press.

Nestle, J. (1987). *A Restricted Country*. Ithaca, NY, Firebrand Press.

Nestle, J. (1997). 'Restriction and Reclamation: Lesbian Bars and Beaches of the 1950's', in *Queers in Space*. G. B. Ingram *et al.* (eds). Seattle, Bay Press.

Newburn, T. (2001). 'The Commodification of Policing Security Networks in the Law Modern City', *Urban Studies* **38**(5/6): 829–48.

Nietzsche, F. (1956). *The Genealogy of Morals*. New York, Vintage Books.

Onken, S. J. (1998). 'Conceptualizing Violence Against Gay, Lesbian, Bisexual, Intersexual and Transgendered People', in *Violence and Social Injustice Against Lesbian, Gay and Bisexual People*. L. M. Sloan and N. S. Gustavsson (eds). Binghampton, Hawthorn Press: 5–24.

Pain, R. H. (1997). 'Social Geographies of Women's Fear of Crime', *Transactions of the Institute of British Geographers* 22(2): 231–44.

Pateman, C. (1988). *The Sexual Contract*. Cambridge, Polity Press.

Perkins, R. (1994). *Transgender Lifestyles and HIV/AIDS Risk*. Sydney, University of New South Wales.

Perry, B. (2001). *In the Name of Hate: Understanding Hate Crime*. New York, Routledge.

Peterson, R. (1993). 'How Musical Tastes Mark Occupational Status Groups', in *Cultivating Differences: Symbolic Boundaries and the Making of Inequality*. M. Lamont and M. Fournier (eds). Chicago, Chicago University Press.

Peterson, R. and R. Kern (1996). 'Changing Highbrow Taste: From Snob to Omnivore', *American Sociological Review* 61: 900–907.

Phelan, S. (2001). *Sexual Strangers: Gays, Lesbians and the Dilemmas of Citizenship*. Philadelphia, Temple University Press.

Pile, S. and N. Thrift (1995). *Mapping the Subject: Geographies of Cultural Trans-formation*. London, Routledge.

Pratt, G., and S. Hanson (1994). 'Geography and the Construction of Difference', *Gender, Place and Culture* 1: 5–29.

Quilley, S. (1997). 'Constructing Manchester's 'New Urban Village': Gay Space in the Entrepreneurial City', in *Queers in Space: Communities/Public Places/Sites of Resistance*. G. B. Ingram *et al.* (eds). Seattle, Bay Press.

Radin, M. J. (1993). *Reinterpreting Property*. Chicago, University of Chicago Press.

Raffo, S. (ed.) (1997). *Queerly Classed*. Boston, South End Press.

Retter, Y. (1997). 'Lesbian Spaces in Los Angeles 1970–90', in *Queers in Space*. G. Ingram *et al.* (eds). Seattle, Bay Press.

Robbins, B. (2001). 'The Village of the Liberal Managerial Class', in *Cosmopolitan Geographies: New Locations in Literature and Culture*. V. Dharwadker (ed.). New York, Routledge.

Robertson, R. (1996) *Globalisation: Social Theory and Global Culture*. London, Sage.

Robson, R. (1992). *Lesbian (Out)Law*. Ithaca, Firebrand.

Robson, R. (1995). 'Convictions: Theorising Lesbians and Criminal Justice', in *Legal Inversions*. D. Herman and C. Stychin (eds). Philadelphia, Temple University Press: 180–94.

Robson, R. (1998). *Sappho Goes to Law School*. New York, Columbia University Press.

Rofel, L. (1999). 'Qualities of Desire: Imagining Gay Identities in China', *GLQ: A Journal of Lesbian and Gay Studies* 5: 451–74.

Rorty, A. O. (1994). 'The Hidden Politics of Multiculturalism', *Political Theory* 22(1): 152–66.

Rose, G. (1993). *Feminism and Geography: The Limits of Geographical Knowledge*. Cambridge, Polity Press.

Rose, N. (1989). *Governing the Soul: The Shaping of the Private Self*. London, Routledge.

Rose, N. (1992). 'Governing the Enterprising Self', in *The Values of Enterprise Culture: The Moral Debate*. P. Morris (ed.). London, Routledge.

Rosga, A. (2001). 'Deadly Words: State Power and the Entanglement of Speech and Violence in Hate Crime', *Law and Critique* 12(3): 223–52.

Rothenberg, T. (1995). 'And She Told Two Friends': Lesbians Creating Urban Social Space', in *Mapping Desire: Geographies of Sexualities*. D. Bell and G. Valentine (eds). London, Routledge.

Rouse, R. (1995). 'Thinking through Transnationalism: Notes on the Cultural Politics of Class Relations in the Contemporary United States', *Public Culture* 7(2): 353–402.

Rubin, G. (1975). 'The Traffic in Women: Notes on the "Political Economy" of Sex', in R. R. Reiter (ed.) Toward an Anthropology of Women', *New York Monthly Review Press*: 157–210.

Rushbrook, D. (2002). 'Cities, Queer Space and the Cosmopolitan Tourist', *GLQ* 8(1–2): 183–206.

Rybczynski, W. (1988). *Home: A Short History of an Idea*. London, Heinemann.

Sandroussi, J., and S. Thompson (1995). *Out of the Blue: A Police Survey of Violence and Harassment against Gay Men and Lesbians*. Sydney, New South Wales Police.

Saraga, E. (1996). 'Dangerous Places: The family as a site of crime', in *The Problem of Crime*. J. Muncie and E. McMaughlin (eds). London, Sage: 184–227.

Sarat, A. (1997). 'Vengence, Victims and the Identities of Law', *Social and Legal Studies* 6(2): 163–89.

Sarat, A. (2001). 'Situating Law Between the Realities of Violence and the Claims of Justice: An Introduction', in *Law, Violence and the Possibility of Justice*. A. Sarat. Princeton, Princeton University Press: 3–17.

Sarat, A. and T. R. Kearns (1991). 'A Journey through Forgetting: Towards a Jurisprudence of Violence', in *The Fate of Law*. A. Sarat and T. R. Kearns. Ann Arbor, Michigan University Press.

Sarat, A. and T. R. Kearns (1993). *Law in Everyday Life*. Ann Arbor, University of Michigan Press.

Sassen, S. (2000). 'New Frontiers Facing Urban Sociology at the Millennum', *British Journal of Sociology* 51(1): 143–59.

Scalettar, L. (2000). 'Resistance, Representation and the Subject of Violence: Reading Hothead Paisan', in *Queer Frontiers: Millennial Geographies, Genders and Generations*. J. Boone *et al.* (eds). Madison, University of Wisconsin: 261–78.

Schroeder, J. L. (1998). *The Vestal and the Fasces: Hegel, Lacan, Property and the Feminine*. Berkeley, University of California Press.

Sedgwick, E. K. (1990). *Epistemology of the Closet*. Hemel Hempstead, Harvester Wheatsheaf.

Sennet, R. (1992). *The Fall of Public Man*. New York, W.W. Norton.

Sibley, D. (1998). *Geographies of Exclusion: Society and Difference in the West*. London, Routledge.

Simmel, G. (1964). 'The Stranger', in *The Sociology of George Simmel* (trans). K. H. Wolff (ed.). New York, Free Press: 402–8.

Simon, J. (2001). 'Entitlement to Cruelty: Neo-liberalism and the Punitive Mentality in the United States', in *Crime, Risk and Justice: The Politics of Crime Control in Liberal Democracies*. K. Stenson and R. R. Sullivan (eds). Cullompton, Willan Publishing: 125–143.

Skeggs, B. (1997). *Formations of Class and Gender: Becoming Respectable*. London, Sage.

Skeggs, B. (1998). 'Matter out of Place: Visibility and Sexualities in Leisure Spaces', *Leisure Studies* 18(3): 213–33.

Skeggs, B. (2000a). 'The Appearance of Class: Challenges in Gay Space', in *Cultural Studies and the Working Class: Subject to Change*. S. Munt (ed.). London, Cassell: 129–51.

Skeggs, B. (2000b). 'The Rhetorical Affects of Feminism', in *Transformations: Thinking Through Feminism*. S. Ahmed, J. Kilby, C. Lury, M. McNeil and B. Skeggs (eds). London, Routledge: 27–33.

Skeggs, B. (2001). 'The Toilet Paper: Femininity, Class and Mis-recognition', *Women's Studies International Forum* **24**(3–4): 295–307.

Skeggs, B. (2002). 'Who Can Tell? Reflexivity in Feminist Research', in *Issues and Practices in Qualitative Research*. T. May (ed.). London, Sage.

Skeggs, B. (2003). *Class, Self, Culture*. London, Routledge.

Sklair, L. (2001). *The Transnational Capitalist Class*. Oxford, Blackwell.

Slater, D. and F. Tonkiss (2001). *Market Society*. Cambridge, Polity.

Smith, A.-M. (1994). *New Right Discourse on Race and Sexuality*. Cambridge, Cambridge University Press.

Smith, N. and C. Katz (1983). 'Grounding Metaphor: Towards a Spatialized Politics', in *Place and the Politics of Identity*. M. Keith and S. Pile (eds). London, Routledge: 67–83.

Smith, S. (1993). *Subjectivity, Identity and the Body*. Bloomington, Indiana University Press.

Solomon, R. C. (ed.) (1999). Justice v Vengeance: On Law, and the Satisfaction of Emotion', in *The Passions of Law*. S. A. Bandes (ed.). New York, New York University Press.

Sparks, R. (1992). 'Reason and unreason in 'Left Realism': Some Problems in the Constitution of Fear of Crime', in *Issues in Realist Criminology*. R. Matthews and J. Young (eds). London, Sage.

Stanko, E. (1997). 'Safety Talk: Conceptualising Women's Risk Assessment as a "Technology of the Self"', in *Theoretical Criminology* **1**(4): 479–99.

Stanko, E. A. (1988). 'Fear of Crime and the Myth of the Safe Home: A Feminist Critique of Criminology', in *Feminist Perspectives on Wife Abuse*. K. Yllo and M. Bograd (eds). London, Sage.

Stanko, E. A. (1999). 'Identities and Criminal Violence: Observations on Law's Recognition of Vulnerable Victims in England and Wales', *Studies in Law, Politics and Society* **16**: 99–119.

Stanko, E. A. (2002). *Understanding and Responding to Hate Crime Project: Homophobic Violence Fact Sheet*. London, Metropolitan Police.

Stanko, E. A. and P. Curry, P. (1997). 'Homophobic Violence and the "self" at risk: interrogating the boundaries', *Legal Perversions, a special edition of Social and Legal Studies* **6**(4): 513–32.

Stanko, E. A. (1990). *Everyday Violence*. London, Pandora.

Stanko, E. A. (1995). 'Women, Crime and Fear', *Annals of the American Academy of Political and Social Science* **539**: 46–58.

Stanko, E. A. (1998). 'Warnings to Women: Police Advice and Women's Safety in Britain', *Violence against Women* **2**(1): 5–24.

Stanko, E. A. (2000). 'Victims R Us: The Life History of "fear and crime" and the Politicisation of Violence', in *Risk and Insecurity*. T. Hope and R. Sparks (eds). London, Routledge: 13–30.

Stein, A. (2001). *The Stranger Next Door: The Story of a Small Community's Battle over Sex, Faith and Civil Rights*. Boston, Beacon Press.

Stolcke, V. (1995). 'Talking Culture; New Boundaries, New Rhetorics of Exclusion in Europe', *Current Anthropology* **36**(1): 1–24.

Streetwatch (1994). *Final Report*. Sydney, Streetwatch Implementation Advisory Committee, Anti-Discrimination Board.

Stychin, C. (1998). *Nation by Rights*. Philadelphia, Temple University Press.

Taguieff, P.-A. (ed.) (1991). *Face au Racism. Vol. 1 Les Moyens d'Agir*. Paris, Editions La Decouverte/Essais.

Taylor, C. (1994). 'The Politics of Recognition', in *Multiculturalism: A Critical Reader*. D. T. Goldberg (ed.). Oxford, Blackwell: 75–106.

Taylor, I. (1999). Crime in Control: A Critical Criminology of Market Societies. Cambridge, Polity Press.

Taylor, J. and T. Chandler (1995). *Lesbians Talk Violent Relationships*. London, Scarlet Press.

Thatchell, P. (2002). 'Some People are More Equal than Others', in *The Hate Debate: Should Hate be Punished as a Crime?* P. Iganski (ed.). London, Institute for Jewish Policy Research: 54–70.

Thompson, K. (1998). *Moral Panics*. London, Routledge.

Tomsen, S. (2001). 'Queer and Safe: Combating Violence with Gentrified Sexual Identities', *Queer City, Gay and Lesbian Politics in Sydney*. C. Johnston and P. van Reyk (eds). Sydney, Pluto Press.

Tuan, Y. F. (1979). *Landscapes of Fear*. Oxford, Blackwell.

Turner, B. S. (2000). 'Cosmopolitan Virtue: Loyalty and the City', in *Democracy, Citizenship and the Global City*. E. F. Islin (ed.). London and New York, Routledge: 129–48.

Valentine, G. (1989). 'The Geography of Women's Fear', *Area* **21**(4): 385–90.

Valentine, G. (1990). 'Women's Fear and the Design of Public Space', *Built Environment* **16**: 279–87.

Valentine, G. (1992). 'Images of Danger: Women's Sources of Information about the Spatial Distributions of Male Violence', *Area* **24**: 22–9.

Valentine, G. (1993). 'Negotiating and Managing Multiple Sexual Identities: Lesbian Time-Space Strategies', *Transactions of the Institute of British Geographers* **18**: 237–48.

Valentine, G. (1998). '"Sticks and Stones may Break my Bones": A Personal Cartography of Harassment', *Antipode* **30**(4): 305–32.

Vance, C. (1984). 'Pleasure and Danger: Towards a Politics of Sexuality', in *Pleasure and Danger: Exploring Female Sexuality*. C. S. Vance (ed.). Boston, Routledge and Kegan Paul: 1–28.

Waaldijk, K. and A. Clapham (1993). *Homosexuality: A European Community Issue*. Dordrecht: Nijhoff.

Walklate, S. L. (2000). 'Trust and the Problem of Community in the Inner City', in *Crime, Risk and Insecurity*. T. Hope and R. Sparks (eds). London, Routledge: 50–64.

Walklate, S. L. (2001). 'Fearful Communities?' *Urban Studies* **38**(5-6): 929–31.

Walmsley, R. (1978). 'Indecency between Males and the Sexual Offences Act 1967'. *Criminal Law Review*: 400–7.

Warde, A. (1994). 'Employment Relations or Assets: An Alternative Basis of Class Analysis', in Paper presented to Lancaster Regionalism Group, 13.12.95, Lancaster University.

Warner, M. (ed.) (1993). *Fear of a Queer Planet: Queer Politics and Social Theory*. Minneapolis and London, University of Minnesota Press.

Weeks, J. (1981). *Sex, Politics and Society: The Regulation of Sexuality Since 1800*. London, Longman.

Weeks, J., B. Heaphy and C. Donovan (1999). 'Partnership Rites: Commitment and Ritual in Non-Hetrosexual Relationships', in *Relating Intimacies: Power and Resistance*. J. Seymour and P. Bagguley (eds). Basingstoke, Macmillan: 43–64.

Weeks, J., B. Heaphy and C. Donovan (2001). *Families of Choice and Other Life Experiments*. London, Routledge.

Weinstein, J. (1992). 'First Amendment Challenges to Hate Crime Legislation: Where's the Speech?' *Criminal Justice Ethics* **11**(2): 6–20.

Werbner, P. (1999). 'Global Pathways: Working-Class Cosmopolitans and the Creation of Transnational Ethnic Worlds', *Social Anthropology* **7**: 17–35.

Weston, K. (1995). 'Get Thee to a Big City: Sexual Imaginary and the Great Gay Migration', *GLQ* **2**: 253–77.

Whittle, S. (1994). 'Consuming Difference: The Collaboration of the Gay Body with the Cultural State', in *The Margins of the City*. S. Whittle (ed.). Aldershot, Arena.

Williams, P. (1991). *The Alchemy of Race and Rights: Diary of a Law Professor*. Cambridge, MA, Harvard University Press.

Williams, R. (1973). 'Base and Superstructure in Marxist Cultural Theory', *New Left Review* **82**: 3–16.

Wilson, E. (1991a). 'Feminism Without Illusions', *New Left Review* **190**: 119–27.

Wilson, E. (1991b). *The Sphinx in the City: Urban Life, the Control of Disorder, and Women*. Aldershot, Ashgate.

Wintermute, R. (1997). *Sexual Orientation and Human Rights*. Oxford, Oxford University Press.

Wotherspoon, G. (1991). *City of the Plain: History of a Gay Subculture*. Sydney, Hale and Iremonger.

Wurff, A. van der, P. Stringer and F. Timmer (1988). 'Feelings of unsafety in residential surroundings', in *Environmental Social Pyschology*. D. Canter, C. Jermino, L. Socka and G. Stephenson (eds). The Hague, Kluwer: 135–48.

Young, A. (1996). *Imagining Crime*. London, Sage.

Young, I. M. (1990). *Justice and the Politics of Difference*. Princeton, NJ, Princeton University Press.

Young, I. M. (1997). 'Unruly Categories: A Critique of Nancy Fraser's Dual Systems Theory', *New Left Review* **222**: 147–60.

Young, A. A. Jr. (1999). 'The (Non) Accumulation of Capital: Explicating the Relationship of Structure and Agency in the Lives of Poor Black Men', *Sociological Theory* **17**(2): 201–27.

Zizek, S. (1997). 'Multiculturalism, or, the Cultural Logic of Multinational Capitalism', *New Left Review* **225**: 28–52.

Zukin, S. (1990). 'Socio-Spatial Prototypes of a New Organisation of Consumption: The Role of Real Cultural Capital', *Sociology* **24**: 37–56.

# Index